The Comprehensive Public High School

Secondary Education in a Changing World

Series editors: Barry M. Franklin and Gary McCulloch

Published by Palgrave Macmillan:

The Comprehensive Public High School: Historical Perspectives
By Craig Campbell and Geoffrey Sherington (2006)

Cyril Norwood and the Ideal of Secondary Education
By Gary McCulloch (2007)

The Death of the Comprehensive High School?: Historical, Contemporary, and Comparative Perspectives
Edited by Barry M. Franklin and Gary McCulloch (2007)

The Emergence of Holocaust Education in American Schools
By Thomas D. Fallace (2008)

The Standardization of American Schooling: Linking Secondary and Higher Education, 1870–1910
By Marc A. VanOverbeke (2008)

Education and Social Integration: Comprehensive Schooling in Europe
By Susanne Wiborg (2009)

Reforming New Zealand Secondary Education: The Picot Report and the Road to Radical Reform
By Roger Openshaw (2009)

Inciting Change in Secondary English Language Programs: The Case of Cherry High School
By Marilee Coles-Ritchie (2009)

Curriculum, Community, and Urban School Reform
By Barry M. Franklin (2010)

Girls' Secondary Education in the Western World: From the 18th to the 20th Century
Edited by James C. Albisetti, Joyce Goodman, and Rebecca Rogers (2010)

Race-Class Relations and Integration in Secondary Education: The Case of Miller High
By Caroline Eick (2010)

Teaching Harry Potter: The Power of Imagination in Multicultural Classrooms
By Catherine L. Belcher and Becky Herr Stephenson (2011)

The Invention of the Secondary Curriculum
By John White (2011)

Secondary STEM Educational Reform
Edited by Carla C. Johnson (2011)

New Labour and Secondary Education, 1994–2010
By Clyde Chitty (2013)

The Comprehensive Public High School

Historical Perspectives

Craig Campbell
and
Geoffrey Sherington

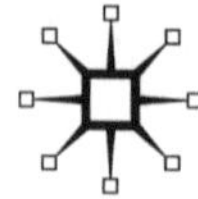

First published in hardcover in 2006 by PALGRAVE MACMILLAN® in the United States—a division of St. Martin's Press LLC, 175 Fifth Avenue, New York, NY 10010.

Where this book is distributed in the UK, Europe and the rest of the world, this is by Palgrave Macmillan, a division of Macmillan Publishers Limited, registered in England, company number 785998, of Houndmills, Basingstoke, Hampshire RG21 6XS.

Palgrave Macmillan is the global academic imprint of the above companies and has companies and representatives throughout the world.

Palgrave® and Macmillan® are registered trademarks in the United States, the United Kingdom, Europe and other countries.

ISBN 978–1–137–03374–1

The Library of Congress has cataloged the hardcover edition as follows:

Sherington, Geoffrey.
The comprehensive public high school : historical perspectives / by Geoffrey Sherington and Craig Campbell.
p. cm.—(Secondary education in a changing world)
Includes bibliographical references and index.
ISBN 1–4039–6489–0
1. Education, Comparative. 2. Comprehensive high schools—History—Cross-cultural studies. 3. Comprehensive high schools—Australia—History. 4. Comprehensive high schools—Great Britain—History. 5. Comprehensive high schools—United States—History. I. Campbell, Craig, 1949– II. Title. III. Series.

LB43.S52 2005
371.01—dc22 2005047556

A catalogue record for this book is available from the British Library.

Design by Newgen Imaging Systems (P) Ltd., Chennai, India.

First PALGRAVE MACMILLAN paperback edition: February 2013

10 9 8 7 6 5 4 3 2 1

Contents

List of Tables

Series Editors' Preface

Among the educational issues affecting policy makers, public officials, and citizens in modern, democratic, and industrial societies, none has been more contentious than the role of secondary schooling. In establishing the Secondary Education in a Changing World series with Palgrave Macmillan, our intent is to provide a venue for scholars in different national settings to explore critical and controversial issues surrounding secondary education. We envision our series as a place for the airing and hopefully resolution of these controversial issues.

More than a century has elapsed since Emile Durkheim argued the importance of studying secondary education as a unity, rather than in relation to the wide range of subjects and the division of pedagogical labor of which it was composed. Only thus, he insisted, would it be possible to have the ends and aims of secondary education constantly in view. The failure to do so accounted for a great deal of the difficulty with which secondary education was faced. First, it meant that secondary education was "intellectually disorientated," between "a past which is dying and a future which is still undecided," and as a result "lacks the vigor and vitality which it once possessed" (Durkheim 1938/1977, p. 8). Second, the institutions of secondary education were not understood adequately in relation to their past, which was "the soil which nourished them and gave them their present meaning, and apart from which they cannot be examined without a great deal of impoverishment and distortion" (p. 10). And third, it was difficult for secondary school teachers, who were responsible for putting policy reforms into practice, to understand the nature of the problems and issues that prompted them.

In the early years of the twenty-first century, Durkheim's strictures still have resonance. The intellectual disorientation of secondary education is more evident than ever as it is caught up in successive waves of policy changes. The connections between the present and the past have become increasingly hard to trace and untangle. Moreover, the distance between policy makers on the one hand and the practitioners on the other has rarely seemed as immense as it is today. The key mission of the current series of books is, in the spirit of Durkheim, to address these underlying dilemmas of secondary education and to play a part in resolving them.

Campbell and Sherington's volume represents a study of comprehensive schooling in Australia's largest state, New South Wales. Their volume considers the origins, development, and impending decline of comprehensive high schools in this region from the early twentieth century until the present day. While clearly a case study located in a particular national setting, the authors are aware of the larger international story surrounding comprehensive secondary education and throughout the volume link their narrative with the development of comprehensive secondary schooling in the other countries, particularly the United States and the United Kingdom.

While these authors identify the important achievement of comprehensive secondary education as a vehicle for enhancing equality and opportunity, they do recognize the array of criticisms that have been advanced, particularly those related to student retention rates and competitive academic examinations. In this vein, they are especially concerned with the emergence since the 1970s of neoliberalism and the resulting emphasis among policy makers and citizens alike of market solutions to public problems. The result in Australia, as they tell their story, has been twofold. First, while both the private sector and the selective academic high school traditions have long histories in Australia, changes since the 1970s have strengthened their appeal and weakened the comprehensive high school. New funding policies have helped to bring into being a variety of private, nongovernmental alternatives to state comprehensive schooling. Even among state comprehensive high schools the ideology of parental choice has become an important factor. Second, the influence of neoliberalism on government policy has led to an increasing tendency among middle-class families to exercise their right to choice often seeking to remove their children from state schools in favor of private options. As a consequence, comprehensive high schools, which were initially promoted on egalitarian grounds, are increasingly under threat of becoming the educational destination of those denied access to selective academic high schools or unable to afford private alternatives.

The Comprehensive Public High School inaugurates our series with one of the most pressing issues facing secondary education worldwide. It sets the stage for further explorations of the kind of important issues that will characterize future volumes in this series.

Barry Franklin and Gary McCulloch
Series Co-Editors

Acknowledgments

The Australian Research Council generously funded the research on which this book is based. We also thank the many public high school principals and policy makers whom we interviewed, and the New South Wales Department of Education and Training for permitting us to talk to them. They shared their valuable insights into the social and educational significance of comprehensive high schooling both in the present and the past. Ms Danni Bouvier from the Australian Bureau of Statistics handled our complex requests for census data with high professionalism.

We are especially grateful to John Hughes, the biographer of Harold Wyndham, who decided to spend his postdoctoral scholarship year on the research project. Dorothy Straesser provided excellent research assistance, keeping an eagle eye on the mass media as its contemporary campaigns concerning public and private secondary education continued to twist and turn. We also thank Bob Connell, David Crook, Terry Haydn, David Hogan, and Tony Vinson for other and varied assistance. None of them bears responsibility for the text or its argument however. We thank our colleagues associated with the conferences of the Australian and New Zealand History of Education Society, the American Educational Research Association, and the International Standing Conference of the History of Education for engaging with our papers in recent times.

We also acknowledge people dear to our hearts, those of our research students who have worked on histories of public education in New South Wales and Australia over the last decade or so. Among them, Catherine Brown, Carl Green, Patricia Jenkings, Alison Nation, Helen Proctor, and Andrew Lynch in particular have contributed in very important ways to this book.

Last, but hardly least, we thank Keith Foulcher and Lisa Sherington, our respective partners, for their loving support—and tolerance.

Notes on Contributors

Craig Campbell is an honorary associate professor in the History of Education at the University of Sydney. His background in education includes high school teaching, teacher union leadership as well as being a research and teaching academic since 1990. From 2013 he is co-editor of the *History of Education Review*. His books include a history of a state high school in South Australia and a co-authored social history of secondary education in Australia from 1850–1925. He is currently writing a new general history of Australian schooling.

Geoffrey Sherington is Emeritus professor at the University of Sydney where he was previously Dean of the Faculty of Education and then Acting Deputy Vice Chancellor. He has an exceptional research and publication record. This includes books on the history of youth, independent schools, educational and youth policy, and migration in Australia and Britain. Co-authored books include *Youth in Australia, Learning to Lead, Fairbridge: Empire and Child Migration* and *Sydney: The Making of a Public University*.

Together, Craig Campbell and Geoffrey Sherington have edited *Going to School in Oceania*, a study of educational history in the nations of the South-West Pacific. With Helen Proctor they have written a seminal study of neoliberal education reform in Australia: *School Choice: How parents negotiate the new school market in Australia* (2009).

Introduction

There is now a general consensus that public education systems in the English-speaking world are at best, in difficulty, or at worst in crisis. For some twenty years in Australia there have been public funding and student population shifts toward private and nongovernment schooling. In other countries, the problems develop differently. One form of public school, the comprehensive secondary school, has attracted a disproportionate share of criticism—the difficulties of the comprehensive high school provide a set of intractable problems to contemporary policy makers. It is this model of secondary schooling which carried the most socially optimistic visions associated with the upward extension of universal elementary schooling. The faltering of that vision has led to a new necessity to reconceptualize what universal secondary schooling should look like in the future.

This book is about the history of that process, how the comprehensive high school emerged in the early and mid-twentieth century as the form of secondary schooling most likely to meet the needs not only of most families, but also of governments responsible for public education. The book might equally have been titled, 'the origin of the present discontents,' because the story which develops, especially from the 1970s through to the beginning of the new century tends to be a story of mounting criticism, despite the achievements of this form of schooling. Not the least of these achievements was increased student retention over the main fifty-year period covered in this analysis. The book takes as its case study of the process, the story of comprehensive schooling in the largest of the Australian states, New South Wales.

The historical trajectory of comprehensive high schools differs from country to country. Even though public high schools in the United States did not really develop along comprehensive lines until the 1930s, the policy base for such development had occurred much earlier.[1] It was not until the 1950s that the practical possibility of such schools emerged as part of an educational 'wave of the future' in Australia and England. In those countries, the comprehensive school was not even part of the immediate post–World War II planning for universal secondary education. England and

Australia both waited until the 1960s before establishing substantial numbers of comprehensive secondary schools. While in both countries they eventually became the dominant form of government or public secondary schooling, the optimistic educational and social visions that accompanied their founding never lacked challenge.

By the last decade of the twentieth century, these schools, especially those in older urban areas in the United States, England, and Australia, were often portrayed in the media and elsewhere as 'residual' in form. They were becoming increasingly deserted by the middle class and increasingly patronized by the families of the poor, and their difficulties were a conspicuous element of a wider decline of state-supported public education in the English-speaking world. The rise of neoliberalism in economics and its influence on public policy, including that of education, challenged some of the dominant visions of how public education systems should be organized and funded. Especially vulnerable was the idea of the comprehensive school as the single or dominant provider of public secondary education in any neighborhood or district.

In the late twentieth century, a renewed emphasis on the utility of free markets to deliver efficiencies and reforms in local and national economies was increasingly applied to education systems.[2] Such thinking not only provided new forms of legitimacy and support to private and nongovernment educational enterprise, but also more vigorous competition from this sector for public education as a whole. The thinking also inspired programs of reform within public education systems. It was believed that by removing regulated monopolies over geographically defined school populations, by increasing levels of autonomy over budgets, staffing, and curriculum in individual schools, competition within public systems might be encouraged. It was possible to envision major public education reform through school competition, through the creation of semi-markets.[3] Schools that failed to compete and lost students might close. Those which grasped the opportunities, which reformed themselves in such a way as to attract competent staff and students, would help reform the public education system as a whole.

Comprehensive secondary schools were always going to be vulnerable in such a reform process. They were invented as universal providers, structured to monopolize enrolments in a given district. They offered a mixed curriculum of a common core and a variety of options. They were a major and 'standardized' vehicle for 'educational uplift' for the majority of young people. One of the reasons for their invention in England and Australia was to deny some of the ill-effects of different secondary schools in public systems, the legacy of 'tripartism.' Such different schools usually selected or were allocated their students at an early age, often locking youth into highly differentiated curricula that too obviously reproduced social divisions and unequal labor-market opportunities between black and white, working and middle class students, and boys and girls.

The creation of new markets in public education was especially problematic at the secondary school level where the contest between the different purposes of schooling was less able to be resolved than at the elementary level. Some of the general purposes of the comprehensive school such as providing for common socialization and citizen-formation experiences and of providing roughly equal opportunities to succeed in an accessible secondary curriculum were not always compatible with the development of competitive markets in education.

Success in a market usually involves the production of commodities attractive to identifiable segments of a market. If a school can persuade such a segment of its relevance to its demands—whether the 'commodity' is high rates of prestigious college and university entrance, moral or religiousl based education, a safe and caring schooling environment, strong vocational programs, responsiveness to the concerns of a parent community, special programs for gifted or disabled students, or even (and such commodities are usually coded) the promise of a socially exclusive student body and a specialist curriculum—then the chances of success in a market are enhanced. If this argument is accepted, then the lesson for a struggling comprehensive school might be to become more specialist, in fact less comprehensive in order to survive in a market.

It is part of the argument of this book that the histories of individual comprehensive schools may play out very differently, and not only as a result of differing responses to new market pressures and opportunities. It is a very old argument, especially in the United States, that the relationship of comprehensive schools to particular populations, and their placement in particular urban, suburban, or rural districts may profoundly affect their character. In the 1960s, in the same period that England and Australia were beginning their bold experiments with the comprehensive school, James Conant was writing about comprehensive schools developing differently in inner cities with large 'Negro' populations and curricula dominated by vocational subjects. In the white suburbs, 'lighthouse' schools had emerged, responding to their communities' demands for curricula dominated by college entrance requirements.[4]

Such tendencies, for comprehensive schools to respond to the local character of schooling populations, were hardly absent in England either.[5] The same phenomenon in Australia was rather more conditioned, at least until the end of the 1970s, by the centralized control that state bureaucracies exercised over public education. The Australian tradition allowed for minimal local influence, whether from parents or local government authorities.

Standard forms of organization, centralized staffing provision, and a curriculum dominated by State boards, State education departments, and public examinations diminished some differences between schools. These extremes of centralized control and hierarchy were the features of the Australian tradition of public schooling that the Americans, Isaac Kandel and then Freeman Butts, had found so confronting during their respective visits in the 1930s and 1950s.[6] Nevertheless, regional differences did appear, and in ways which were recognizable to observers from Britain and the United States.

By the 1990s, the disruptions of neoliberal-influenced policies saw some inner-urban comprehensive schools sink very low. Indeed, in England the phrase "sink schools" was used to describe some failing schools that had disproportionate shares of problem populations and inadequate human and material resources with which to educate.[7] Such problems also occurred in the larger Australian cities.

The purpose of this book is to trace and explain the invention, rise, and decline of the government comprehensive high school in New South Wales. In doing so there are two ideas that are crucial to our analysis.

The first is the idea of 'regional difference.' Histories of comprehensive secondary schools, even in a centralized system as large as that of New South Wales can be very different. Rural and urban locations produce some of the differences, but there is plenty of variety within these broad categories as well.

The second idea is that of 'residualization.' From its apparently social-democratic conception in the 1950s and 1960s in England and Australia, the public comprehensive high school now appears to be an increasingly 'residual' school. This is a school that collects students and families who are relatively poor and somewhat powerless in an education system. Such families often do not, or cannot, operate effectively within an education market.[8]

Both these ideas emphasize the social history of the comprehensive secondary school that becomes the main focus of the last chapter in this book. In the earlier chapters, the development of the idea of the comprehensive school in Australia, the transformation of the idea into public policy, and then the politics of its implementation are the main focus. We argue that in the late twentieth century the gap between the intended operation of comprehensive schooling and the social realities of such schooling in communities widened. A history of the comprehensive secondary school in Australia demands a transition from a policy focus to a sociological focus, and the plan of this book reflects that demand.

In the United States, schooling remains overwhelmingly public in character. While there are highly selective and wealthy private schools and substantial Catholic parochial systems, the issue of 'residualization' is played out for the most part within an extraordinarily diverse public school system. Many decades after Conant, David Labaree pointed to the effect of markets and the role of educational credentials in creating and sustaining private educational advantages even within public school systems in the United States.[9] In England the public (government) school system is also very strong, but with its traditions of incorporating church-controlled schools and semiautonomous grammar schools into the national system, schools which might be described as 'private' in Australia, are part of the public system in England.

Consequently, comparisons of the relative health of public education systems across the United States, England, and Australia must be circumspect. The example of how Catholic school populations are treated in each country demonstrates the point. In Australia, with the introduction of comprehensive high schools in the 1950s, Catholic high schools were almost totally outside public education. They received no funding from the state. By the end of the period, in the early 2000s, they were substantially funded from federal and state government sources, but retained relative autonomy from state regulation. Ideologically and popularly they remained determinedly part of the 'private' or 'nongovernment' sector. In the United States, the place of the Catholic parochial sector is ultimately driven by interpretations of the Constitution that separate church and state. Unlike in Australia, the consequence is a limitation on the potential expansion of the Catholic sector, despite the presence of a rapidly growing Hispanic, usually Catholic population. In England, religious schools, including the parochial Catholic, are often part of the public education system, though their presence and degrees of autonomy may still be seen as challenging to some county, now community, schools controlled by Local Education Authorities.

In recent times, both England and the United States have experimented with the development of government-funded schools that have been detached from direct control. The charter schools of the United States, though still limited in number and distribution, are an obvious example of this development; similarly in England, the 'direct grant' and 'independent' schools, still within the 'mainstream state schools' category, have increased in number. As nonsystemic schools, in most respects they are free to develop specialist curricula and in many cases, develop specific student and family markets for their services. In England, some are 'faith' schools, serving particular ethno-religious communities. Therefore, they are not comprehensive public schools.

The question of what defines a comprehensive high school for the purposes of this book needs some clarification. An Australian attempt at this in the 1970s argued that it was a school which "admits all children of appropriate age in a given area and provides a range of courses to suit their whole range of interests and abilities."[10] It is useful though limited. It points to the idea of a school which is not specifically oriented to populations defined by specific characteristics such as wealth (i.e., ability to pay fees), religious attachment, ethnic or racial origins, or indeed previous academic attainment or 'ability' and 'intelligence.' In order to be such a school, it is likely to be part of a public, tax-supported school system. The quotation also points to the necessity of an accessible curriculum for all students. How this might be organized has been subject to long disputation. The 'multilateral' school provides different courses for a range of students in the one institution, but opportunities for easy transference from one course to another might be limited. The comprehensive school is in theory more likely to provide common core subjects and a range of options. In theory, mobility across the curriculum should be easier in a comprehensive school, but tracking, streaming, and separate courses have commonly existed in comprehensive schools. Mobility across the curriculum groupings cannot be taken for granted.

A lack of certitude over the essential components of comprehensive schools has enabled such schools to meet a variety of pressures from different populations. In the United States such flexibility has caused conservative backlash to 'shopping mall high schools' that, it is argued, have consistently met the curriculum demands of pressure groups by expanding curriculum offerings and lowering academic standards.[11] In England, the Black Papers debate, coincident with the early expansion of comprehensive schools, represented a determined criticism of falling academic standards as grammar schools began systematically to be converted to comprehensives.[12] Nevertheless, flexibility in curriculum offering and organization has enabled comprehensive schools to meet changing demands in different historical periods, such as the upgrading of science programs in the Cold War period, or the incorporation of community languages during the rise of multicultural priorities in public policy, or the 'back to basics' and renewed vocational training pressure in a more recent period when governments sought to link schooling outcomes more efficiently to national economic and technological development objectives.

Where curriculum pressures such as these could often be accommodated by comprehensive schools, less able to be accommodated were changed expectations of the middle class in public schooling in all three countries. The idea that there could be a common secondary school, not just for the meritorious or youth of the wealthier and more powerful classes, but for all youth regardless of their talent or social background was a peculiarly twentieth-century idea. Its emergence early in the century required a great range of favorable social and intellectual circumstances. One of the most important was the discovery of 'adolescence.' The work of the American scholar, Stanley Hall identified youth as having certain psychological characteristics and social needs that extended beyond those of the biological. Moreover his depiction of adolescence tended to downplay the significance of class or social background (though not gender). Hall and his popularizers advocated the invention and adaptation of organizations, including schools, which might protect adolescents from too early an entry into adult society, and which might encourage their talents in creative and good-citizenship directions. The idea of a universally accessible secondary school in which the universal biological, social, and psychological needs of adolescents might be met was a logical consequence of such thinking.[13]

By the end of the twentieth century, the role of the high school in the lives of young people had changed considerably from thirty to forty years before. A consequence of youth labor markets failing to absorb as many school-leavers meant that school retention rates increased. But many of these students experienced prolonged high school attendance as unwelcome. Youth also fled the older adult-supervised recreational organizations such as church, youth and to a lesser extent, sporting clubs, making the high school an even more forceful institution in the lives of young people. As high schools developed a more universal and custodial character as a consequence, and as ever greater proportions of the labor market became sensitive to the claims of educational credentials—while youth entertainment and culture was mainly experienced outside it—the comprehensive high school was decreasingly likely to contain the social pressures at work.

One feature of this phenomenon has been the developing anxiety of the middle class for the futures of its young people. For much of the middle class in the United States, England, and Australia, heightened attention to school choice is clearly present. The peculiar dependence of the new middle class in modern societies on the credentials that schools can provide is an old theme in educational historiography.[14] That it has entered a new phase, often detrimental to the support of public comprehensive secondary schools, is a rising issue not only in the academic literature, but the news media.[15]

Such anxieties, not only confined to the middle class, are also sustained by newly current conceptions of good citizenship in the neoliberal era. Contemporary citizen-parents plan the schooling of their children carefully. In Australia, governments support those who do so by subsidizing their choices if they occur outside the public school system. A consequence is that there is no particular objection to the privileging of private interest above the public. Indeed the citizen-parents who choose the nonpublic school are often represented as more caring, even wiser, parents than those who do not. This tendency produces a fundamental problem for the public comprehensive high school with its historic tradition of serving an undifferentiated 'community' or 'neighborhood' and providing a mainly common curriculum. An education market responsive to private needs depends on the development of differentiated curricula and schooling ethos.

The problems of working classes in economies subject to deindustrialization have been less well studied. Recent work by Thomson has shown the disastrous consequences for an old industrial area in one of Australia's major cities, of the conjunction between the closing of the factories and the rise of working-class unemployment with the loss of government support for state comprehensive schools. Such literature links with a much older literature exposing the problematic relationships between state secondary schooling and the working class.[16] Parallel debates on these questions exist in Britain and the United States.

This discussion has established some of the issues that the following chapters explore in more detail. It remains to introduce the Australian site and methods of the study.

New South Wales produced a nationally significant program for comprehensive secondary school reorganization in the late 1950s.[17] The 'Wyndham scheme,' named after its principal author, Harold Wyndham, was justified as part of the process of postwar reconstruction. The emerging schools were to be socially integrative and coeducational in form. The scheme was conceived in a period when 'assimilation' and the 'White Australia' policies remained the dominant approach to migration and migrant re-settlement. By the end of the century, the vision of socially integrative schooling of the 1950s would be transformed. By this time 'White Australia' had been displaced and Australia had clearly become, and been recognized as a multiethnic and multiracial society.

Wyndham's career in the New South Wales Education Department owed its success to his leadership of research and testing units that supported a highly differentiated secondary school system.[18] To him, comprehensive schooling in New South Wales suggested the possibility of an escape from the dominance of intelligence testing and its role in distributing students into academic high schools, and then the various junior technical, home science, intermediate, and other post-primary schools.

As is the case with many reform programs involving comprehensive schools, the implementation process was flawed. Though promising new opportunities for children in public schooling from the 1960s, in effect the scheme preserved a dominant academic curriculum within the comprehensive schools. It also allowed for the continued existence of academically selective high schools within the public system.[19] (This was also true for the introduction of comprehensive schooling in England.) The notion that comprehensive schooling might mean 'grammar schooling for all' accounted for some of the support the new schools received. That several academic high schools in New South Wales, as did many grammar schools in England, survived the patchy process of comprehensive reorganization had important consequences for the future.[20]

The historical trajectory of these new schools, given the compromises involved in their foundation, is complicated by the contemporaneous and dramatic reversal of Australian school funding policies. From the early 1960s, for the first time in nearly a century, Australia's 'private' schools, including an extensive Catholic system, began receiving government financial assistance. In the long term, this was to weaken public comprehensive high schools as 'private,' but in fact 'state-assisted' schools, would become more accessible to a broader range of Australian families. Such difficult and messy circumstances for the foundation of comprehensive school systems are hardly unique, especially in comparison with England.[21]

Because the New South Wales public school system was and is one of the largest in the Western world, it provides an excellent opportunity to study the foundation and progress of a single comprehensive reorganization across a very large number of schools—in a wide variety of rural, urban, and suburban circumstances. It also provides an opportunity to add to the current comparative study of the different policy and ideological foundations of comprehensive schooling. As in England, the attitude of the Labor Party was crucial to the foundation of comprehensive schools, yet the strength of Catholicism in Australian Labor led to the production of rather different school reform discourses. In Australia, the socialist left was neither as strong nor as vocal as in England. The English defense of comprehensive schooling led by author-activists including Simon, Benn, and Chitty over many years remains distinctive, and mainly unparalleled in Australia.[22]

The New South Wales case not only illustrates the relationship between support for comprehensive schools and labor educational traditions. There were reasons why non-Labor political parties might also support comprehensive schools from time to time. This occurred in England, although it was more likely at a local than national level.

The author of the New South Wales scheme, Wyndham, received his doctoral education at Stanford University in California. In many respects his career may be interpreted in terms of 'administrative progressivism.'[23] Though Scottish and New Zealand comprehensive reorganizations are usually cited as the most significant influences on Wyndham, he was also responsive to American influences.[24] The attack on progressivism in American public education systems, sustained over much of the second half of the twentieth century, came late to New South Wales. The legitimacy and relevance of the original charter of comprehensive secondary schooling in the United States, *The Cardinal Principles of Education* (1918), had been subject to sustained criticism for some time.[25] In New South Wales the first major assault on the progressive foundations of comprehensive schooling came in the late 1980s, with a Liberal National coalition government apparently seeking to strengthen the public secondary system as a whole by rapidly increasing the numbers of specialist and academically selective secondary schools. The debate over this reform program in education was intensive. Hostility toward these and other reform measures led to mass demonstrations of teachers, students, and parents and the eventual resignation of the Minister in charge, but more significantly, not the revocation of the reform program itself.[26]

Since the 1980s, the fate of the public comprehensive high school of New South Wales has been the object of intensive scrutiny from mass media, political and educational interests, and from the population at large. To a great degree, this scrutiny is sustained by a centralized public examination system. Having imported from England, with local variations, the ritual of publishing State-wide 'league tables' of school success, the inevitable categories of comparison were not only individual schools, but blocks of schools, usually the public comprehensives, public selectives, and nongovernment schools. Unsurprisingly, but nevertheless the cause for great alarm, the public comprehensives were usually the least successful schools, where the measure of success was the production of students who attained very high scores in the Higher School Certificate examinations and the various indexes for university entrance.

Thus, New South Wales provides a case study of comprehensive school history that has not only been responsive to common international pressures on public education systems. It also provides a unique opportunity to study the comprehensive secondary school's interaction with some uniquely Australian phenomena such as the collapse of the century-long political settlement that denied government financial assistance to nongovernment, usually church-owned schools. As a consequence, the problems of the Australian comprehensive school are not merely to do with curriculum or performance. In Australia, the comprehensive school has been subject to intensive competition from within and without the public education system. A significant task of this book may be to explain the survival of comprehensive schooling as much as its decline, given the present crisis in public education.

This study relies upon the analysis of data collected from four research activities. The first has been a survey of policy formation and its implementation in the 1950–2003 period. The second has been the collection of data concerning the changing patterns of school participation and provision over the same period. The third has been a survey of public and media perceptions of the changing fates of public comprehensive schooling. Fourth was the collection of interviews with some ninety principals of public comprehensive and selective high schools in New South Wales. Each of the activities has contributed unique perspectives on the historical problem of the comprehensive school. The policy analyses which might interpret this modernist form of schooling as 'social engineering,' or perhaps an expression of social democratic policy, need to be understood in relation to the questions of who used the schools and why. They need to be understood in the context of their representations in the media. The schools themselves need to be understood as very material, operating institutions, which have organized not only the lives of their students and teaching staffs, but the communities to which they have been attached.

The idea that the needs of all young people might be met by one standard and comprehensive institution, the comprehensive high school, was radical and contradicted the dominant schooling tradition in New South Wales. As old as New South Wales itself was the idea that children and youth came from very different social backgrounds, and that their educational needs were very different. The provision of different and separate schools—for orphan girls and boys, for Aborigines, for poor children, for children of powerful elites, for the middling classes, for the laboring classes, for Roman Catholics, for Protestants, for boys, for girls, for the able, for the disabled—was commonplace, and few had sought to challenge it. The provision of National, then public elementary schools from the mid-nineteenth century began a process of reducing some of the divisions but more significant change had to await the emergence of an idea which elevated the common needs and characteristics of youth above those which divided them in terms of family, class, religion, gender, ethnicity—and ability. The discovery and invention of 'adolescence' was the key phenomenon, aided by the growth of new and adapted institutions and professional practices to manage this potentially volatile group whose transition to responsible adulthood was seen to be fraught with danger. The common and comprehensive high school emerged during the twentieth century as one of the key institutions for the governing of adolescents. How this occurred in the United States, Britain, Australia, Canada, and New Zealand, each of which was responsive to the social discourse emphasizing the perils of adolescence, varied enormously. But some common patterns are discernable.

The question of how the 'comprehensive' high school emerged as the solution to the problem of providing universal secondary schooling in New South Wales has significance beyond that one Australian State. The New South Wales solution was widely studied and in some cases influenced reform in other parts of Australia. However, this book is not only about the emergence of systems in Australia. It contributes to a study of how educational ideas, practices, and institutions travel and adapt from one part of the world to another. Under the circumstances of increasing globalization, the emergence of common world histories of public policies and institutions is a significant issue for the future development of local schooling patterns and systems.

As well as tracing the origins of the comprehensive high school, we also seek to explain the form that it took. There is no universal model of comprehensive schooling. In each locality, let alone each country, such schools develop and are invented differently. They respond not only to prevailing educational ideas but also to the needs of local economies and the attitudes toward schooling by local communities defined by class, gender, ethnicity, and other elements of a local culture and their interactions with youth labor markets. Broad demographic movements, including those associated with migration, can also be highly significant. It will be argued that in Australia the conjunction in the 1950s and 1960s of a 'baby boom' with an expanding economy requiring greater levels of education from its workforce was as significant as any of the other explanations for the emergence of the comprehensive high school.

There are also the hard politics associated with public policy formation to be accounted for—the demands of the labor movement for fair opportunity for working-class children; the impact on the Labor Party of Catholic pressure to support a Catholic system of education as well as a public, secular system; the attachment of different elements of the middle class to private education, or a sternly meritocratic and hierarchical public system; the demand of agricultural communities from the 1920s through the highly effective Country Party for secondary educational opportunity in rural areas—each of these provide explanations for a local history of secondary school provision. Then there was the strange mix of ideas with consequences for public education in the various Nationalist, United Australia, and Liberal parties that included degrees of Protestant triumphalism and protectionist forms of liberalism. From the 1970s it was changes in the approach of this side of politics, but increasingly Labor as well, that would see a substantial loss of faith in the efficacy of public bureaucracies and their instruments, including the government comprehensive school.[27]

This brings us to the final aim of the book, which is to explain the beginnings of the decline and perhaps survival of the government comprehensive high school. How did the 'wave of the future' become an increasingly residual form of secondary education and where might that development lead? Again the explanations need to be wide ranging, and never absent from them can be the conjunctions of pressures arising from new economic policy approaches, changing youth labor markets, and demographic and cultural change.

This book thus combines a political and social analysis of the history of public secondary schooling during the twentieth century, with a particular consideration of the period since the 1950s—and their relationship to the fate of an idea—that the best form of universal secondary education was the comprehensive public high school.

Chapter 1

Origins

The public comprehensive high school was a development of the twentieth century. Its origins lay much earlier in time. The idea that a school could include students of any background and talent—but restricted to a certain age—only slowly emerged with the transformation of schools that took place over the nineteenth and twentieth centuries. The idea that a school could be detached from particular religious denominational influence on curriculum and governance took long enough to develop also, especially in the schools of Britain and its Empire. Even the term 'secondary school' was virtually unheard of until almost the eve of the twentieth century. Rather than being seen as a 'stage' of education, the boys' schools that became known as 'secondary' were initially influenced by educational traditions drawn in part both from the long standing predominance of classics and the classical curriculum as well as the more commercial and vocational subjects that had emerged in the eighteenth century. In the English-speaking world those schools associated with the classical tradition often assumed the title of a 'grammar school'; those offering a more vocational or practical curriculum were often described as 'academies.' In practice, these distinctions sometimes carried little substance. The creation of new and reformed secondary schools in the nineteenth century was closely associated with the formation of the middle classes in Europe, Britain, and the 'new world' of North America as well as those other mainly English-speaking 'settler societies' which emerged in the nineteenth century.

The association of secondary education with specific gender and class formations had a profound impact on the development of secondary schools. While national education systems emerged to provide elementary 'schools for the people,' secondary education was often the province of the private sector. In the English context, at the beginning of the nineteenth century, local private ventures, sometimes in an incorporated form, were the main provider of schools for the professional and commercial middle classes. Clergy and others set up schools for boys. They were for private profit and operated under various names, sometimes under the title of 'grammar school' even though their curriculum was often only composed of elementary subjects. For girls there were private schools offering the 'polite accomplishments' including music and literature. Small in size these private venture schools provided much of the education available to the children of the middle class of England in the nineteenth century.[1]

Secondary Education for the Few

Many 'private schools' had confined life histories opening and then closing within a short period. Of longer and more continuing establishment were the 'endowed' grammar schools created initially through private philanthropy and operating under corporate governing bodies. The 'grammar school' academic tradition would be the major influence on how the formal secondary school curriculum was conceived not only in England but also throughout much of the English-speaking world. Of equal influence was the emerging and related male 'English public school' tradition found initially in the older endowed schools such as Eton College and Winchester College. Drawing boys from a wide geographic area, such schools had assumed the 'public' role of educating the sons of the aristocracy as future political and social leaders.

By the mid-nineteenth century, this tradition had been emulated in other endowed grammar schools as well as new foundations set up to cater for the English middle class. Associated with a mid-nineteenth century educational 'revolution' which involved a focus on 'character formation' as much as formal academic studies, and stressing the importance of 'athleticism' and organized games, the expanded English public schools were one of the most significant developments in the creation of the idea of secondary education. By the end of the nineteenth century, a new 'public school tradition' in secondary education had been established influencing both boys' and girls' schools in England and overseas, particularly in the British colonies of settlement, including Australia.[2]

In contrast, the United States soon offered a different conception of a 'public school' despite some lingering English influences. In the prerevolutionary era, town grammar schools had been established in some of the American colonies. Following the American Revolution, a variety of grammar schools and academies were established, sometimes private ventures, sometimes schools funded by community, philanthropy, or authorities from the different levels of local through to state government. In the older colonies of the East a very few private boarding academies for boys were established, catering to those 'born to rule' in the republic, formally being 'prep' schools for university and college, but also assuming values and a curriculum that developed on similar lines to the English public schools.[3] In the South and elsewhere private venture schools often turned into 'chartered' academies under a governing body and were often supported by public funds. Such schools often flourished in rural areas as much as in the larger towns and cities. Generally single sex, they helped to create a form of racially exclusive middle-class culture for both males and females.[4]

The Boston English High School established in 1821 assumed an iconic status as a new type of foundation. It was a day school for boys, still offering an academic curriculum but as part of the emerging public school system in Massachusetts. Like Philadelphia Central High established a few years later, its curriculum elevated in status the English or commercial subjects. These new public high schools became closely associated with the aspirations of the developing urban and commercial middle class, and with republican virtues.[5] By the late nineteenth century, with development of the common school idea, the concept of the public high school in the United States was seen more generally as "a school established by the public—supported chiefly by the public, controlled by the public, and accessible to the public under terms of equality, without special charge for tuition."[6] The possibility that girls and boys could attend the same public schools, especially those offering an advanced or higher education than elementary, took hold much earlier in the United States than in Britain, or parts of its Empire such as Australia.[7]

The Australian colonies initially shared more with the British experience than that of America. Established in the wake of the American Revolution as both a penal colony and a new outpost of the British Empire in the 'East,' the colony of New South Wales initially had none of the established grammar schools and academies that were to be found in both Britain and North America at the end of the eighteenth century. Rather, at least during the early nineteenth century, groups of tutors, governesses, and private venture schools catered to the needs of the small elite of administrators, large owners, and commercial entrepreneurs. This became part of an informal and unregulated market albeit one that was highly gendered. Clergy and others established tuition in their own homes to provide elements of classical learning or to teach commercial practices to males. Governesses from Britain set up ladies' academies to teach the 'polite accomplishments' of art, music, and literature.[8]

The Australian colonial landscape of 'secondary schools' was thus initially diverse. One example of a private venture for boys was the Caledonian

Academy that the Presbyterian Minister J. D. Lang established in 1826. Closing after only one year the Academy offered both elementary subjects and classical and modern languages. The teaching was nondenominational. In 1831, Lang then created the Australian College. Initially headed by Henry Carmichael, Scottish-educated and influenced by Jeremy Bentham, the Australian College lasted a decade, leaving a legacy of secular instruction and the nonclassical curriculum in Australian secondary education.[9] Moreover, there was the general influence of the Scottish democratic 'myth' that suggested a poor boy from the parishes could still climb the ladder to enter university even though many Scottish secondary schools were being increasingly Anglicized during the nineteenth century particularly among the urban middle class.[10]

Eventually, the dominant influence on middle-class education in Australia was the grammar school and the reforms in the English public schools for boys and the new schools for girls from the 1840s. The small Australian private venture schools were supplanted by schools with 'corporate' governing bodies generally being foundations of the various churches. This was most clearly seen in the colony of Victoria during the 1850s to 1880s that expanded with the impact of the gold rushes and where all the major churches established schools. Attempting to emulate the reformed English public schools for boys the new 'corporate' boys' schools also aspired to produce the future leaders of society. Not only an academic grammar school tradition but also the new emphasis on character building and organized games, which formed part of the changes in the English public schools, would become an important feature of nineteenth-century Australian secondary education. Similarly, though a little later, new girls' grammar schools under corporate governance were also developed. Recent research has shown the strength of the curriculum continuities with the private ladies' academies rather than arguing for a sharp adoption of the male, or public examinations-oriented curriculum—an argument that characterized the older historiography.[11] Almost all these new corporate schools were single sex, so consolidating the segmentation of Australian secondary education.[12]

Of particular significance was the fact that many of these Australian secondary schools were founded after the mid-nineteenth-century reforms in the English public schools. They soon inherited a particular curriculum and other educational traditions that would have a major impact on the future of Australian secondary schools. Among the boys' secondary schools sporting and other associations were created in each of the Australian colonies so establishing the basis of a system of differentiation and status similar to the English public schools.[13] Such associations often crossed the barriers of faith and ethnicity, but with different consequences on grounds of gender.

Catholic boys' schools found common ground with those of Protestant faith in sustaining a culture of colonial middle-class masculinity that owed much to the ideology of the expanding British Empire in Australia and elsewhere.[14] In girls' schools there were often major differences in the ways femininity was espoused and supported. The major Protestant girls' schools often had male heads and male governing bodies. Other girls' schools arose out of the aims and foundations of a new generation of headmistresses who were in part drawing upon the nineteenth-century English feminist movement to create different forms of education and opportunities for women. Finally, convent schools, run by female religious orders, taught a specific form of domesticity and religiosity that drew upon the traditions of the Catholic faith.[15]

The colonial corporate schools established a powerful legitimacy for the private sector in Australian secondary education. They created and helped to maintain cultural and social capital for the small ruling class in Australia while serving as educational models for members of the colonial middle class who aspired to social status. Moreover, the emerging colonial state often assisted this process. By the 1850s, public funds established and endowed the single sex male Sydney Grammar School that came to follow curriculum and other traditions generally modeled on the English public schools.[16] Elsewhere, state endowment supplemented local endeavors. In the newly established colony of Queensland state funds were provided for regional grammar schools that were under their own governing bodies charging fees but which also provided bursaries. In Western Australia, the colonial government endowed Perth High School in 1875.[17] These schools, though in the main socially exclusive, also and significantly, legitimized secular secondary school foundations in the Australian colonies.

Creating Systems of Public High Schools

State endowment of individual 'public' schools raised the possibility of founding *systems* of public secondary schools. In Australia, the concept of 'public education' emerged out of a contest between state-supported church schools, as in the European tradition, and an emerging secular system of schools.[18] There was a long and protracted debate over the form that public education should take culminating in the 'compulsory, free and secular' education acts of the colonial parliaments, and the ensuing legislation and regulations that were introduced over the period from the mid-nineteenth century to the early twentieth century. Prior to the 1870s, public, tax-raised funds had usually been available for church schools. This aid was now withdrawn. In contrast with England and Canada, and much of Western Europe, these educational settlements in the Australian colonies refused to recognize the social and religious diversity of the population in the interests of establishing a common civic culture in elementary schools funded by the state. This educational settlement was generally accepted and supported by most of the Protestant churches in Australia. Predictably, the Catholic Church regarded the withdrawal of state funding for its schools as a denial of social justice. It also condemned public education as 'irreligious' and even immoral. Public education in Australia would carry this legacy of a sectarian divide well into the twentieth century.[19]

This new settlement was the first of the factors that would re-orient the development of Australian secondary education from parallel development with Britain more toward that of the United States. The reasons for the separation of church and state in Australia were rather different from the Enlightenment-inspired arguments that influenced the writing of the Constitution of the United States however. A consequence of this was the relatively uncontested reversal of the settlement in Australia in the 1960s.

There was also the importance of centralization in the colonial context. The idea of the 'common school' in Australia was generally not founded on local government control through such agencies as school boards. In some colonies such as South Australia local communities in the 1830s and 1840s supported schools assisted by state funds but central control was soon established as elsewhere in the Australian colonies.[20] Overall, the establishment of state-provided schools was associated with new administrative arrangements in public education that strengthened the controls of centralized bureaucracies in each colony and then state in post-1901 federal Australia. Whereas schools became part of community-building in much of North America, the role of local communities in the formation of public schools was usually weak in Australia. The public education systems that emerged in Australia soon became highly centralized with inspection of local schools and teachers. Central state administrations both funded public schools and ruled in such matters as staff provision, curriculum and textbook determination, and most other areas of organization.[21]

The first secondary school to be established as part of a public school *system* in Australia was the Advanced School for Girls opened in Adelaide in 1879. Offering an academic curriculum oriented toward public examinations set by the local university, and catering principally for the urban middle class, the school attempted to follow the new forms of English public schools for girls created during the second half of the nineteenth century.[22] In 1883–1884, in New South Wales and in the wake of the Public Instruction Act (1880), public high schools were established in Sydney and in a number of major regional centers. In the main, the curriculum and values of the new public high schools were modeled on the existing Australian church and corporate secondary schools. All were single sex institutions and the boys' schools in particular eventually followed Australian versions of the traditional grammar school curriculum as well as the ethic of leadership and character-building through organized games and such devices as the prefect system. Sydney Boys' High even joined the elite Athletic Association of Great Public Schools that was designed to regulate sporting competitions.[23] Some have also seen Sydney Girls' High as catering to the same middle-class clientele who were patronizing the elite private girls' schools, although more recent research of early enrolments would suggest that many pupils were the daughters of widows, with others coming from families which were either on the way up or sliding down the social scale, a possible contrast to those attending church and other corporate schools. Sydney Girls' High, like other 'modern' girls' schools founded in the late nineteenth century, arose from two essentially middle-class movements—female emancipation and the concept of 'meritocracy,' with the school offering an education which could lead to university and the professions.[24]

However, all the early public high schools in New South Wales charged tuition fees. This reinforced their relationship to the middle class but it also proved a disadvantage in some local educational markets. Only the two high schools in Sydney, and two in the regional center of Maitland north of Sydney, where there was no local corporate school, survived into the twentieth century.[25]

Unlike the United States, the Australian public high schools did not therefore develop out of a 'common school' tradition. Rather, these new high schools were highly selective, introducing a form of meritocracy into secondary education. Students qualified for them by a process of competitive examination. They also interacted in a variety of ways with the existing corporate and church schools even adopting many of the features of the reformed English grammar and public school traditions while challenging schools of the private sector in terms of academic performance.[26]

Of great significance in the development of colonial public high schools was the emerging relationship between secondary and higher education in Australia. The Australian colonies generally followed the model of the local public examinations for schools established by Oxford and Cambridge. Even before founding a local university in 1890, Tasmania had been the first of the Australian colonies to adopt a system of providing credentials for secondary schools that maintained connections between the secondary curriculum and universities.[27] Established in 1850 with state funds, Australia's first university, the University of Sydney was a secular institution, but with provision for denominational residential colleges. The University's constitution was developed along the lines of the new Queen's University in Belfast in an effort to satisfy the need for a colonial university but with some recognition of the claims of the various churches.

The creation of the University occurred at the same time that the colony of New South Wales achieved responsible and broadly representative parliamentary government. The University of Sydney was to provide a political and civic elite drawn from the emerging middle class in the colony. By the late 1860s, the University had created and was administering a system of 'junior' and 'senior' public examinations designed to influence and improve the standard of secondary education in the colony. By the 1880s, the curriculum of the University included new professional schools in such areas as medicine and law while women could also now matriculate and graduate. The University became the 'pinnacle' of the education system in New South Wales establishing and long maintaining a dominance over the curriculum of the secondary schools through its centrally administered examinations.[28] With the opening of the University to women, girls from Sydney Girls' High soon came to predominate among females sitting for the public (university) examinations and many of its alumni became early graduates of the University.[29]

Given this colonial context for the foundation of secondary schools, corporate and public, it is difficult to discern any early state interest in the idea of comprehensive secondary education. However, there was one nineteenth-century development that heralded the possibility at least of *universal* secondary schooling, if not *comprehensive*. Higher grade schools were established in England from the 1870s under local school boards created by the 1870 act for elementary education. Offering both scientific and liberal studies, the English higher grade schools often met local needs for secondary education in urban areas. By the 1890s they were even challenging many of the older endowed English grammar schools.[30] In mid-nineteenth-century Australia, the colonial state had sometimes allowed the teaching of post-elementary subjects, including the classics, within elementary schools. With the passage of the secular education acts such practices generally ended particularly in the colony of Victoria where a clear border was now established between public elementary schools and secondary education. The colonial government provided a very limited number of scholarships to the existing corporate schools.[31]

In New South Wales, however, 'superior public schools' continued as part of the public elementary school system and with the advantage of not having to charge high fees as did the new public high schools. Pupils were often allowed to stay on beyond the statutory leaving age, in both Sydney and regional rural areas. Significantly the superior publics were mainly coeducational. They offered an academic curriculum that enabled their pupils to matriculate to the University.[32] Emerging from the public elementary system, the superior public schools had the potential to become more comprehensive in curriculum offerings and inclusive in enrolments. In practice, some became elite academic institutions. This was partly because, as with the English higher grade schools, some of the superior public schools were the source of teachers and teacher training for the expanding public education system. The most celebrated of the superior publics was the Fort Street School in the heart of Sydney. Founded initially as a 'model school' and teacher training institution in 1848, by the late nineteenth century Fort Street had almost 2,000 pupils and had developed high prestige in the public system through its students' successes at the examinations administered by the University.[33] It provided another example of the meritocratic social basis and competitive academic tradition that commonly dominated the most prestigious institutions of the emergent public education systems of Australia.

Reform and the Possibility of Universal Secondary Schooling

The period of the early twentieth century marks a major transition in the concept of secondary education. Some have attributed this principally to the emergence of the universalization of the idea of adolescence. While the middle class may have been the first to have 'discovered' adolescence the concept was soon applied more generally as school progressively displaced work in the lives of all young people. The emergent modern secondary school with 'appropriate' age graded and gendered curricula became one of the major institutions structuring experiences of youth.[34]

These changes were associated with the rise and growing influence of the education profession and the emergence of educational expertise in the central education bureaucracies as well as in the teachers' colleges and related university departments that were established in the late nineteenth and early twentieth centuries. The decades from the 1890s were also those of the 'New Education' and its efforts to change schools to prepare future citizens and workers for a world being transformed by science and industry—and increasing economic competition between empires and nations. Of great significance also were the development of educational knowledge as 'scientific,' and the related claims to be able to measure human differences and specifically human intelligence.[35] The emerging concept of adolescence and the efforts to measure and then differentiate children and youth scientifically had major implications for the creation of new systems of Australian secondary schools that began in the decade preceding World War I.

The changes were most dramatically seen first in the United States. At the end of the nineteenth century one of the most pressing issues was the relationship of the high schools with colleges and universities. In 1893, the Committee of Ten of the National Education Association, under the chairmanship of Charles Eliot, President of Harvard, had tried to construct programs of study that would first provide parity of esteem to all academic subjects and then define a secondary school as being tied to college and university entrance through forms of accreditation in the recognition of high school diplomas.[36] Over the next two decades the expansion of high schools in the cities and elsewhere raised the issues of appropriate studies for *all* students and therefore 'preparation for life' as well as college entrance for the minority. The early attempts to introduce vocational and other nonacademic subjects into the secondary school curriculum have been seen as part of the 'educational efficiency' movement and other forms of scientific management in schools as they were impelled to respond to the economic and social changes marking the progressive era.

A culminating point was the national Commission on the Reorganisation of Secondary Education which issued its famous report in 1918 calling for the secondary school curriculum to be organized around seven cardinal principles that included: the promotion of health, command of fundamental processes, worthy home membership, vocation, citizenship, worthy use of leisure and ethical character.[37] A recent interpretation maintains that the 'cardinal principles' of this report were not necessarily designed for national efficiency and social control as suggested by revisionist historians of the 1960s and 1970s. Rather, this internationally significant report was both democratic in recommending a local 'comprehensive' school for all, and progressive, but not necessarily anti-intellectual, in proposing curricula adapted to individual student needs. With its advocacy of the comprehensive high school, named as such, as the best way to allow pupil choice of subjects while ensuring a common school experience for all, the 'Cardinal Principles' report can be seen as the progressive manifesto and foundation of the comprehensive ideal in the United States.[38] Eventually, its influence would spread well beyond North America.

Over the next three decades, the public comprehensive high school increasingly became the most common form of secondary school in America even though regional differences persisted. Some of the older urban public high schools such as Central High School, Philadelphia, maintained an emphasis on academic credentials and selective entrance. In a large metropolis such as Chicago, the urban comprehensive high schools began to fulfill their 'progressive' mission, not always completely successfully, of absorbing into the Republic's 'melting pot' the sons and daughters of the immigrants who had arrived from Europe in the early twentieth century.[39] In rural and small town America, local comprehensive schools evolved from more exclusive institutions or were newly established. In line with the aims of the Cardinal Principles report, more subjects were introduced into the school curriculum. For schools large enough to offer curriculum choice, 'tracking' or ability grouping became a major feature of organization, generally justified from the new science of intelligence testing, and assuring middle-class parents that there would be continuing opportunities for their children to follow paths leading to college entrance. The Depression of the 1930s and the erosion of jobs for youth led to greater student retention and more comprehensive curriculum offerings. By the end of World War II, a high school education had become the norm for most young Americans who remained in school until at least age fifteen. They attracted the interest of social scientists in the new styles of youth culture within and outside school.[40] Recent critics of the American public comprehensive high school thus often point to the 1930s and 1940s as the period of growth of a supposed 'custodial' or 'warehousing' function for the American comprehensive school as it attempted to cater to all students and a variety of curriculum offerings.[41]

These developments in the United States have been elaborated in some detail because eventually they would become highly significant for mid- and late-twentieth-century high school development in Australia. Outside America the influence of national and educational efficiency movements led initially not to public comprehensive high schools but to a highly differentiated system of state post-primary and secondary schools. The social and educational deficiencies of British and Australian recruits for the Boer War and the threat from Germany in the lead up to World War I drove many of the changes in British Empire education in the Edwardian era. There were also the ideas of the New Liberalism and Fabian socialism and those influenced by their concerns for administrative reform at all levels of government.[42]

There is a general view that the changes in English education in the early twentieth century interrupted progress toward common secondary schooling in a number of local areas. From reasonably undifferentiated local systems embracing a number of possibilities there developed a national system that was highly differentiated.[43] A 'grammar school' tradition closely associated with the exclusive 'public' schools was created. Moreover, with the end to the former pupil teacher system the new secondary schools provided an academic education to future teachers who would now go on to training colleges. While some working-class children were able to access such schools, and even become teachers, it was the urban middle class who principally benefited.[44] Only slowly did the idea of the secondary comprehensive school begin to be glimpsed at a national level in England. One start in the early 1920s occurred when the Labor Party, under the guiding hand of R. H. Tawney, was propounding the idea of 'Secondary Education for All' proposing primary and secondary education as successive rather than separate stages of schooling.

Such a view helped to begin the debate over whether secondary education for all could mean a local comprehensive school or different schools according to student 'abilities,' now increasingly defined in terms of the results of intelligence testing.[45] The importance of measuring ability certainly influenced the Hadow Report (1926). Titled *The Education of the Adolescent*, the report sought to create debate over defining different forms of post-primary education while leaving the existing secondary schools untouched. Change could come through administrative reorganization and developments in the higher elementary schools: a pattern followed in government proposals for educational reform in the interwar period.[46]

As in England, the reorganization of state secondary education in early twentieth-century Australia can be related to issues of social class, gender and age relations as well as state formation and school culture.[47] As part of the British Empire, Australia was also drawn into the discussion about national and imperial efficiency and the implications this held for educational change. There was certainly a demand to extend public education for all beyond the elementary stage.[48] Although Australia became a federation in 1901, responsibility for education remained with each of the six states. With the creation of Directors of Education in all the Australian states, power to influence change was more concentrated than ever in the hands of centralized state bureaucracies.

These developments were closely associated with increasing state intervention in education as much as in other areas of social and economic policy. Historians have long recognized a standard list of Australian reform achievements from the 1890s and early national period that usually include industrial conciliation and arbitration, women's suffrage, old age pensions, and the basic wage for all workers. During these years, Australia became recognized as a 'social laboratory' offering the world new experiments in social and economic reform through state intervention.[49] The newly appointed Directors of Education such as Frank Tate in Victoria, Alfred Williams in South Australia, and Peter Board in New South Wales held uncomplicated visions of the potential efficacy of the state to produce educational reform and social improvement.[50]

In the area of education reform there was an unusual dependence in Australia on ideas drawn from overseas. This marks it out as qualitatively different from much of the other turn-of-the-century reform effort. The achievement of nearly secular, nearly compulsory, and nearly free public schooling had been a homegrown development of the late nineteenth century in most of the Australian colonies. Many now believed that further educational progress could only come by engaging with the debate emerging internationally around the New Education. Under the general umbrella of the international progressive education movement a specific idea of universal secondary education, and eventually the comprehensive high school began to emerge within Australia.

Some of the ideas for change emerged from higher education. By the late nineteenth century, a new generation of professors had been appointed at the University of Sydney. Often influenced by the New Liberalism in Britain some were seeking to frame discussions about future social and educational policies in New South Wales. One was Francis Anderson, Professor of Logic and Mental Philosophy. Educated in Scotland and a philosophic idealist, Anderson was actively engaged in a number of areas of social reform in the 1890s including the women's movement. He was also passionate about the importance of education developing the whole personality of the individual student. Invited to address a mass meeting of the local public teachers' association in 1901, he used the occasion to launch a severe critique of the existing public school system.[51]

The shock, even brutality, of Anderson's attack on the public education system of New South Wales remains fresh today, well over a century later. His main argument was against the rigidities of a state education department that conceived the process of education as systems and mechanisms. Neither the human spirit nor true learning were served by a system where a hundred children would learn their geography like parrots: "New Guinea—North of Australia—birds of Paradise—gold."[52] Anderson railed against the enslavement of teachers to pedantry, inspection, examination, and apprenticeship modes of training.[53] Much of the speech addressed the problems of the public elementary schools. Anderson's major comment on secondary schooling simply exposed the idiocy of charging high fees for public high schools when superior public schools such as Fort Street offered much the same curriculum for practically nothing. Nevertheless, as part of the same comment he cynically asked: "Surely it is not the intention of the Department to establish a *social* distinction between the different classes of schools."[54]

We can identify from the issues that Anderson raised those that may have contributed to the establishment of the Australian comprehensive secondary high school a half century later. First, the argument was made that different kinds of secondary schools might deliberately encourage social privilege. Second, he suggested that coeducational schooling might be desirable, even encouraging "healthy human companionship."[55] Third, he argued that the New Education curriculum, through such means as object lessons, might profitably be extended to all students. Though directed toward elementary school reform, it potentially set curriculum reform in the direction of greater accessibility and general utility.[56] Fourth, Anderson maintained that the purpose of education was greater than producing industrial strength. The purpose was also to produce "good men and women and the good citizen."[57] The last of these, the citizen-producing aim remained a constant through the main waves of reform in twentieth-century Australia and eventually became a major justification for the common, comprehensive secondary school.

There were limits to Anderson's vision however. At times, some of his arguments may be read in opposition to such a common school. As a eugenicist of sorts, he certainly demanded more specialist schools for deficient and backward children.[58] He made a strong case for technical schools; there is no reason to disbelieve that on the whole his vision of a reformed secondary system would be differentiated to a high degree.[59] His idea of examination reform was that examinations should be centralized, made more powerful, not less. The benefit would be to free inspectors, that they might become guides and friends to teachers, not their punitive assessors.[60]

Within a year or two, in response to the furor surrounding Anderson's intervention, the New South Wales government had established a Royal Commission to investigate matters concerning public education. George Knibbs, later official statistician for the new Commonwealth of Australia, and John Turner, Principal of Fort Street School, were appointed Commissioners. They traveled extensively through Europe and North America seeking enlightenment on the matter of educational reform. The language of the various Knibbs–Turner report sections was almost as blunt as that of Anderson. Education in New South Wales was in a very bad way. The terms of reference had included not only technical and elementary education, but secondary as well. As was the case for Anderson we can assess Knibbs and Turner's report on secondary education for the ideas that might eventually make it possible to imagine the comprehensive high school a half century later.

Knibbs and Turner demanded that secondary education be incorporated as a further and necessary *stage* within public education; the state could not continue to neglect it. Secondary education was becoming primarily a state, not a private or church responsibility.[61] They argued that England (but not Scotland) was mainly the wrong place to look for inspiration in the building of new institutions; England's present weaknesses were similar to those of New South Wales.[62] Here also was a direct criticism of 'vested interest' in education. Only public secondary schools could avoid perpetuating the circumstances producing inferior systems of education and their dangerous national consequences.[63] This line of thinking was crucial for the eventual commitment by the state to the comprehensive public high school.

The United States was admiringly considered; its schools seemed marked by an absence of class prejudice, a resolution of the 'religious difficulty' and forms of educational practice that were altogether more humane. Knibbs and Turner bravely turned their backs on the tradition that made classics the core of the secondary curriculum. Neither Latin nor Greek should be a compulsory subject, and surely modern languages and science had justified their place.[64] This also was a crucial step toward imagining a more useful and accessible secondary curriculum, though it hardly overturned its competitive and academic character. They also argued for the expansion, though not the universalization of secondary education.[65]

As was the case for Anderson's speech, there was plenty of argument and absences of argument that would send New South Wales down different paths than those leading to comprehensive secondary schooling. Knibbs and Turner provide an Australian equivalent to Eliot's *Report of the Committee of Ten*, although unlike the United States, Knibbs and Turner had not only to imagine the proper work and organization of public high schools, but also their very establishment.[66] Knibbs and Turner drew back from coeducation.[67] Their main effort was to provide high schools that recognized talent, that rewarded the claims of merit built on sustained effort. What was required was "an aristocracy of intellect and character," not "the maintenance of an exclusive caste founded upon birth or wealth."[68] Knibbs and Turner provided a manifesto for selective academic high schools, the sort that would benefit the new middle class most of all. Nevertheless, the secondary school that recognized the merit of its students before their birth or wealth was still a step toward common secondary schooling. On the other hand, there was no imagining by Knibbs and Turner of the secondary school catering in one way or another to the newly discovered 'adolescent' with social needs of schooling beyond the provision of an academic curriculum. The report of Knibbs and Turner only predated that of Williams in South Australia by three years. Unlike Knibbs and Turner, Williams had absorbed the message of Stanley Hall's great work on adolescence, which formed part of his argument for a public system of free high schools in that Australian state.[69] There was no criticism of the role that University-controlled public examinations might play. Rather, there was an enthusiastic acceptance of the University's potential contribution to teacher training in the building of a public high school system.[70]

The progressive impulse in early twentieth-century New South Wales was thus mainly about the building of new institutions and pathways, indeed ladders of opportunity. Progressivism in this phase of Australian secondary reform apparently had little to say about pedagogic matters, though more about issues of curriculum content or 'syllabuses.' As Director of Education in New South Wales from 1905 to 1922 Peter Board was not only a co-architect of 'the renaissance' in secondary education with Knibbs and Turner. (The reports and recommendations he produced from his European and American travels were less voluminous, and more widely read.) He was also the great builder, having the Department of Education and its resources at his disposal, and the confidence of the ministers of state responsible for education. Board emphasized the arguments about the relationship of secondary education to national prosperity and the making of good citizens.[71] He closed the superior public schools as competitors to the high schools, reopening some of them as single sex high schools. For the mass of pupils he established boys' junior technical, girls' domestic science, or commercial schools and evening continuation schools for youth who had already entered the workforce. Rather than being conceived as full secondary schools many of these institutions were seen as 'post-primary.' In contrast, the high schools would be academic; they would provide no resting place for "the lazy boy."[72] New South Wales high schools should be recognized as had those in the United States, as essential places of training for the boy who wished to 'get on,' to build a career.[73] Though girls would fully participate in the new high schools, they seldom appeared as 'representative students' in the official discourses of the time.

At the same time, there are moments when Board peers beyond the building of a meritocracy. He imagines the effect of secondary schooling on the lives of many city youth:

> It is as a city problem that the subject of the training for industrial efficiency of the youths of the city who now drift aimlessly and wastefully in what should be the most educative period of their lives, has to be considered in its bearing upon the welfare of the State as a whole.[74]

At another point, Board even argues against the separation of students oriented toward technical secondary education from those in the general (academic) course. The "association of students of differing tastes and ambitions" can be conceived as a good thing.[75] Might this be considered a faint precursor of the later call to the comprehensive high school, to provide a 'little society' in which all the classes might mix in order to know one another and become a united citizenry? It was at least a vision of the multilateral school where different courses might coexist under the same school roof. Board's other efforts aimed to increase by a year the time spent in the high school, and to replace the University's public examinations with the new student-oriented Intermediate and Leaving examinations and certificates. While the University still dominated the examination boards such certificates were expected to have more general utility than university matriculation alone, and were thus important steps in the imagining of the secondary school as a suitable place for many more youth than previously thought possible.

The focus on centralized public examinations would have major consequences. By making the reform of secondary school examinations and credentialing a principal object of his attention, Board began a long twentieth-century tradition in New South Wales of substituting the reform of assessment and credentialing practices in particular for educational reform in general, leaving meritocratic assumptions at the heart of any reform process.

By 1914, Francis Anderson recognized the previous decade and a half as characterized by "reform and reconstruction."[76] He summarized the reasons for rejecting the English mix of secondary schools as a model, with their encouragement of class distinction, but he consolidated the demand for diverse secondary schools as a perfectly sensible Australian response to the problem of building a system of secondary education:

> The ideal of special training for special functions is not inconsistent with a unitary organic scheme of national education in which the democratic features of freedom of access to the highest positions, and freedom of promotion by merit and proved capacity, will be preserved and strengthened.[77]

Nevertheless, the problem of early school leaving had not been solved. Children still waited to be protected "from the results of their own ignorance and from the selfishness of parents and employers."[78] There was no form of secondary school that could deal with this yet, nor the 'weedy' youths of the metropolis for whom a solid period in the school cadets might provide both moral and physical good effects.[79]

Imagining a Comprehensive Secondary School

Alexander Mackie, the Scottish-born Professor of Education at the University, and the Principal of the Teachers College, summarized much of the progress in an essay published in 1920. But Mackie also introduced a new note; here was a call to consider the works of John Dewey, and the fitting of the child for "complete citizenship," though the "aptitude" of the child is also to be considered.[80] Mackie also used another term that had not been used in the earlier reform discourse. The "drop out" pupil was becoming a real problem, as was the lack of connection between schools and their local communities.[81] Could a form of secondary school be imagined that reduced the likelihood of "drop out," which really connected with the local community, and which really responded to the diverse 'aptitudes' of its students? 'Not yet!' is the necessary answer. Writing their history of the post-1901 period in 1924, S. H. Smith, the newly appointed Director of Education in New South Wales, and G. T. Spaull, a teacher, identified 1911 as the great year dividing the old from the new regime in secondary education. The problems of the retreat from reform in the post–World War I period were typified by the reactionary introduction of fees for high school attendance in 1923.[82]

A low level of steady reform proceeded during the 1920s. Beginnings were made to develop intelligence testing as useful for school organization. Schools were also used for medical inspections. Vocational guidance began its history in Australian public schools. New schools for mainly working-class children commenced. These central, junior technical, domestic science, and intermediate and district schools may be thought of as secondary, although in more than one place in Australia they were referred to as super-primary, upward extensions of elementary education and its spirit.[83]

Such reforms fall mainly into the realm, to use David Tyack's phrase, of the 'administrative progressives.'[84] These reforms were led by the 'sorters and selectors' whose primary vision was for a socially, economically, and nationally efficient population.[85] Even Frank Tate, the former Director of Education in Victoria and a major architect of early twentieth-century reform, agreed with the view that the educational reform process had stalled. A more liberal view of the function of the school in a democratic society was required: "for a while, in the years before the Great War, we had done reasonably well in developing our school system, we had not since then realized sufficiently how remarkable and how far-reaching were educational developments elsewhere."[86]

There is rather little that might be taken from the 1920s as a precursor for the post–World War II emergence of the comprehensive high school—with two major exceptions. The first was the idea that working-class youth were in the main entitled to some form of secondary education. The second was not really an idea, but the actual beginnings of an adaptable institution. That institution was the developing coeducational rural high school. No particular reform program informed the development of some rural high schools from the 1920s as community schools.[87] They were less academically selective than metropolitan schools. They were also coeducational rather than single sex as in the city high schools and other forms of urban post-primary schools. They tried to be multilateral in their approach, but low numbers ensured that students who would never have been taught together in the large city high schools came together in the rural. Such schools were looked to as proof in the 1950s and 1960s that an Australian version of a 'comprehensive' high school was possible.

These developments were not unnoticed at the time, but they made little impact on dominant theories in Australia about what the good secondary school should look like. Few young people in the Australia of the 1920s and 1930s, including the rural areas, saw their way into a secondary school of any kind. Very few of the rural schools went through, or took many students through to senior high school. Overwhelmingly, in the 1920s and 1930s, and through to the 1940s and 1950s, secondary schooling was dominated by the impulse to select and differentiate.

In New South Wales, there was one government inquiry (1934) that is occasionally held to be the great precursor of the scheme for comprehensive schools that would emerge in the 1950s. Chaired by R. S. Wallace, the Vice-Chancellor of the University of Sydney, the inquiry promised a great deal. Its seven subcommittees canvassed a range of important issues.[88] But the report was a disappointment; the despair associated with the stringencies of the Great Depression inhabits the low expectations associated with its recommendations. There is no particular educational vision associated with its recommendations. The report is a prime example of when having nothing to say on substantial educational reform, the focus becomes restricted to tinkering with the public examination system. The Committee recommended that a supervisory council of secondary education be established in New South Wales. It would be representative of the 'stake holders,' including the Education Department, University, government and non-government schools.[89] It would "provide a continuous clearing-house for the consideration of educational problems and for the observation and discussion of all educational movements in other States and abroad." It aimed to liberate secondary schools from the domination of University matriculation requirements, enabling more general secondary courses of study to be introduced. In the final stage of secondary studies more specialization might occur.[90]

In the year following the Wallace report, Peter Board, the former Director of Education, reflected with pride on the efficient and differentiated secondary school system of which he had been chief architect. He listed the nine different kinds of public secondary or post-elementary school New South Wales had produced. They were formally differentiated according to the gender of their students, their region of residence, the predicted vocational paths of its students, the measured intelligence, capabilities, and aptitudes of its students—and these were just the formal means of differentiation.[91] The system remained much as he had created it two decades earlier.

As in the early twentieth century, many of the ideas for reform in the decade prior to World War II, originated outside Australia. In 1930, the Australian Council for Educational Research (ACER) was established with the aid of a

Carnegie Corporation grant. The founding executive officer was K. S. (Kenneth) Cunningham. He had studied under John Dewey and Edward Thorndike at Teachers College, Columbia, in the 1920s.[92] By the end of the 1930s ACER publications advocating educational reconstruction had begun to flow. Cunningham and another employee of the ACER, William Radford, helped sustain interest into the war years and beyond. One of Radford's publications on the role of schooling in rural communities finally took on one of the key tenets in Australian school organizational thinking. It was not a good idea to build separate secondary schools, at least in rural towns, one technical, and the other "high schools."[93] By 1940, using somewhat primitive quantitative research techniques, another author, J. A. La Nauze, had even 'proven' the relationship between differentiated schooling, public and private, and unequal access to the universities and the professions.[94]

As ACER Director, Cunningham was the major force in organizing the New Education Fellowship (NEF) conference in 1937. This was the most significant group of international educational expertise that had ever gathered in Australia. Convening in the various capital cities of the Australian states from August 1937, the NEF conference involved prominent speakers from Europe, Britain, and the United States, most of whom were committed to the principles of progressive education.[95] The proceedings of the NEF conference enable us to identify the ideas which helped clear the way for the comprehensive secondary school (not all of them necessarily compatible):

1. The peril of the coming war and the various crises of the industrial nations required better forms of schooling that were more committed to democracy, and very much committed to producing practical training in good citizenship.[96]
2. The school must do more than transmit the knowledge and culture of the past. It had the duty of preparing for a new, better, reconstructed world. Schooling for a new social and world order was required.[97]
3. Human wastage could no longer be tolerated; schooling needed to apply itself to the development of all, not the few.[98]
4. The school must become a genuine community school, 'owned' by the people whom it served, and anchored in a particular locale.[99]
5. Education could no longer be tied to the aims of syllabuses and examinations. They were a deadening hand on the new tasks of education.[100]
6. Nor could education afford to be tied to the narrow demands of the universities. Too few students went on to study at universities. The needs of all children had to be recognized and schools must adapt accordingly.[101]

7. The secondary curriculum needed expansion into the arts and the cultivation of the senses and emotions. A new kind of curriculum as well as school was required. The 'whole child' should be the subject of attention. The education of the 'adolescent' required such an approach.[102]
8. Education was required for the general purpose of learning to "live well." In the light of technological and industrial progress, the demand for education for leisure as well as work was already immanent.[103]
9. The 'normal' child should become the object of attention. An appropriate curriculum for such a child should include attention to health, the arts, general literacy in the vernacular, numeracy, and science, with attention to citizenship and religious, spiritual, and moral education as well.[104]
10. The study of society, social studies, must become part of the school curriculum.[105]
11. The curriculum and schools needed to be responsive to new knowledge about human development. The slow and quick learner could be equally accommodated with new curriculum approaches such as the Dalton plan. The old 'subjects' needed to be integrated into new forms responsive to the interests and needs of the young.[106]
12. The education of the 'adolescent' required attention to health and emotions as well as intelligence.[107]
13. Education needed to become anti-competitive. No child should 'fail' in a school. Schools should become cognizant of the child's emotional development. There was a new role for the child psychologist in the school.[108]

The report of the NEF proceedings of 1937 concluded with a brief and pointed criticism of contemporary approaches to schooling in Australia. Isaac Kandel, Professor of Education, Teachers College, Columbia University, shared the responsibility for the critical summary. He underlined the need for 'all-round' education, the criticism of the role of the examination in Australia, the domination of centralized public school bureaucracies and university matriculation requirements. He asked the question: "Do the schools, especially the secondary schools, introduce the pupils to things that they will love and admire throughout their lives, or are they dominated by traditions which no longer have psychological justification and by the demands of the universities . . ."[109] A new kind of secondary schooling was clearly required for Australia, and the grammar school, or selective academic tradition was clearly not the answer.

This summary of ideas that could have led to the idea of the comprehensive high school could also have led to other kinds of schools. There were many problems with the NEF analysis of what needed to be done in school reform. There was no attempt to deal with the issues of public and private schooling. There was a natural assumption that educators would accept changes to practice on the basis of their disinterested professionalism. There was no attempt to provide a class analysis of schooling diversity, simply a naïve assumption that progressive educational reform might ensure communal solidarity around notions of good citizenship and democracy. There was little attention to the different worlds of girls and boys, or dominant and minority ethnic groups. In one way or another these were issues that would not disappear, even when the comprehensive secondary school with its idealist reform program came to be established.

Some of the authors of papers were also clearly out of tune with Australian traditions in their approach to reform. The distrust of the state and its centralized approaches was an important issue for many of the progressive visitors.[110] For most Australian reformers there was no question that the state itself and its centralized educational bureaucracies would not be the key agent in producing reform. The state was still reform's customary agent in the Australian tradition. In terms of the comprehensive school ideal, the general thrust of the Conference, however, was to doubt some of the old rigidities in the selecting and differentiating of students. The central idea was toward communal, holistic, child-oriented, and citizen-forming education. And some of these ideas would be taken up in the discussion that occurred during World War II.

There is now a significant literature on the effect of the educational proposals of the interwar years and the subsequent debate over 'reconstruction' that occurred not only in Australia but also Britain and the United States during and after World War II. Debate continues on the significance of the 1944 Education Act for England and Wales and how far even the postwar Labour Government reinforced prewar ideas of 'tripartism' involving grammar schools for the academic elite, technical schools for future technicians and 'secondary moderns' for the majority of adolescents—rather than local comprehensive secondary schools for all.[111] In the Australian context, Bessant and Spaull have summarized much of the pressure toward universal, if not comprehensive secondary schooling.[112] There was the pressure arising from rapid industrialization, and the requirement for better-educated technicians and managers. There was the increasing advocacy of 'secondary education for all.'

Wartime pamphlets produced by the Australian Council for Educational Research were bold: "A democratic society must in the future be dependent for its existence upon the effective presence of two things—equality of educational opportunity and the provision of practical lessons in co-operation."[113] The author of this tract was scathing toward the support given to private secondary schools. They affronted the obvious needs of nation-building, and the anticipated social reconstruction effort to follow the war: "far too many private schools . . . do not provide adequate education in any sense and exist precariously on a basis of snobbery . . . This kind of individualism must cease. All education is a matter of public concern."[114] In New South Wales, various individuals and organizations pressed for a more common form of secondary school. The Board of Secondary Studies, belatedly established in 1936, following the Wallace committee inquiry, argued in 1946 for a secondary school of two levels, the first four years providing a general education and only the final two, for university entrance.[115]

Much of the debate took place within an Australian national context. For a period it seemed that the wartime federal Labor Government may have been tempted to move toward a national policy on schools. Hopes for such an outcome soon faded in the immediate postwar years. Federal aid was extended to universities but denied to schools on constitutional grounds. Responsibility for public schools would remain with individual Australian state governments—which were decreasingly able to find the resources to meet enrolment demand in the early postwar years.[116]

Despite the fading hopes of the wartime years, a direct argument for the comprehensive high school, though still not named as such, was made by the ACER in 1953:

> At present Australia adheres somewhat uneasily to the traditional selective view of secondary education. It is advocated that entrance to secondary education be based on age only and not on educational achievement. For all children four-year courses should be provided in a single institution combining the resources at present found in high schools of the academic type and in junior technical schools. In country districts there would be some bias towards rural interests, but only from the point of view of linking school work with life.[117]

The connection had been made at last, between the citizen-forming aims of socially reconstructed schooling, with the invention of a new kind of secondary school.

The origins and development of the idea if not the substance of the public comprehensive secondary school often involved contradictions. In part this related to different views of the role of 'public education' itself as much as changing conceptions of the secondary school. As Robert Anderson has recently pointed out in respect to European secondary schools, in the wake of the French Revolution an idealized model did emerge: an elite public 'secular' institution, run by the state or local authorities, with few links to the developing systems of mass public elementary education. Ostensibly, the main aim of nineteenth-century secondary schools was to prepare students for higher education through a curriculum oriented to a school leaving examination. In practice, the secondary school in Europe and elsewhere continued to serve many purposes catering to different sectors of the middle class.[118] Conceived principally in terms of the needs of middle-class boys, it was not until the very late nineteenth and early twentieth century that secondary education was regarded as being appropriate for an entire age group. This new view of universal secondary education did not necessarily lead to the one school for all. Even in the North American context, a strong academic tradition in secondary education remained until well into the twentieth century despite the growing influence of the comprehensive high school ideal. As Lawrence Cremin and others have pointed out, by the 1950s, there was even a view that progressive education and the comprehensive high school ideal were undermining the important work of educating the academic elite in the United States.[119]

In Britain and its Empire of settlement, including Australia, the role of the state in secondary education initially reinforced differentiation in the provision of schools while emphasizing the creation of a meritocracy. Public secondary schools served to sustain and create a significant section of the Australian middle class. Except for a brief period in the early 1920s the new expanding high school system in New South Wales was free. As such it was popular with many of the urban middle class. Recent research has revealed that throughout Australia, the expansion of state secondary education in the early twentieth century was closely associated with the aspirations of the new middle class of professionals, small businessmen, and white-collar workers. Specifically, the children of the 'employed' middle class were generally those who remained in the new state high schools to complete the new credentials that had been established.[120]

What marked out New South Wales was the strength of the public sector in secondary education, particularly when compared with its main rival in population and wealth, the state of Victoria. There the older private and corporate schools remained predominant. In New South Wales, the public academic high schools were soon celebrated as creating new educational opportunities for those of talent while challenging the older corporate and church secondary schools. By the 1940s, more than half the future social and political elite of New South Wales had attended public high schools. Many of these successful high school graduates were concentrated in such areas as the universities and public service administration, a reflection perhaps of the creation of a new civic-minded elite employed within the public sector.[121]

Specific national and local contexts were thus highly significant in the creation of the public secondary school systems. Yet, the movement for change toward the public comprehensive high school also owed much to the influence of the 'educational progressives' whom public education systems had fostered through state bureaucracies and the academic intelligentsia found in universities, teacher colleges, and the research institutes of the early to mid-twentieth century. Increasingly, many looked to the idea of the comprehensive school as providing an all-purpose institution that could reconcile older meritocratic, nation-building and newer social reconstruction, and equality of opportunity aspirations in education.

Chapter 2

Postwar Planning

In 1959, James B. Conant, a former President of Harvard, published *The American High School Today*. Commissioned by the Carnegie Corporation, this was designed as a report directed principally to school board members and educational administrators on the state of the American comprehensive high school. In the context of the Cold War in the 1950s and the challenge of the USSR, demonstrated with the launch of Sputnik in 1957, it was the aim of Conant to defend 'Democracy's High School' but in ways that would respond to those critics who were suggesting that the comprehensive high school under the influence of educational progressives over the twentieth century had become too concerned with the social adjustment of students and less focused on matters of the mind and the intellect.[1]

Conant defined the 'three main objectives' of a comprehensive high school as being: "*first*, to provide a general education for all the future citizens; *second*, to provide good elective programs for those who wish to use their acquired skills immediately on graduation; *third*, to provide satisfactory programs for those whose vocations will depend on their subsequent education in a college or university."[2] Seeing the comprehensive high school as *the* "American development" of the twentieth century, providing opportunities and catering to the needs of all in a local community, he posed the question as to whether it was still possible to provide an "adequate education" for the minority of students who wished to pursue further education in college and university.[3]

Recognizing the regional differences in secondary schools that still existed in the United States, Conant had surveyed eighteen states. He was particularly concerned to see that adequate provision was made for those of "academic talent" wishing to proceed to higher education. Because he recognized a need to expand elective options that included the study of more academic subjects, Conant proposed an end to "small" high schools still found in much of regional America. This was principally to allow for the concentration of the academically talented so that there could be adequate provision in science, mathematics, and languages.[4] At the same time, Conant favored individual student choice rather than 'tracking' in defined courses such as "college preparatory," "vocational," and "commercial." With appropriate counseling he believed that it would be possible to guide all students into appropriate studies, including the academic. The core program of studies should include four years of English, three or four years of history, and a senior course in American problems or American government and at least a year of science and mathematics. All students would be urged to include art and music among their elective choices. Significantly, in both the core curriculum and the electives, Conant argued for ability grouping.[5]

By the end of the 1950s, what Conant had identified as America's original early twentieth-century solution to the provision of universal secondary schooling seemed almost to have been achieved. The postwar generation of young Americans was overwhelmingly a generation within the American comprehensive high school. As Conant recognized, the proportion of seventeen-year-old Americans in high school had more than doubled from 35 percent in 1910 to more than 70 percent in 1959. By the 1960s, those who left before high school graduation were being defined as 'dropouts'; an apparent sign of social and institutional failure.[6] Despite the initial concern of Conant for those of academic talent, it was obvious even in the 1950s that there was an emerging racial divide in educational provision. While the early twentieth-century city high schools had absorbed and assimilated the European migrant young it was now apparent that many of the postwar 'dropouts' were increasingly the sons and daughters of those black Americans who had migrated to Northern industrial cities for work. This movement was accompanied by the early signs of 'white flight' to the suburbs. Between 1940 and 1960 the population in the suburbs of American cities had grown by 27 million leading to a major decline in the share of the metropolitan populations living in the central cities.[7]

Conant himself admitted that less than half the high schools in the United States in the 1950s fitted his proposed model of providing opportunities for all in a large school drawing upon different social and racial groups. He thus devoted specific attention to the small high school, the large city high school, and the suburban high school, all of which had a "limited degree of comprehensiveness."[8] In a further report published in 1961, Conant contrasted the high school in the suburbs where 80 percent of students graduated to college with the schools in the city slums where more than half the students dropped out in grades 9, 10, and 11. He was increasingly concerned with the emerging problems of the black inner-city unemployed youth. While still committed to the importance of early guidance and maintaining academic programs for those of talent, he now called for more resources to improve inner-city schools.[9] Six years later in 1967, Conant published his second report on the comprehensive high school. Claiming that many of his original recommendations had been achieved, including more choice of academic subjects, he now called for extended educational opportunity to be achieved through more resources and such measures as vocational programs in schools.[10]

Conant's reports and his definition of the function of the comprehensive high school had moved discussion well beyond the 'cardinal principles' policy of 1918 and its view of secondary schooling being "essential to all youth." His vision was democratic but retained a meritocratic element, drawing as he did on contemporary understandings of ability and intelligence deriving from the intelligence-testing movement of the early to mid-twentieth century. In place of the ideal of the comprehensive high school as a 'democratic community' serving small town America he had attempted to come to terms with the industrial and social changes of postwar America, and its new place in world affairs.[11] More generally his reports reflected the growing concern in the years following World War II to find ways of reconciling provision for all within a comprehensive school while not neglecting the academic elite.

In 1959, the same year that the first Conant Report was published, in England the Central Advisory Council for Education, under the chairmanship of Sir Geoffrey Crowther, Deputy Chair of The Economist Newspaper Ltd, released its report titled *15 to 18*. This was a review of the provision that should be made for those students leaving school at age fifteen. The Council surveyed the changing nature of secondary education in England. It noted the future impact that demographic change would bring. The low birthrates of the 1930s and wartime years had been followed by rising rates in the postwar years. It was estimated that from 1959 to 1965 the size of the age-cohort 15 to 18 would grow by a third. The report noted that of those in full-time education in this age range there was a marked social class bias. Working-class children left school much earlier than their middle-class peers. This, the Council suggested, was also an indication that many young people of high ability were not receiving an education of which they were capable. At the same time, the Council recognized growing parental expectations for their children across the social classes, with many students being the first generation from their families to attend a grammar school.[12]

Secondary education in England during the 1950s became more complex. The 'Eleven Plus' examination sorted primary students into secondary schools. The Crowther Committee identified six forms of these. About 20 percent of students attended the grammar schools; about 7 percent were in secondary technical, comprehensive, and bilateral and multilateral schools and a similar percentage remained in 'all-age' schools. The vast majority of students, approximately two-thirds of the age-cohort eleven to fourteen, were in secondary modern schools. Secondary education in England had become principally bipartite, divided between the academic elite who had been selected to attend the grammar schools and the mass of students who were sent to the secondary moderns. Some of these were simply converted higher elementary schools. While the grammar schools were mainly single sex, the secondary modern schools were increasingly coeducational as were the few newly established comprehensive and bilateral schools offering academic and other studies.[13] At the same time, with rising standards of living, the growth in demand for educational qualifications and the impact of technology requiring more adaptable skills, many students in the secondary modern and comprehensive schools were remaining longer at school and even completing the General Certificate of Education previously only open to those in the grammar schools.[14]

The Crowther Report was released in a period of growing disquiet over the policy of early selection for secondary education. The Marxist academic Brian Simon had already published in 1953 a critical account of the dominance of the intelligence-testing movement. He highlighted the later success of students who had not passed the Eleven Plus examination, arguing that mental testing had failed.[15] In the second volume of its Report, the Crowther Committee included a detailed survey of the social distribution of educational opportunity. Based principally on the testing of national service recruits, this demonstrated that educational opportunities were still skewed toward the middle class.[16] It seemed that there was a clear social bias in the selection process involved in the Eleven Plus examination that favored middle-class children. At the same time, there were growing complaints from many middle-class parents whose children had 'failed' the Eleven Plus.[17]

Concerned at 'educational wastage,' even in the senior forms of grammar schools, one of the recommendations of the Crowther Committee was to establish County Colleges for the 15- to 18-year-old population so providing more vocational options.[18] Such a proposal contributed to the continuing debate over the development of comprehensive education. There was increasing argument that not only were comprehensive schools a more democratic solution to the provision of universal secondary schooling but that comprehensive school students could achieve academic results equivalent to those in the grammar schools. A number of Local Education Authorities, including the London County Council, had moved cautiously in the postwar period to introduce plans for comprehensive schools.[19] By the mid-1950s, the County of Leicestershire, partly under the influence of the academic Robin Pedley, one of the major proponents of the comprehensive school, was establishing a two-tiered system of comprehensive education. The plan involved transforming some of the County secondary modern schools to comprehensive schools taking in children at age eleven and then turning existing grammar schools into upper schools taking students at age fourteen.[20]

Brian Simon has identified the late 1950s as the period prior to the comprehensive school "break out" which would soon follow. A Conservative government had come to power in 1951 determined on 'educational cuts' to support the British commitment to the Korean War. There was also a strong campaign in the mid-1950s to defend the grammar school ideal as many Local Education Authorities began to consider plans to go comprehensive. By the end of the decade, there was a growing recognition that extended education was necessary if Britain was to achieve the necessary scientific and technological revolution associated with modernization and in accommodating the loss of Empire.[21] In this context, the Crowther Committee had identified a number of the demographic, social, and economic conditions that had given rise to this emerging movement for comprehensive schools. The aspirations of families for their children were matched by what was seen as the waste of educational talent. As the Committee suggested, there was an increasing need to see education as both a social service in the emergent welfare state and a form of national investment.[22]

Proposing Comprehensive Schools in Australia

The social and economic changes in the industrial democracies of the United States and the United Kingdom had echoes in Australia. In the postwar years Australia became a modern industrial state building up secondary industries under policies of protection and with an expanded program of migration that brought in many skilled and unskilled workers from Britain and Europe. By 1960, Australia was turning from being a population of predominantly British and Irish origin and culture to becoming an increasingly multiethnic society. With most immigrants being concentrated in the cities, Australia was undergoing a version of the transformation that had marked the United States in the late nineteenth to early twentieth century when so many migrants had arrived from Europe.[23]

Population growth from both new arrivals and the increasing birthrate stimulated economic growth and prosperity. Essentially an urban society since the late-nineteenth-century Australia became increasingly so. By the early 1970s, 86 percent of Australians lived in towns or cities.[24] Young middle and working-class Australians increasingly grew up in the expanding suburbs of Australian cities. They also attended school in growing numbers. By the late 1950s, only one-third of students left school by age fifteen, about half the proportion of two decades earlier. There was an increasing demand for school qualifications as postwar prosperity prompted the growth of middle-class and white-collar occupations. The number of the various secondary schools in New South Wales doubled during the 1950s with students increasingly staying on to complete their studies. By the mid-1950s, almost one-sixth of students remained to undertake the Leaving Certificate at a variety of schools. Included among these schools were local public 'high' schools catering to all students in an area. The first two opened in the metropolitan areas of the regional cities of Newcastle and Wollongong in 1953. An important symbolic change was the nomenclature of 'high school' being applied universally to the new secondary schools. The earlier known junior technical and other post-primary schools became technical high schools and agricultural high schools, and domestic schools became home science high schools, all tending to follow the same core academic curriculum of the other existing high schools. Former intermediate high schools were usually upgraded into full high schools.[25]

As in England, there remained a distinct social class bias in the numbers of students remaining to complete secondary school in Australia. Those in the corporate, church, and private sector represented two-thirds of those still at school at age seventeen. Beyond school, only about 4 percent of the age group 17–22 was in University.[26] Even among this group there were high failure rates in the first year of university: a problem identified from the 1940s as a result of the younger age at which students were now entering university studies compared to earlier generations.[27]

Despite growing affluence for many in the postwar years, the question of 'educational wastage' was becoming as much an issue in Australia as in the United States and Britain. A study of the "holding power" of Sydney high schools conducted in the early 1950s suggested that many students were leaving school before completing their Leaving Certificate. Drawing on a work of Conant titled *Education and Liberty*, this study pointed out that in 1951 only 14 percent of seventeen-year-olds in New South Wales were still in school compared to more than 60 percent in America. While this proportion was almost double the figure in England, and was slightly more than that of those staying on in the Australian States of Victoria and South Australia; it was still less than in Australia's smaller neighbor New Zealand. A comparison between eight Sydney high schools suggested the possible influence of social class. North Sydney Boys' High School, mainly serving the middle-class northern suburbs of Sydney, had the highest retention at over 85 percent while some of the high schools in the West of the city, associated with lower middle and working-class suburbs, had only one-third of students completing secondary school. However, the study suggested that rather than simple economic factors leading to students leaving school early, the more important reasons were feelings of failure, a desire for personal and financial independence, and the belief that school was irrelevant.[28]

Faced by rising birth rates, and an ageing teaching force, all Australian state governments faced challenges to expand and maintain public education. By the mid-1950s, there were reports of a growing 'crisis' in Australian secondary schools as a result of increasing student numbers projected to expand by one-third within a decade. The crisis would involve teacher shortages as well as lack of schools and school buildings.[29] Demographic pressures alone would force changes in the pattern of secondary schooling. Rather suddenly, it now seemed much less feasible to hold to the principle of building multiple schools for different groups of students, particularly in those areas of rapid suburban expansion on the fringes of Australian cities. One large public secondary school to serve a new group of suburbs seemed the only sensible solution to the approaching secondary student population crisis. The word 'crisis' was justifiable. Not only would there be thousands of new students, but they were expected to stay at school longer, intensifying the pressure on inadequate or nonexistent facilities.

As the smallest state of the Australian federation, Tasmania had already begun in the 1930s to experiment with a series of multilateral 'Area Schools' in rural districts. Following a visit of the Tasmanian Director of Education to England, Scotland, and the United States, Tasmania moved to introduce comprehensive schools. First year high school classes organized on comprehensive lines were introduced into the area schools; by 1960 metropolitan schools in Tasmania had also become comprehensive.[30] In Western Australia, Thomas Logan Robertson, the Director General of Education from 1951 to 1966, was a strong supporter of comprehensive schools. An English immigrant, and a former scholarship holder he was a critic of the influences of caste and class. As a Carnegie Fellow he had spent time in England in the 1930s and was disturbed by the Spens Report that had rejected the comprehensive model in favor of more concentration on specialist technical schools.[31] In 1956, Robertson undertook a visit to the United States and Canada on a further Carnegie Fellowship, a trip that convinced him of the need for change. By the mid-1950s, Western Australia was moving toward introducing comprehensive schools in the metropolitan area of Perth as well as in the rural districts. The selective high school, Perth Modern, which had a long reputation for producing a meritocracy, also became a comprehensive school.[32]

The centralized and bureaucratic character of the Australian public school systems allowed for the development of universal plans for change in ways that were not possible in either the United States or the United Kingdom. In New South Wales, the move toward a system of comprehensive schools would be prompted by the release of a major report that provided a justification for a new pattern of organization.

The Wyndham Report

For much of the twentieth century in Australia, Labor Governments had been regarded as the major source of economic and social reform. In New South Wales, most of the early twentieth-century reforms in secondary education directed by Peter Board had been introduced under the Labor governments from 1910 to 1922. Over thirty years later, in 1953, the Minister of Education in a New South Wales Labor Government that had been in power since 1941, established a committee with the following terms of reference:

> (1) To survey and to report upon the provision of full-time day education for adolescents in New South Wales.
> (2) In particular, to examine the objectives, organization and content of the courses provided for adolescent pupils in the public schools of the State, regard being had to the requirements of a good general education and to the desirability of providing a variety of curriculum adequate to meet the varying abilities of the pupils concerned.[33]

This Australian 'committee of ten' was chaired by Harold Wyndham, Director of Education in New South Wales. Previous commentators have suggested that from the outset the Committee was essentially designed to legitimate a model of the comprehensive school that would be acceptable to Wyndham and the State's educational bureaucracy. While the Committee was nominally representative of interest groups outside the Department of Education, including industry and Catholic and other non-state schools, the major ideas in the Report came principally from Wyndham and his departmental colleagues on the Committee.[34]

The data-gathering process and the official launch of the Report in 1957 can also be seen in part as a public relations exercise. Over four years the Committee had held 92 meetings, 57 as public hearings, with a million words of evidence recorded and a further one-third in written submissions. The Report had been long awaited and the press and electronic media were there at the launch. While tabled as an official report in the New South Wales Parliament, it was also printed as an octavo size book available for purchase by the public. The Public Relations Officer of the Department of Education soon titled the Committee the 'Wyndham Committee.' Despite his later protestations, the Report itself was soon known after the chairman who was assumed to be its prime author.[35] The reforms that followed became known as the Wyndham scheme.

Appointed Director-General of Education in New South Wales in 1952, Wyndham was part of that generation of the Australian educational bureaucracy and intelligentsia that was associated with the overall progressive movement in educational and public policy during the mid-twentieth century. Of Methodist background, he was a graduate of Fort Street High School, Sydney Teachers College and the University of Sydney. He had obtained his doctorate in education from Stanford University in California in 1934 and was certainly exposed to contemporary school and educational policy in the United States. During the 1930s, he established a reputation in educational research working in the field of ability grouping. In 1935, he was appointed to inaugurate research and guidance services in the New South Wales Department of Education. Two years later he was appointed secretary to the sessions of the New Education Fellowship Conference held in Sydney (discussed in the previous chapter). During World War II he was assigned to the Commonwealth Department of Post-War Reconstruction, returning in the postwar period to the New South Wales Department of Education where he helped to oversee a limited decentralization of educational administration. When he was appointed Director-General of Education in New South Wales he was undoubtedly one of the most influential members of the educational intelligentsia in Australia.[36]

While he had made his research career in the area of measuring individual differences and educational grouping, by the 1940s Wyndham had become convinced of the futility of the attempt to find efficient ways of selecting primary school children for differentiated secondary school entry. This affected the Wyndham Report, as more generally did the discussion about the future of the education of the 'adolescent' that had taken place in Britain and North America over the first half of the twentieth century. By the 1950s, the ideas and influences leading to the comprehensive high school were becoming ever more complex and diverse. Some have suggested that the 1947 Fyfe Report in Scotland, which proposed reorganization of secondary education to achieve comprehensive secondary schools, while maintaining a central leaving certificate, was more influential in Australia than the 1944 Education Act in England and Wales.[37] Across the Tasman Sea, in New Zealand there was also the example of a Labour Government in 1945 introducing a common secondary curriculum following the wartime Thomas Report. Wyndham had visited Sweden as well as Scotland while compiling the final report of the Committee. He was impressed by what he saw as the 'democratic' nature of secondary education in Scotland but saw the proposed 1950 Education Act in Sweden as being too cautious and preserving too much of the old system of selective schools.[38]

The Report was reasonably brief. Among the appendices was a part review of secondary education in the United States. The opening chapter placed the Report clearly in the context of the development of secondary education in New South Wales, from the elite system of the nineteenth century to the moves toward universal secondary education in the twentieth century. Much was made of the reforms of Peter Board and his efforts to create differentiated forms of schooling. There was also a review of the proposals for change which emerged from the 1930s and specifically the recommendations of the Board of Secondary School Studies in 1946 calling for new principles of secondary education being adapted to the "needs and capacities" of adolescents and a curriculum "related closely to the interests and experiences of life." The Board had proposed that secondary schools be organized into two stages of general secondary education of four years and higher secondary education of two years: a proposal that would now influence the recommendations of the Wyndham Committee.[39]

The second chapter outlined the dilemmas associated with recent developments in New South Wales public secondary education. Selection beyond the primary schools depended not only on the wishes of parents but also on the results of scholastic exams and two intelligence tests conducted two years apart in the final years of primary education. In Sydney and the other major centers of Wollongong and Newcastle and also in the outer Sydney suburban center of Parramatta students were then admitted to "selective" high schools offering a five-year academic program of studies. In Sydney and Newcastle, there were also technical and home science schools for which entrance was competitive. In Sydney and the country areas there remained the "intermediate" high schools from which students could then graduate to a full high school. Of most significance was the development of new "comprehensive" high schools in the newer suburbs of outer Sydney offering full five-year programs of studies. These schools had often developed "twin schools" for boys and girls on the same site, so challenging the single sex tradition in the Sydney metropolitan area. Finally, the Report noted the existence of not only "district rural schools" extending the primary school curriculum but a large number of high schools in country New South Wales, not so much comprehensive in form but rather "streamed" and multilateral, offering different courses of study which could be primarily academic, junior technical, home science, or commercial.[40]

What held this system of post-primary or "secondary schools" together was the formal examination process. All the public secondary schools, as well as the non-state schools, prepared their students for the Intermediate Certificate taken after three years of study and now examined internally in schools. Increasingly, not only the "selective" high schools but also other secondary schools were preparing their students for the externally examined Leaving Certificate taken after five years of study. From 1925 to 1955 the number of Leaving Certificate candidates had grown eightfold and was predicted to increase to almost tenfold by 1960. For the Wyndham Committee such growth not only placed a strain on the examination system but was also associated with educational 'wastage.' Only 16 percent of those entering secondary school in New South Wales in the 1950s successfully completed the fifth year with only 7.5 percent matriculating to University. The Report suggested that this indicated a serious failure with "any attempt to provide a sound general education for adolescents" being affected by the number of students leaving school early.

The Committee was convinced that more than one-sixth of students were capable of remaining to undertake the higher academic studies in the latter years of secondary school. At the same time, the recent lowering in the age of university matriculants and the high failure rates of first-year students at University suggested that they also could benefit by a further period in school.[41]

The second half of the Report attempted to provide a solution to such dilemmas. The third chapter provided a statement of "Aims." Brief in content this could be said to represent the Committee's own 'cardinal principles' for the reform of secondary education. Harold Wyndham took responsibility for writing this section of the Report.[42] This chapter reveals Wyndham's familiarity with the ideals of twentieth-century progressive education. While there was only indirect reference to the origins of the "Aims," they undoubtedly reflected much of the thinking of progressive education in the twentieth century and the efforts to relate schooling to both preparation for living as citizens in the modern world as well as accommodating to the development of young people. The eight stated aims were thus based upon notions of broad individual needs, differences, and interests as well the necessity of learning to live within social groups. They were:

Health
Mental Skills and Knowledge
Capacity for Critical Thought
Readiness for Group Membership
The Arts of Communication
Vocation
Leisure
Spiritual Values.[43]

The fourth and final chapter in the Report was intended to reveal how these aims would be achieved. The "central problem" of reform was outlined as the "emergence of the view that secondary education is the education not of a select minority, whatever the basis of selection, either social or intellectual, but of all adolescents, irrespective of their variety of interests, talents and prospects." The problem of contemporary secondary education and its solution lay in the meeting of "the needs of all adolescents without impairment to the potentialities of any."[44]

When secondary education had been conceived as an education of the elite, the main point at issue was the criterion upon which that elite should be selected. Organization, curriculum, and method were also issues, but they largely followed from the determination of the student body. The issue was now not so straightforward. "The education of all adolescents" implied a proper provision for all types and levels of ability and for the wide variety of interest and need to be found in any entire school generation. The "age" of the potential secondary student would become the last significant discriminating factor determining secondary school enrolment. The Committee argued that what was sometimes overlooked is that this definition of secondary education made it obligatory for the community to provide suitable education not only for the "average" adolescent, but also, and on the same social and moral grounds, the "adolescent of talent" and "the adolescent who is poorly endowed." Nor, the Committee argued, could any community afford, in making general provision for all its adolescents, to lose sight of the need for identifying and cultivating talent of every kind, wherever it may be found among its youth.[45]

In some respects this was a statement of the same dilemma that Conant would reflect on in his first report. But the difference here was that the Wyndham Committee would propose a centralized solution to change rather than the diverse forms of comprehensive schooling that existed in the United States in the 1950s.

This fourth chapter of the Report began with a rejection of the view that it was possible to select students at the end of primary school for specific and different forms of secondary education. Rather, the choice of a course of study appropriate to individual students must be progressively developed at stages throughout the secondary school. For a minority of students, in order to meet academic objectives and the demand to prepare students for university studies, it was necessary to extend the course of study to a sixth year. This, the committee implied, meant that "all pupils in a locality will proceed to the same school without selection and that those who wish to proceed to university will pursue their secondary school studies for six years."[46]

This effort to argue and legitimate a new approach to the delivery of universal secondary education, while still catering to an academic elite, had a number of implications. The Committee had considered and rejected the American model of junior high schools as well as the New Zealand 'intermediate school.' Instead, it proposed a 'transition' year in the first year of high school with students being able to adjust to the new environment and then through guidance, choosing an appropriate course of studies. As such, the Committee was generally opposed to the concept of 'streams' in secondary schools but the question of providing students with an adequate choice of subjects raised the issue of the size of the future secondary school. While many witnesses to the Committee had advocated schools no larger than 500 to 700 pupils, the Report drew upon the views of the Advisory Council of Education in Scotland that it was still possible to provide a satisfactory organization with schools about 800 in size, as well as the American experience where the majority of schools was somewhat smaller.

> Our general position is, therefore, that the arguments both against selection and segregation at the point of entry, and for a progressive determination of the shape of a pupil's course, are so strong that we recommend the provision of a type of secondary school, which may be best called 'comprehensive,' even though such provision may mean having schools with enrolments in excess of 600 or 700.[47]

This qualified statement is one of the few sections in the Report where the Committee attempted to define its understanding of a comprehensive school. A friendly critic later suggested that in the New South Wales context the Committee meant to say: "A comprehensive school . . . is one that caters for all children of a defined area—excluding those who go to private schools—of both sexes, of all shades of ability, in such a way to engender in the pupils a high degree of unity of outlook and identification with the school, while providing for the wide range of ability and interest present."[48]

In fact, the Committee was not even convinced as to whether all comprehensive schools would be coeducational, commending the recent practice of the New South Wales Department of Education for establishing "twin schools" for males and females.[49] Nevertheless, metropolitan coeducational high schools became more than possible, and the experience of coeducational rural high schools, and that of the selective Parramatta High provided models of practice.[50]

The recommendations for curriculum reorganization were more decisive. The Committee argued for a common core of studies along with elective subjects. To some degree the common core was aligned with the earlier defined "Aims of Education" although the subjects chosen were mainly academic in content and disciplinary in focus: English, Social Studies, Science, Mathematics, Music, Art, Crafts, Physical and Health Education, and, Religious Education. While opposed to broad streaming in the school on the basis of intelligence testing, the Committee also accepted that within this core, students would most likely be grouped by ability for the study of English, Social Studies, Science, and Mathematics.[51]

In the area of electives, as with the Conant Report, the Wyndham Committee was anxious to assert the principle of student choice. It suggested that the provision of "electives" had a threefold objective: to provide as comprehensive a choice of courses as possible; to free the secondary school while offering a general education to all, to allow the "most able students" to progress to the top of their special field; and, to provide for other students to achieve some success in some aspect of their schoolwork. In contrast to some of the curriculum developments in some American comprehensive schools during the 1940s and 1950s the Committee saw all electives as being "courses of study of adequate duration and demanding adequate standards." Ideally, the Committee looked for parity of esteem between all courses with the main question being whether the course adequately tested the abilities and interests of individual pupils.[52]

While providing a reaffirmation of progressive curriculum principles, this section of the Report was framed in such a way that it was doubtful if its views on student choice and a school catering to individual differences would actually result from their recommendations. The Committee admitted that while the list of electives could be quite extensive they would be limited by the facilities available in each school. Even then the range of subjects that the Committee expected each school to provide was principally a list of academic units, that is: art, commerce, geography, history, home science, languages (ancient and modern), manual arts (e.g., drawing, metalwork, and woodwork), mathematics, music, and science (e.g., agriculture, biology, botany, chemistry, geology, and physics).[53]

Ultimately, the Committee must have been aware that the question of student choice and electives would also be subject to one of their major recommendations: the establishment of two new externally assessed credentials administered by new boards of studies representing not only the universities of New South Wales, but also teachers. The School Certificate would be taken after four years of study. It was expected that this credential would mark the end of secondary school for the majority of students. Those intending to proceed to a university would remain to complete the Higher School Certificate after a further two years of study.[54]

It was this provision for an academic 'top' on the proposed comprehensive high school, similar in intention to a grammar school, that has led a number of critics of the Wyndham Report to suggest that it was inherently an elitist solution enshrining a "competitive academic curriculum." Equally, the provision for ability grouping even from the first year of the secondary school seemed to betray the comprehensive principle.[55] While not necessarily rejecting such a critique, his recent biographer suggests that Wyndham himself saw the three main features of the Report as being the abandoning of selection for secondary schools, the introduction of four years of universal "junior secondary schooling" with a core curriculum, and the effort to cultivate the talent of all students through the proposed system of electives.[56]

In defense of the Wyndham Report it could also be said that in the 1950s, of those who supported the introduction of comprehensive schools, few criticized the nature of the proposed curriculum. In its submission to the Wyndham Committee the New South Wales Teachers' Federation, the union of the public school teachers, supported a core curriculum similar to what the Report eventually proposed although it did wish to see up to one quarter of the first year of the high school curriculum devoted to optional subjects. These could have included "informal education" in settings outside the classroom such as library study or visits to industry, local government offices, and dramatic performances. The one major difference between the Federation and the Wyndham Committee was the suggestion that the School Certificate examination taken after four years of study should be internally assessed with each school awarding the credential.[57] The Committee was not prepared to move toward that level of decentralized control over the curriculum process. Moreover, it should be remembered that even though the Report chiefly addressed the reorganization of public secondary education, the proposals for new credentials affected the nongovernment private, church, and corporate schools as well. Control of public examinations and credentials were a well-established means by which the state forced a degree of coherence over education in New South Wales as a whole.

On the question of ability grouping, there seems little doubt that overall the Wyndham Report did not advocate the teaching of all students of whatever ability in the same class. In this way, it was in accord with the views of Conant but differed from what was assumed to be the American model of the comprehensive school and approximated more to the form of comprehensive school being slowly introduced in Britain in the 1950s. As the Crowther Report argued, a comprehensive school in the English context took in pupils of all ability ranges but once inside the school there was no attempt to teach them all together. Students were placed in forms or sets according to their abilities. It was in outside class activities, in games and the extracurricular activities that students came together, rather than in their studies.[58]

It should be stressed, however, that the Wyndham Report was not necessarily at odds with the supporters of progressive education in Australia during the 1950s. As President of the local New Education Fellowship, the

Scottish-born George Howie, a senior lecturer in Education at the University of Sydney, provided one of the few locally originated published statements justifying the introduction of the comprehensive high school. Drawing upon Conant's report of 1959, Howie argued that the comprehensive high school provided for the educational needs of all youth in the community while accepting provision for the special treatment of the "educational sub-normal" and "handicapped" children as well as the rights of parents to send their children to 'independent' or denominational schools. He also suggested that "multilateral" and "comprehensive" schools were almost synonymous but that the term "comprehensive" stressed the "organic unity and interconnection of the various strands which make up the whole society of the school."[59]

On this basis, Howie and the New Education Fellowship were generally supportive of the Wyndham Report. In keeping with most of the sympathies of Wyndham himself, Howie emphasized the tenets of the educational progressives that the purposes of schools were not "merely instructional" but "social" in teaching students "how to live." Influenced by the philosophies of Dewey and Tawney, Howie argued that in a democratic society schools must reflect democratic values providing "full educational opportunity."[60] In accord with the Wyndham Committee, his main concern was to review and reject "selection" of students for different secondary schools. In terms of their future organization he argued that this would mean that the comprehensive schools would need to be about 1,000–1,500 pupils in size but he suggested that English experience showed that it was still possible to maintain "intimacy" in such schools through the "House" system under the pastoral care of a House Master or Mistress aided by other staff. He was also prepared to see ability grouping as students moved through the stages of secondary education. As with Conant, and reflecting the views of the Crowther Report in England, Howie, perhaps even more than the Wyndham Committee, urged that the interests of those of "ability" and "talent" could be pursued within the comprehensive school:

> Those who support the claims of the comprehensive high school on broad educational grounds set before themselves two principles which they regard as equally important. On the one hand education is more than the progressive assimilation of organized subject matter. On the other hand, there is an equal insistence that the thorough intellectual training of the able child in the academic subjects, which really stretch him, must not be neglected. Enough has already been said to show that it is a fantastic misunderstanding of the curriculum of the comprehensive school to say that it provides the same subjects and courses to all its students, or that pupils are lumped together for instruction without regard to differences of innate ability or direction of interest. In the comprehensive school the bright child is still nurtured on the

> disciplines which are most appropriate to him. He receives the intellectual stimulation he needs from his association with his intellectual peers in subject 'sets.' At the same time, on the school council, in the sports field, in the school societies, he learns to respect talents of a different order from his own, and comes to know that the on-going life of a free community requires the pooling of many individual contributions.[61]

As had Conant and the Crowther Committee, Howie continued to think of 'ability' in rather static terms even though he had firmly rejected the validity of intelligence testing at an early age as a projection of ability. Judged in these terms, the Wyndham Report was in general accord with mainstream views on progressivism in education in 1950s Australia and beyond.

In summary, while it may not been seen as producing a one best model for 'Democracy's High School' in Australia, the Wyndham Report represented a culmination of development in public secondary education over almost three quarters of a century, and in public education as a whole over more than a century. From an elite form in the 1880s public secondary schools had moved toward a comprehensive form that theoretically would embrace all students from a neighborhood. Some have argued that as a consequence it was indirectly if not directly 'assimilationist' in intent, ignoring such issues as gender difference in the rush to privilege the forming of 'citizens' for a modern Australia.[62] Others argued that Wyndham simply refused to recognize the growing ethnic diversity in Sydney and other metropolitan regions. Instead he maintained that students should be assessed on *individual* achievement and with no necessary recognition of their *group* related cultural and related backgrounds. For most of the 1950s, the Department of Education under Harold Wyndham tended to ignore the educational and social needs of the children of recent immigrants particularly those from non-English speaking backgrounds.[63] The Wyndham Report itself certainly enshrined parts of the Protestant British-Australian background from which Wyndham himself came. The study of English in particular was given a special recognition with the proposal that it occupy the attention of at least one quarter of the timetable for the curriculum core. Not only was English the natural medium of instruction and communication in a school but its teaching held a special place "ensuring that all adolescents can understand and use both spoken and written English as members of a community assumed to be literate."[64] More tellingly, the Report was anxious to highlight the joys of English literature and the importance of poetry that could "appeal to the minds and feelings of most pupils."[65] In this way, the Wyndham scheme was designed to form a specific form of English-speaking citizen and subject as well as promising enhanced educational opportunities for all youth.

The Opposition

Four years elapsed between the release of the Wyndham Committee Report and the presentation to the New South Wales Parliament of legislation that sought to enact most of its recommendations. The delay arose from two issues that would have a significant bearing on the future development of comprehensive schools in New South Wales. The first concerned the fate of the existing 'selective' high schools. The second related to the impact on families of the proposed extension of the 'junior' years of high school from three to four. Each was taken up by constituencies with influence in the ruling Labor Government in New South Wales.

Supporters of Academically Selective High Schools

The Wyndham Committee Report proposed that all students in a neighborhood or area would proceed directly without selection to a local high school. While the Committee did not recommend specifically that selective high schools would be phased out, the scheme implied that all forms of previous academic selection and testing would cease once the scheme was in operation. Indeed there is little doubt that Wyndham himself assumed that the era of the selective high school would come to an end.[66]

A number of commentators have drawn attention to the support for the grammar school ideal that prevailed within the postwar Atlee Labor Government in Britain, so hindering plans for the introduction of comprehensive secondary schools there.[67] In New South Wales, support for selective high schools came initially from an alliance of parents' groups in association with a number of academics. A High Schools Parents and Ex-Students Association was formed to protest about the prospective closure of selective high schools. As with many of the critics of the comprehensive high school in the United States, the Association couched its case in terms of Cold War politics suggesting that while the USSR was producing 322 scientists for every one million of population Australia was only producing 79. The Association argued that under the proposed Wyndham scheme high ability students, representing about one-sixth of the student population, would be spread across all schools in the State, rather than being concentrated in specialist academic high schools with qualified staff. "We feel that comprehensive schools will raise the standard of average pupils, but this should not be at the expense of the ablest children in the State."[68]

These views were supported by academics such as Dr. John Mackie, senior lecturer in philosophy at the University of Sydney and son of Alexander Mackie the former Principal of the Sydney Teachers' College. Mackie composed a pamphlet putting forward arguments for the selective high school to counter those of Howie and the New Education Fellowship. While accepting the moves toward the establishment of comprehensive schools he also claimed that it was still possible to maintain some selective high schools. The justification for such schools was on the basis of the "cultivation of talent." Intellectual abilities were displayed in the "systematic study" of academic subjects (such as those contained in the traditional grammar school curriculum). There were, he suggested, "very great differences" in intelligence and aptitude for the study of academic disciplines. What was appropriate for the ablest 10 or 15 percent of students would be beyond the majority. The view that selective grading could be achieved in comprehensive schools failed to recognize that such a policy would merely dilute the top academic classes which would have to cater for up to 20 percent of the ability range. The advantages of early and accurate selection of able students to place them in separate schools were not only obvious but also possible. Moreover, rather than being undemocratic, the selective high schools of New South Wales were a "democratic achievement" representing the "career open to talent." The other view of comprehensive high schools providing a rich experience in cooperative living was merely "a slogan" that was liable to support conformity and dull mediocrity.[69]

In 1960, and in defense of his Committee's recommendations, Wyndham argued that apart from ten specialist high schools selecting on the basis of the courses offered (such as the agricultural high schools or the Conservatorium High School in Sydney) only 14 of the 111 high schools in New South Wales were "selective." Nor were any of the 174 secondary departments that had grown up in other post-primary schools "selective." The "selective" high schools were confined to metropolitan areas and were thus "not representative of the whole public secondary system." Nor indeed, was selection on the basis of intelligence and attainment a great issue for the rival nongovernment sector.[70]

Parent groups defending the selective high schools also admitted that the overall principle of selection had been lost in the changes that had already occurred in public education in New South Wales. Through the 1950s, the Department of Education had introduced a 'zoning' system whereby children would move from local primary schools to the local high school. Increasingly, selection for high school related to neighborhood not merit.[71] Moreover, this practice seemed to suit most parents. As the New South Wales Teachers' Federation informed the Wyndham Committee, every year parents protested when their children were sent to junior technical or home science schools rather than high schools. There was a view that their children were being "discriminated against" by not being given the same educational opportunity as children who attended the high schools. In the metropolitan area, where students traveled long distances to attend either the selective high schools or junior technical or domestic science schools, such schools were not part of the local community, "nor have they the same status in the local community as country high schools."[72]

The defense of the selective high school principle thus came to focus more on the 'traditional' high schools established in the late nineteenth or early twentieth century. These schools often drew upon students from a wide area in Sydney and in the metropolitan centers of Newcastle and Wollongong. Some had even established idiosyncratic forms of selection, suiting 'private' rather than the public purposes of public education. Even before the release of the Wyndham Committee Report there were complaints that sons of old boys at Sydney Boys' High School and Fort Street Boys' High School received preference in admission even over those who had a record of better academic performance in the same primary school. The then Acting Minister for Education agreed that the Department of Education had extended the privilege of enrolling at 'competitive' high schools to the sons and daughters of ex-pupils provided their children were qualified and their parents agreed to pay the costs of travel to the school. In defense of this position it was maintained that the Department appreciated the efforts of Old Boys' and Old Girls' Unions and their interest in their former schools by providing equipment, prizes, and awards. The headmaster of Sydney Boys' High said he was keen to admit the sons of old boys because they "showed loyalty, and helped build up a family tradition at the school."[73]

The defense of such 'traditions' received strong support from those associated with Fort Street Boys' High School, the public high school with the longest established record of success at the public examinations. This was the school that had produced many of the male elite of New South Wales including Harold Wyndham himself. The Old Boys Union and the Fort Street Boys' High Parents and Citizens Association were at the center of the campaign to retain the traditional selective high schools.[74] This appears to have had particular impact on the ruling Labor Party, many members of which had a close association with either Fort Street or other traditional selective high schools.[75] When the Labor Government finally introduced the Education Bill of 1961 that would implement the Wyndham Report, the new Minister of Education, E. J. Wetherell, a former trade union leader but coming from a family of teachers and a strong supporter of the overall thrust of the Wyndham scheme, announced to the Parliament:

> The review has made it clear that the location of certain schools in Sydney would make it well nigh impossible to constitute them as local area secondary schools. Moreover, certain of these schools are schools with a long-established

> history which no sensible person would wish to ignore. It is proposed, therefore to retain a limited number of such schools, for boys and for girls, serving a broad metropolitan area and to limit entry accordingly. It is important to bear in mind, however, that entry to these schools will not constitute any predetermination of the particular secondary courses the pupils will follow.[76]

Harold Wyndham later admitted more candidly to the Minister that in New South Wales, as a general policy "we have set our face against preselection on the basis of primary school attainment." Nevertheless, there were exceptions in regard to schools like Fort Street and Sydney Boys High. Wyndham argued that there were two reasons for this. The first was that "with the growth of other high schools nearby, the remaining feeder areas for Fort Street would be very small and in the case of Sydney Boys'High almost non-existent, since the school is surrounded by parklands." The second was pragmatic, the reorganization should avoid making "violent changes in regard to schools with a long historical tradition." The resulting compromise allowed students who had qualified to proceed to secondary school and who lived in for example, the present feeder zone for Fort Street, to proceed to Fort Street. At the same time boys living outside that zone and whose achievements at the end of primary school were superior, had the option of seeking enrolment at a school such as Fort Street. Wyndham added that in the case of Sydney Boys' High, the wider area from which students were drawn was limited to the Eastern suburbs and in the case of Fort Street, to the western suburbs of Sydney. He continued: "I should also add that it has always been the practice for our Department to permit the enrolments of the sons of the old boys, provided that the son meets the usual requirements for entry into high school."[77]

In effect, this policy retained eight selective single sex high schools in Sydney and a further four in Newcastle and Wollongong. In the case of Sydney Boys' High, and Sydney Girls', which were on neighboring sites, the range of selection allowed for entry of the top 25 percent of 'ability' in their 'neighborhood' area of much of the Eastern suburbs of Sydney while provision was made for children of former students and even brothers and sisters of existing students.[78] It was a compromise that satisfied most of the supporters of the selective high schools. It would also have major implications later for the future of the overall comprehensive school system in New South Wales.

The Catholic Opposition and the State Aid Question

The question of selective school survival as much as the issues associated with determining appropriate curriculum plans and ability grouping were the matters which linked the planning of the comprehensive high school system to the international educational debates of the 1950s and 1960s. Of more specific Australian context were the issues of political attachment and religious faith that would have an equal if not more profound impact on the creation of the Australian version of the public comprehensive high school.

Of great significance were legacies inherited from the nineteenth century concerning the development of 'public education' in Australia. Denied taxation-raised funding from 1880 in New South Wales and at other times elsewhere, the Catholic Church throughout Australia had set out to create its own systems of schools. This had been achieved by organization at the local parish and diocesan levels, and through the expansion and importation of Catholic religious orders of nuns and brothers. Catholic schools tended to replicate the state system in several respects. They mainly followed the same secular curriculum that provided opportunities for Catholic students in New South Wales to undertake public examinations such as those for the Junior and Senior, and then Intermediate and Leaving certificates. The system of state bursaries introduced in Queensland during the nineteenth century, and in New South Wales from the early twentieth, had actually continued to assist students in Catholic secondary schools. By the immediate postwar years Catholic schools were educating one-fifth of the Australian school age population. They also represented more than four-fifths of enrolments in the schools outside the public sector.[79]

With the growth of post–World War II immigration, including a large number of migrants from Catholic Europe, there was increasing pressure on Catholic schools. They already faced growing teacher shortages as the religious orders failed to recruit in sufficient numbers to keep pace with enrolment growth. A survey in the mid-1950s indicated that enrolments in Catholic schools had risen by almost two-thirds since the end of World War II. Within a decade it was projected that enrolments would have more than doubled since the war. Costs had been contained by the relative cheapness of a religious order based teaching force, but the new demand could not be met from this source. The prospective introduction of a new pattern of secondary education with four rather than three years spent by students in the 'junior years' before the first public examination would place a further strain on resources particularly as nongovernment schools now educated more than 30 percent of all students in secondary education and of these 60 percent were in Catholic schools.[80] Moreover, in New South Wales, Catholic schools had long sustained higher retention rates than the public schools. Catholic students almost doubled the proportion of public students who remained to complete secondary school.[81]

Since its formation in the 1890s there had been a close association between the Australian Labor Party in the eastern states and the Catholic

Church. In part this related to Australians of Irish origin feeling excluded and alienated from the British-Australian Protestant establishment. It also derived from the strong representation of Irish-Australians in the working-class and labor movement. This association had been accentuated when the Labor Party split over the issue of military conscription in World War I. Many Catholics of Irish background came to prominence in the Labor Party that managed to sustain its anti-conscription policy at the cost of losing government. A recent analysis has even suggested that the Labor Party, especially in eastern Australia, almost became the party of Catholicism as Catholics shied away from the non-Labor parties that were associated with Protestantism.[82]

This relationship between the Labor Party and Catholicism assumed new forms in the domestic politics of the Cold War of the 1950s. Many observers had noted that in contrast to the First World War there had been a decline of sectarianism during World War II as all Australians came together to support the war effort. In the early 1950s, the federal Labor Party, contrary to tradition, was even sympathetic to the prospect of introducing state aid to Catholic schools as part of the general campaign to secure federal funding to education.[83] This politics of growing support changed with new tensions within the Australian labor movement. With the fear of an expansionist Soviet Union and 'godless communism,' Catholic-inspired 'industrial groups' were formed throughout Australia to oppose what they saw as the growing influence of Communists within the Australian trade union movement. This led to increasing conflict within trade unions, the Labor Party and the labor movement as a whole.[84] By the mid-1950s the Party was splitting, leading to the collapse of Labor governments in more than one State. A new Democratic Labor Party (DLP) was formed. It mainly represented Catholics who were strongly opposed to any Communist influence in the trade unions, there still being several that were closely associated with the Labor Party. The creation of the new party that now directed its voting preferences toward the ruling federal Liberal-Country Party coalition helped to keep the government led by Robert Menzies in power until the mid-1960s. The DLP was also aligned with Catholic Social Action in Australia that had emerged out of the Catholic Social Movements in the 1930s. The educational policy of the new party included support for the re-introduction of state aid for Catholic schools. In part rejection of Catholic influence and with determined opposition to the DLP on any ground, the federal Labor Party now adopted for the next decade an official policy opposing the introduction of state aid to nongovernment schools.[85]

In New South Wales there had been a long and close association between the leadership of the Catholic Church and the leadership of the Labor Party.

J. M. Cahill, Premier of New South Wales, was a Catholic and friend of Cardinal Gilroy the Primate in Sydney. Unlike the situation in Victoria and Queensland, the New South Wales Labor Party did not split, partly because the Catholic hierarchy in New South Wales opposed the creation of the Democratic Labor Party. At the same time, and despite the views of the federal Labor Party, the New South Wales Labor Government introduced and continued a series of measures that indirectly supported Catholic education. They included subsidized transport for students and allowing Catholic schools to gain access to government stores and supplies.[86]

The rising issue of restoring state aid to Catholic schools added a new dimension to the introduction of the Wyndham scheme of comprehensive secondary education. While the selective high school issue generated much of the public debate and acrimony, the delay in introducing legislation into the Parliament was due more to factional opposition organized by some members of the State Labor Party who were concerned over the possible impact of the scheme on Catholic working-class families. Furthermore, R. J. Heffron the Minister for Education when the Wyndham Report was released was also reluctant to move quickly because of his ambition to become Premier of New South Wales. It was only when Heffron succeeded to lead the Labor Party and government, and E. J. Wetherell was appointed Minister for Education that the supporters of the Wyndham scheme, including the New South Wales Teachers' Federation, were able to bypass the Parliamentary Labor Party and present the scheme for adoption as policy to the 1961 State Labor Party Conference. The Conference accepted the scheme on the basis of retaining the Intermediate Certificate as a credential at the end of the third year for those leaving school prior to the completion of four years of study. The Conference also called for senior bursaries for students remaining in school. This protective action and concern by many Labor Party members and Parliamentary representatives was not only directed toward students in the increasingly stressed Catholic schools but also for those in public schools. The further prospect that the opposition State Country Party would now support a policy of state aid for church schools was another probable reason that the State Labor Government finally agreed to support the introduction of the legislation enacting the Wyndham scheme.[87]

By the early 1960s, the issue of state aid was thus influencing the politics of public education. While the New South Wales Labor Government was reelected in 1962 the new administration faced an immediate crisis when the Catholic Bishop of the regional center of Goulburn ordered the closure of Catholic schools in his diocese. This decision followed a requirement of the State Department of Education that certain Catholic schools in the Goulburn area meet appropriate standards of health in the provision of toilets. The truth was that this 'Goulburn school strike' was intended to force the State Labor Government into negotiations on the question of aid—or it could look forward to chaos in the public schools as very large numbers of Catholic children presented themselves for enrolment. Teacher and building shortages were endemic in the public as well as Catholic schools. In the short term, what was achieved was a promise of more bursaries for senior students in the last years of high school.[88] In the long term there was the possibility that the new public comprehensive system of high schools would be delivered a group of serious competitors in new and restored publicly funded Catholic and other nongovernment secondary schools. These developments on the funding of nongovernment schools in New South Wales were the lesser part of the unfolding state aid story. In the next chapter, we discuss the far more significant developments at the federal government level.

The immediate postwar years saw increasing attention given to the promise of the public comprehensive high school. In many ways, this was prompted by the demographic, social, and economic changes in all postwar industrial democracies. There was a general growth of participation in education at all levels during the 1950s. Increasingly, the generation of postwar youth, not only in the United States but also in Britain and Australia, was a generation in school, with many staying to the end of secondary education and even graduating to higher education. With the onset of the long postwar economic 'boom,' governments in most industrial democracies supported the comprehensive school as part of the continuing process of modernization meeting the postwar expectations for expanded educational and social services. As a mass and universal institution the public comprehensive high school seemed to provide a solution for expanding educational opportunities. It appeared to meet many of the aspirations raised in education by the social democratic character of postwar plans for social and economic reconstruction.

What united the supporters of the comprehensive school was the proposed end to early selection and differentiation. As Conant came to recognize, the extension of the comprehensive ideal could not by itself overcome social and other disadvantages, but it could at least be seen as delivering opportunities and choices to individuals. It could simultaneously deliver on collective social goals, specifically the forming of future citizens in a democracy.

While in theory, democratic in intent, it is also clear that the proposed extension of the comprehensive ideal accommodated the interests of the academic elite. This was certainly the intention of Conant in his defense and promotion of the comprehensive high school as 'democracy's high school.' In the British and Australian contexts, the comprehensive school was generally conceived in terms of being a 'multilateral school' with continuing provision for ability grouping and streaming. The Australian solution, at least in New South Wales, also provided for a continuing academic curriculum with a continuing central place for public examinations. There was also the fact of the continuing existence of the small group of public selective high schools that maintained a 'grammar school' tradition similar to many of the Australian corporate schools and even that of the English grammar and so-called public schools.

This introduction of the 'new' schools, while providing for an accommodation with the past traditions of secondary education requires further explanation. The demands for working-class educational opportunity and national development through educational expansion are only partial reasons for the change. The demands and expectations of the middle class in general as much as the aims and objectives of the educational intelligentsia prompted much of the movement toward the comprehensive high school in Australia, and in New South Wales in particular. Only through the expansion of comprehensive secondary education did it seem possible that the rapidly expanding aspirations and demand for secondary school qualifications might be met. They provided the entry point to higher education and expanding white-collar employment. In the Australian context, it was not only the leadership of the Catholic Church and the Catholic population that were confronted with a challenge from an expanding demand for secondary education, apparently to be met by a new system of public comprehensive high schools and an additional year of school enrolment. Combined with fortuitous pressures of the Cold War on the Labor Party, the old issue of public funds for schools outside the public system was reopened. In turn, this would eventually confront the supporters of the public comprehensive ideal with an even more fundamental challenge.

Within these contexts, the proposed introduction of the public comprehensive high school was not quite the fundamental reform it appeared. In New South Wales there was a continuation of the meritocratic principles that had long governed secondary schools. As has been suggested by W. F. Connell, the traditional practice of Australian education had created an educational meritocracy through early selection using four main instruments: academic and then intelligence testing, the streaming and tracking of students, a formal public examination system and systems of differentiated schools.[89] The Wyndham scheme was to end early testing and the differentiation of secondary schools (with minor exceptions), but for the most part would preserve streaming and in every part, the central public examinations. Perhaps the scheme's greatest achievement was to propose an all-purpose school that could meet with fair satisfaction the rapidly rising demand for secondary education from the post-war 'baby boom' youth and families, as they began to arrive in high schools in very large numbers from the new suburbs in the late 1950s.

Chapter 3

Going Comprehensive

During the 1960s and early 1970s much of Europe and Britain prepared to 'go comprehensive,' building on the educational debate and discussion about the future of secondary education that had been developing for more than half a century. In Europe, France and parts of Scandinavia led the way in turning their former differentiated secondary schools into comprehensives, though each system adapted to local conditions. The comprehensive school seemed to be the 'wave of the future.'

Despite the features of comprehensive schools that would appear to make them more acceptable to the Left, the labor, and social democratic parties of Europe, they were certainly not confined to those political origins. In Britain, political support initially cut across party lines, beginning well before Labour came to power and issued the famous Circular 10/65 requesting Local Education Authorities to prepare plans for comprehensive schools. Central acquiescence in local plans for comprehensive schools continued at a pace under Margaret Thatcher, the Conservative Minister of Education in the Heath Government 1970–1974, despite her issuing Circular 10/70 effectively withdrawing the earlier Circular 10/65.[1] It was only in the late 1960s and the early 1970s that the authors of the 'Black Papers,' with close associations to the Tory Right, began to attack the introduction of 'the comprehensive disaster' as leading to a decline in educational standards.[2]

Political Ownership of the Comprehensive High School

The Australian example of the 'comprehensive revolution' also presents some apparent political contradictions. At the federal level of politics,

Liberal–Country Party coalition governments remained in power until 1972. In place of the collectivist ethos of the wartime years, the postwar Australian Liberal–Country administrations, under the general influence of Keynesian economic theory, saw their role as providing prosperity whereby individuals could pursue aspirations for themselves and their families.[3] Robert Menzies, Prime Minister of Australia 1949–1966, was the dominant political figure representing these values. In helping to establish the Australian Liberal Party in 1944 he had made a clarion call to the 'forgotten people'—the Australian middle class.[4] Educated in an Australian corporate school as a 'scholarship boy,' Menzies held distinctive social values that tended to favor the private education sector. During his first period in government, he allowed tax concessions for nongovernment school fees and provided interest concessions on loans to nongovernment schools in the Australian Capital Territory that was under federal government jurisdiction.[5]

While continuing the wartime Labor government's policies of financial support for universities and university scholarships, Menzies initially refused the requests of the states for financial assistance for public schools. As Prime Minister he maintained that under the Australian federal constitution public education was the responsibility of the states. With income tax powers transferred to the federal government as a result of a wartime decision, the individual state governments in the 1950s became virtual supplicants to the federal government seeking annual grants to operate their budgets. Services such as public hospitals and public schools were among their most expensive responsibilities.[6] It was only following the revived debate over state aid for Catholic schools, the establishment of the Democratic Labor Party and other Cold War pressures that led to federal support for schools. With an obvious appeal to the Catholic vote, in 1963 the Menzies Government promised an expanded federal scheme of scholarships for students in the senior years of high school. It also committed to a proposal for the introduction of funds to support science laboratories in both public and private secondary schools. (This latter proposal resulted from the ideas of the Industrial Fund for the Advancement of Science, an organization of businessmen and headmasters of corporate schools who had been concerned at the scientific threat of the USSR.[7]) Thus began a major federal government commitment to all secondary schools that was continued with funds to establish school libraries in 1969 and also recurrent grants to private schools, so matching the forms of direct 'state aid' that were already occurring in the individual Australian states.[8]

Despite this emerging federal involvement, the development of public school education in the 1960s still resided within individual state administrations, most of which were Liberal and Country Party coalition governments. The introduction of comprehensive schools in the smaller states of

Tasmania and Western Australia in the 1950s was soon replicated. In Queensland, a Country–Liberal Party coalition government came to power in 1957 after 40 years of Labor governments that had virtually ignored public secondary education. Under this new administration during the 1960s Queensland began to develop a system of public comprehensive secondary schools.[9]

In New South Wales, it was a Liberal–Country Party coalition government, elected in 1965 after a period of more than a quarter of a century in opposition, which would assume responsibility for implementing the Wyndham scheme. The commitment of this new government to the comprehensive school experiment can be explained from a number of perspectives.

First, with its close associations with middle-class Protestantism and the major Protestant churches, the New South Wales branch of the Liberal Party had been traditionally committed to supporting public education and the overall educational settlement between state and the churches that had been reached with the Public Instruction Act of the late nineteenth century. Many of its leaders had been educated in public schools. There was also a strong and continuing suspicion of any measure that seemed to aid the Catholic Church and its schools. Robin (later Robert) Askin, the leader of the New South Wales Liberal Party since 1959 and then State Premier and leader of the government 1965–1975, had been educated at Sydney Technical High School. He was also a Freemason and member of the Church of England.[10] On being elected Leader of the Liberal Party he publicized his working-class parentage, his father having been a tram driver. He described himself as "a Liberal spelt with a little 'l.' "[11] This also meant initial opposition to state aid for Catholic schools. In the early 1960s, he even threatened to close down the 'Young Liberals' section of the party when it passed a resolution supporting state aid to church schools.

Ever a pragmatist Askin eventually came to accept state aid that became official policy of the state Liberals at the 1965 election, but the shadow of past sectarianism still lay over his Party.[12] As the junior partner of the Coalition Government, the Country Party had agreed to support the principles of state aid from the late 1950s but it also had a commitment to public education and its own 'Drummond legacy.' Formed in the 1920s throughout Australia, the Australian Country parties had a specific agenda to protect rural interests and sponsor the concerns of those living outside the major metropolitan areas on farms and in country towns. During its previous period in office in the 1920s and 1930s with the then conservative National Party and then United Australia parties (the predecessors to the Australian Liberal Party), the New South Wales Country Party had held the education portfolio in cabinet. The Minister of Education from 1927–1930 and 1932–1941, and Deputy Leader of the Country Party from 1932 to

1949, was David Drummond, member for a rural electorate on the northern tablelands of New South Wales. While educated at The Scots College, one of Sydney's elite corporate schools, Drummond was committed to extending educational opportunities to those in the 'Australian bush'. He saw to the establishment of a University of New England in his own electorate but he also promoted the rural high school movement. These schools were part of the practical foundations of the Australian version of the multilateral and then comprehensive high school.[13] On its return to government in 1965, the Country Party continued its commitment to public education in rural New South Wales. The party's leader and Deputy Premier Charles Cutler, himself having attending Orange High School in country New South Wales, became the Minister for Education and Science.[14]

Overall, the new coalition government ultimately supported the Wyndham scheme because it suited the constituencies that it represented. For the Country Party there was a continuation of long standing support for and further development of the rural high school. For the Liberal Party there were only a few critics who argued that the introduction of comprehensive schools would lead to a decline in standards and thus disadvantage the urban middle class. The most prominent opponent of the Wyndham scheme was Douglas Darby, Member of Parliament for the principally middle-class seat of Manly, one of Sydney's Northern Beaches, suburbs. A former teacher in public schools, he had become a strong opponent of all forms of 'progressive education'. He was one of the few members of Parliament who had given evidence to the Wyndham Committee opposing comprehensive schools. Something of a maverick in his own party and first elected to Parliament in 1945, he had lost party pre-selection in 1962 only to be elected as an Independent Liberal before being re-admitted to the Liberal party in 1966. Darby continued to criticize the Wyndham scheme over the next decade while the Liberal Party was in office.[15] But in the mid-1960s such voices within his party were little attended.

Liberal Party support for a scheme of comprehensive schools was best expressed by Premier Askin who represented the middle-class seat of Collaroy adjacent to Darby's electorate. In his speech supporting the 1961 Education Act, Askin outlined the reasons why his Party endorsed the earlier Wyndham Report:

> The advantages I see under the report may be listed in this way: first, the report aims to provide a satisfactory secondary education for all adolescents, irrespective of aptitudes and abilities. Second, it aims to seek talent and to cultivate it wherever it is found. Third, it does away with preselection at the primary school level and thus lessens the margin of error. Fourth, selection of

> pupils for various courses at secondary schools will be a continuous process. Fifth, it will be easier to transfer pupils from one course to another. Sixth, there will be equality of opportunity for all pupils. Seventh, more tolerance will be developed in pupils generally. Eight, cultural enhancement should follow. Last, more children will remain at school for a longer period.[16]

Viewed from this perspective, the Liberal Party support for the comprehensive school was founded on the assumption that an apparent commitment to a 'universal' reform was compatible with fostering talent and opportunities, and serving those whom it represented politically. The selective high schools had not been able to meet the expectations of all those middle-class parents who sought academic credentials for their children. The Wyndham scheme held out a new promise to such parents, particularly through the provision for two senior years of study being based on an academic curriculum that could lead to university.

While Wyndham had hoped to carry forward his idea of individual choice of electives into the final two years of the secondary school, this had met strong opposition from the universities that were concerned at the possible effect on academic standards in the Higher School Certificate examination. Students could elect to take subjects at three levels according to their interest. The universities interpreted these levels as relating to standards of attainment and refused to consider subjects taken at the third level as being appropriate to matriculation. Wyndham was forced to concede. It was an indication that external academic examinations, under university influence, had long determined much of school curriculum and would continue to do so.[17]

The academic nature of the upper years of the New South Wales version of the comprehensive high school had a marked impact on the question of the continuing selective high schools. If the comprehensive high school had an 'academic top,' was there any further need for the old principle of selection? Immediately on coming to office in 1965, the new government accepted the Departmental compromise that had been reached over the selective high schools issue, at least in the metropolitan center of Sydney. There, the minimum entry requirement would be "slightly reduced" so as to "assist in building up the comprehensive schools in the metropolitan area." Students in the Sydney selective high schools would be drawn from the local area while children of former students of the selective high schools and "immediate members" of the family of any student attending these schools would retain right of entry.[18] As Minister and Leader of the Country Party, Cutler had a different view of selective high schools outside of Sydney but even here he was essentially endorsing departmental policy. In answer to a question about the future of the remaining two selective high schools in the center of Newcastle, the industrial city north of Sydney, he reassured the Parliament in 1967 that he had long been concerned about the "sibling rule" whereby younger members of a family could attend schools where the older children in the family or either parent had attended. While this rule had existed since World War I there were many problems in its operation and there were now more applications for attendance at comprehensive schools than at selective schools. Moreover, in his hometown of Orange where there were two high schools, there was no sibling rule applied and children were required to attend the school on their side of town.[19] In this way, the Coalition Government had come to accept the prevailing Department of Education view that the introduction of comprehensive schooling had to be associated with a 'zoning' rule in which the local neighborhood school was defined by central rules rather than specific wishes of parents.

By 1973, a new Minister for Education, Eric Willis (later Leader of the Liberal Party) had accepted the advice of his Departmental officials to end selective secondary education in Newcastle. His decision came in the face of opposition from the Parents and Citizens Associations of the existing selective high schools in the Newcastle area. As he informed the local media, there was a "definite need for reorganization and modernization of schools in Newcastle" and the view of his Department was for comprehensive, coeducational schools and the abandoning of selectivity.[20] Despite continuing pressure, Willis indicated six months later that the matter was a dead issue and there was no way he would review his decision.[21] In correspondence later cited in Parliament, he provided a justification of the comprehensive high school that appeared to go beyond even the Wyndham committee in its promotion of democratic ideals:

> The policy of the Department of Education is to provide that form of organization which best suits the community which the school serves. In what is generally considered to be a 'classless society' in which educational opportunity should be offered, that form known as the comprehensive, co-educational local high school is favoured. The major concern must now be the total educational experience available for children. The comprehensive, co-educational school of the size envisaged for Newcastle provides a broad curriculum in a natural, community setting where a child can receive appropriate academic stimulation while learning to appreciate the points of view and modes of thinking of a wide spectrum of his peers. The comprehensive high schools in the outer suburbs of Newcastle and Lake Macquarie are visible examples of success.[22]

Even within the city of Sydney it appeared that the fate of the selective secondary schools might be sealed. With the senior years of the secondary school under the Wyndham comprehensive scheme remaining essentially academic in nature it seemed that the old selective schools were now less popular than before. By 1973, the Liberal Country Party government had agreed to amalgamate Fort Street Boys' and Girls' High Schools despite an initial campaign of opposition to keep them on separate sites.[23] By 1975, there were vacancies for places in all the surviving selective high schools except the long established Sydney Boys' High. At North Sydney Boys' High School alarm was expressed with a decrease in the proportion of new pupils with an IQ over 125. The Council of Sydney Boys' High School, concerned at the future impact on its enrolment, now requested the Minister to allow for the school to draw on a wider geographic area and permit a "wide range" of activities as a criterion for entry (an obvious reference to the associations based on sport that Sydney Boys' High shared through its membership of the elite Athletic Association of Great Public Schools). The Council of the School suggested more generally that as five of the eight remaining selective high schools in New South Wales were serving areas of "dwindling population and declining socio-economic status", it would be necessary for the Minister to modify enrolment policies so as to "raise the academic standard of the intake."[24]

The idea and fact of the comprehensive public high school now seemed well accepted. The issue remained as to how systematically and how well the ideal would be implemented.

Comprehensive Reorganization

It is as well to establish the quantitative dimensions of this period of public secondary school growth and reorganization in New South Wales. Though table 3.1 does not specifically identify the comprehensive schools or their students, it demonstrates the problem of 'accommodation' faced by the governments of New South Wales as the numbers of public secondary students grew rapidly from the early 1950s.

The table points not only to the sheer growth in students, but the growing proportion of students attending secondary school in comparison with primary. Not only were the greater retention rates responsible for this, but following the implementation of the Wyndham scheme, there was the addition of a further (sixth) year to the secondary program.

In 1970, the Australian Council of Education Research published a review titled *The Secondary School at Sixes and Sevens*.[25] By then most Australian states were in the process of transforming their various secondary schools into comprehensive systems. Victoria, with its technical high schools would be the

Table 3.1 Government secondary schools, and primary and secondary students: New South Wales, 1945–1970 (*N*, %)

Year	Separate secondary schools (*N*)	New secondary schools from previous 5 years (*N*)	Public primary students (*N*)	Public secondary students (*N*)	Proportion of sec. student comp. with primary (%)	Growth of sec. student population (%)
1945	83	17	252,376	86,492	34.3	8.6
1950	90	7	299,286	86,017	28.7	−0.6
1955	126	36	387,516	109,034	28.1	21.1
1960	184	58	435,348	160,307	36.8	32.0
1965	266	82	466,830	201,800	43.2	20.6
1970	310	44	520,143	266,331	51.2	24.2

Source: New South Wales Department of Education and Training, *Government Schools of New South Wales 1848–2003* (Sydney: 2003), pp. 210–214.

last to change. According to its author, the Wyndham scheme in New South Wales initially seemed at the forefront of this process, attracting wide attention throughout Australia with its "explicit rationale contrasted with the more piecemeal approach to problems in schooling customary elsewhere in Australia. Therein lies the scheme's chief significance."[26]

Actual comprehensive reorganization was much less easily achieved. Going comprehensive in Australia involved curriculum change certainly, but attention to issues of staffing and resources was also required. Much occurred in haste. During the debates over the Education Act 1961, the new Liberal Premier and Country Party Deputy Premier had indicated that they foresaw problems with the Department of Education finding resources for implementation of the Wyndham scheme.[27] In office for the decade from 1965 to 1975, the Liberal–Country Party government constantly reiterated the view that the former Labor Government had not planned for change and as a result the new government had inherited the difficulties of making the new system function. There is some justification for the claims.

In the mid-1960s there were still firm hopes for the effective planning and implementation of change. As an example, one of the intentions of the Wyndham scheme was to provide a new framework giving schools more independence and flexibility. School principals were to be allowed the freedom to experiment with new grouping patterns responsive to student ability and interest. Despite the continuing significance of centralized exams, it was hoped that individual student programs would replace the older forms of 'streaming' in the former multilateral schools. 'Cross-setting' would allow more able students to take subjects at an advanced level while less able students would take corresponding studies at the pass level. Students would not necessarily belong to a fixed class or form, but would move about the school according to their own timetables.[28]

These ideas were also reflected in the way the Department of Education conceived the architectural plans for the new comprehensive school. The intention was that greater student movement would replace the older style single classroom routine of a school 'form' being mainly in one place. From 1965, high school design consisted of self-contained blocks of buildings, each housing one or two year levels or forms. These blocks became known as 'doughnuts' because of their shape with four sides and a courtyard in the middle. These 'doughnut' schools had problems with student traffic and noise from specialist rooms. By 1969 an arrangement known as the *Study 2 High School* had been introduced. Classroom blocks were still based on year levels but specialist rooms were arranged in separate blocks allowing for the Wyndham scheme's provision for the junior years' core of music and art, as well as provision for home economics facilities and science laboratories. Even this design did not leave enough room for flexibility and increasing use of audiovisual aids. By the late 1970s, a new *Study 3 High School* design had been created exemplified by Cromer High School established on the Northern Peninsula of Sydney in 1977. Classrooms for a particular subject were now grouped next to a subject resources center with staff studies near by, much in the manner of Faculty arrangements in Universities.[29]

Accompanying the proposed reorganization of school design, programs, and timetables was some effort to encourage other flexibilities. From the late 1960s, a number of Australian states experimented with school-based curriculum reform. Many Victorian schools embarked on local curriculum experimentation designed to accommodate increasing school retention rates and the diverse nature of school populations.[30] In New South Wales, curriculum reform remained for the most part controlled by the central bureaucracies of Department and Board. By the early 1970s, the newly established Studies Directorate in the Department of Education in New South Wales had issued a statement on "The Aims of Secondary Education." This was the first attempt since the Wyndham Committee Report to clarify the purposes of the secondary school. In contrast to the Wyndham Report, with its implied if not direct reference to the social purposes of the secondary school, the emphasis here was on individual development and more particularly, the skills of cognition as well as encouraging students to develop their own values while understanding the values of others. Some teachers also compared this document to the Wyndham Report and criticized its lack of focus on the comprehensive school as a social institution.[31]

The issue of these new "Aims of Secondary Education" was associated with other changes. From 1973, the external examination of the School Certificate taken at the end of four years was abolished and the number of 'levels' at which subjects could be taken was reduced from three to two. The Board of Studies formally responsible for the public examination also issued a "Base Paper on the Total Curriculum" suggesting that individual schools could be more "flexible" in organizing the curriculum within the general policy guidelines of the Board.[32] The academic Alan Barcan, a long time critic of the comprehensive reforms and participant in the politics of the reorganization of the secondary schools in Newcastle, prematurely suggested that the Wyndham scheme itself had concluded.[33]

Continuing the process of implementing change required increased resources. During the 1960s, expenditure on education increased to about one-quarter of the budgets in all states.[34] All Australian states also faced the prospect of teacher shortages. This became a factor in the growing levels of industrial conflict following the introduction of another senior year in the secondary school. As the union of the teachers of New South Wales, the Teachers' Federation had a longstanding working relationship with the Department of Education even though the leadership of the Federation in the 1950s was associated with the Communist Party.[35] The Federation had supported the introduction of the Wyndham scheme and the development of comprehensive schools even though it had warned of the impending crisis in the areas of staffing and resources. The Federation also supported the establishment of an Education Commission that would include representatives of the Federation and assume general responsibility for staffing and employment of teachers.[36]

In opposition, during the 1950s, and early 1960s both the Liberal and Country parties had supported the establishment of such an Education Commission. As a result, and despite its long-term association with the labor movement and the Labor Party, the Teachers Federation gave tacit support to the policies of the Liberal–Country Party Coalition at the 1965 election. In Government the Liberal–Country Party coalition government reneged on the commitment to establish an Education Commission. The Federation was angry with the new government for breaking this promise, and was frustrated by the growing staffing pressures emerging from the implementation of the Wyndham scheme. It was also emboldened by a new generation of young teachers and soon came into conflict with Cutler, the new Minister of Education. In October 1968, for the first time since its formation in 1918, the New South Wales Teachers' Federation instituted a one-day strike.[37]

In part answer to the charge of resourcing failures the Minister established a committee of enquiry to investigate and advise on class sizes and teaching loads in public secondary schools. The Committee paid particular attention to such matters as centralized and inflexible staffing policies that both limited the discretion of individual principals and hindered cooperation between schools, an outcome of which may have been to consolidate curriculum offerings and electives. In effect, the Committee defended the Department of Education and its officers against most criticisms but admitted that in the metropolitan areas there could be further cooperation between schools in close proximity. Essentially, the Committee framed its findings within the traditional framework; that in order to meet the needs of all communities across the state, public education was best organized from the center. Drawing international comparisons, it pointed out that while class sizes of up to 35 pupils per teacher in some schools were much higher than in the United States or many European nations, the overall pupil–teacher ratios were lower. An analysis of the reasons for this apparent paradox highlighted some of the problems of education in New South Wales. Many arose from the object of providing the kind of curriculum envisaged by the Wyndham scheme through the Education Act, for all children wherever they lived. They were the consequence of the need to provide a broad curriculum taught by trained teachers, often in small schools in small towns, and the need to provide a fairly wide range of electives in almost all schools, wherever they were situated.[38]

As these arguments developed in the late 1960s and 1970s, the origins of some of the later problems for government comprehensive schools can be discerned. There were the beginnings of public education being associated with industrial unrest, and the problems of resourcing a broad curriculum demanded by comprehensive education.

With the Minister of Education being Leader of the Country Party the new Government was hardly likely to change the state's longstanding policy on the centralization of public education. The Committee on Class Sizes considered a number of future options for the implementation of the comprehensive ideal in New South Wales. Significantly for the future, they included a possible introduction of "senior high schools" or colleges for the final two years leading to the Higher School Certificate similar to the "matriculation colleges" already introduced in Tasmania. But both the Department of Education and the Teachers' Federation opposed such a suggestion as "a radical departure from the departmental concept of its responsibilities under the 1961 Act, to provide comprehensive, district-based high schools in which all adolescent pupils in a neighborhood would be educated."[39] The Committee was skeptical of the possible advantages of "senior high schools" arguing instead that consideration be given to developing a "school park complex" in New South Wales.[40] Its major recommendation was a long-term objective to reduce secondary school class sizes in the junior secondary school to no more than 30 and to 20 to 25 in the senior years: an objective to be achieved by recruiting and training more teachers.[41] Such a long-term aim did not satisfy the Teachers' Federation that continued to press for immediate reductions in class sizes, leading to continuing conflict with the Coalition government. By the 1970s, the relations between the government and the Federation were in continual crisis.[42]

Finally, and perhaps of most significance for the efficient implementation of the Wyndham scheme, was the fact that the comprehensive schools of New South Wales were not all created anew. The reorganization necessarily involved the existing differentiated secondary schools that had been established over more than half a century. Comprehensive reorganization involved not only establishing a new curriculum and providing newly trained and re-trained teachers, but also the adaptation of older schools and their grounds. This was particularly difficult for the making of coeducational comprehensives from older single sex schools. While the plans for purpose-built comprehensive schools in the new suburbs were straightforward enough, the bringing of single sex schools together as comprehensives on old city sites was a process that often took a decade and more. Other single sex 'comprehensive' schools that had only just opened in the 1950s prior to the final acceptance of the Wyndham Report had also adopted a rather ambiguous approach to coeducation. As late as 1980 there remained 70 secondary schools in New South Wales which were still single sex representing about 16 percent of the total number of public secondary schools. The vast majority of these single sex schools were in the Sydney area.[43] This was just one indication that from the outset, comprehensive reorganization was highly responsive to regional differences.

Regional Patterns of Reorganization—and Social Class

Recent literature has identified the different regional patterns of comprehensive schooling that occurred in Britain during the 1960s and 1970s. The British experience of comprehensive reform rested much on the relationship between central government and local authorities. In some respects, ever since World War II, the initiative to develop the comprehensive high school had originated from the Local Education Authorities that had the task of dealing with the wishes of local constituencies as well as the interests of such groups as the 'voluntary sector' including the Roman Catholic schools receiving local aid.[44] There was no necessarily uniform system of comprehensive schools established by the various Local Education Authorities in England.

The metropolitan center of London and urban areas such as Manchester proceeded at different paces and with different ideas of what constituted a comprehensive school compared with developments in rural areas. Some counties were adventuresome; some cautious. Some local authorities followed the earlier Leicestershire model of transferring pupils into a two-tiered system of 'lower' and 'upper' comprehensive schools; others created full-scale unified comprehensive schools; a few established comprehensive schools without sixth forms.[45]

In New South Wales, there was some minor concession to regionalism with the creation of new regional directorates even though these remained under central Department of Education control. While organized by the central bureaucracy, the 'on the ground' implementation of the Wyndham scheme in the decade from the mid-1960s to the mid-1970s responded to regional differences that already existed in public education as well as the patterns of suburban development in postwar Sydney. These regional variations can be considered in the following ways: the consolidation of the rural high schools, the reorganization of secondary education in the inner western still predominantly working-class suburbs of Sydney, the expansion of high schools in a number of the middle-class suburbs of Sydney and the extension of public high school education to the outer western new working-class suburbs of Sydney. Most of the development of comprehensive schools occurred after the Education Act of 1961 although in some regions, changes had occurred even prior to the release of the Wyndham Report.

The Rural High School

As already indicated, the rural high school in country towns had become in part an early Australian precursor of the comprehensive school. The implementation of the Wyndham scheme allowed for these former multilateral high schools in country towns to be consolidated into fuller versions of the comprehensive high school creating a full six years of secondary education. Few new schools were established. Rather, where necessary, a new two-year 'top' to prepare students for the Higher School Certificate was added. This can be seen by examining two contrasting rural regions.

The first is in the Central West of rural New South Wales that embraces a number of country towns including Orange which Cutler, the Minister of Education, represented in Parliament. In the major towns in the Central West, those with populations, by the 1960s, generally in excess of 10,000 inhabitants, such as Orange, Bathurst, Parkes, Cowra, Young, and Dubbo, coeducational high schools had been established prior to 1950. There were also a number of 'Intermediate High Schools' in smaller towns such as Temora, Forbes, Cootamundra, and Wellington offering three years of high schooling up to the then Intermediate Certificate. During the 1950s and 1960s these had been converted into High Schools offering five years and then six years of schooling under the Wyndham scheme. In some of the more outlying settlements further away from the major country towns, in such centers as West Wyalong, Grenfell, Condobolin, Crookwell, Naromine, Blayney, Canowindra, and Oberon there were Intermediate High Schools and 'Central' and 'Rural District' Schools, the latter two offering limited forms of post primary education. All these smaller schools were converted into full high schools during the 1960s and 1970s. These post-1965 changes also saw second high schools established in some of the larger country towns such as Orange, Bathurst, and Dubbo in order to meet population growth.

In some of the Central West country towns the Catholic Church had established secondary schools since the late nineteenth century. In major centers such as Bathurst and Orange there were also Protestant secondary schools. But in the smaller rural towns it was more likely that the public high school was the only secondary school. Where there were small Catholic schools with secondary classes, they terminated at the Intermediate, or later, with the School Certificate (Year 10). As such public education under the Wyndham scheme in the 1960s still often offered the only possibility of a full secondary education to all youth in a rural district.

The other rural region of interest is the coastal strip beginning approximately 200 miles north of Sydney. While the Central West in the 1950s and 1960s was a region of large sheep and wheat farms with generally prosperous country towns the Mid-North Coast of New South Wales still had many small dairy and other farms, many of which struggled to survive. Regional prosperity varied. In the major coastal towns such as Taree, Kempsey, Coffs Harbour, and Macksville, high schools were already established by 1950. Inland from the coast, generally areas of dairying or timber felling, the smaller centers such as Wauchope, Bellingen, Wingham, and Dorrigo, or along the coast, Port Macquarie and Woolgoola, had Intermediate High Schools, Central Schools, or Rural High Schools. These were all converted into full high schools from the 1950s, principally during the 1960s and 1970s. The expansion of Coffs Harbour as a major regional center led to another two high schools being established there by 1980.

The establishment of the Wyndham scheme also had a marked effect on rural schools in the private sector. By 1970 it was noted that many of the Catholic parish schools were closing their former secondary 'tops' and Catholic students were traveling to the local public high school. Other non-Catholic schools were also finding it difficult to compete with the local high schools. Required to provide extra facilities and staffing for a more diversified curriculum some of the smaller country colleges were being forced to consider amalgamation or closure.[46]

Suburban Comprehensive Schools in Sydney

The Australian public comprehensive high school of the 1960s and 1970s was essentially an urban phenomenon. For New South Wales it was in the state capital, Sydney, that the greatest changes took place; the scale of reform implementation was enormous. Throughout the early to mid-twentieth century the provision of secondary education in Sydney was responsive to the social, demographic, and geographic development of the city. Social class was a major determinant of what, if any, kind of secondary education would be accessed by families. Access to schools was restricted by factors that included patterns of urban transportation through to the state policy of academic selection for high schools. The older corporate, principally church-affiliated schools, predominated in the established upper middle and middle-class suburbs of eastern and northern Sydney. The new public high schools were more to be found in the inner city of Sydney or in selected areas of the expanding southern suburbs. But the vast majority of students in Sydney during the interwar period had either left the public schools at the compulsory leaving age of fourteen, or attended a variety of post-primary schools, including single sex intermediate and emerging junior high schools, commercial and junior technical schools for boys, and home science schools for girls, all of which had come to supplant the earlier superior public schools. Many of these 'post-primary' secondary schools were in working-class areas where the main competition to public education came from the Catholic schools that educated about one-fifth of the total school population.[47] The legacy of this organization of schooling remained in the Sydney of the 1960s and 1970s.

There was also the major impact of demographic change. By the 1966 census the population of Sydney was 2.5 million, double what it had been at the end of World War II. Over three quarters of the postwar population growth had come from immigrants and their children.[48] Urban growth was associated with expansion on the suburban fringes and demographic and social changes in the inner city where postwar immigrants replaced many of the Australian-born. Private home ownership jumped from 40 percent of properties being owner-occupied in the 1940s to more than 70 percent in the 1960s. A housing boom took place in the suburbs. In 1947, 38 percent of the population of Sydney lived in the inner city and nearby suburbs; by

1961 only one-quarter did so. In contrast, the outer suburban areas expanded from 44 percent of the total population in 1947 to over 60 percent in 1961. Suburban expansion occurred not only through private ownership but also from a policy of 'slum clearance' in the inner city and the creation of public housing estates on the outskirts.[49]

Sydney in the 1960s thus remained a city much divided by region and social class, and was also fast developing an increased ethnic diversity, with its own pattern of spatial concentrations. A study of social status and prestige published in 1969 suggested that of the then 368 suburbs in Sydney one-quarter could be given the status of 'middle' rank, just over one-quarter had a higher rank than the middle but almost half had ranks lower than the middle. Most of the higher status suburbs were still in the east and north; most of the lower status suburbs were in the south and west.[50] Social divisions intersected with long-established voting patterns. Those living on the 'North Shore' of Sydney Harbour, along with those in the more affluent eastern suburbs along the southern fringes of the Harbour, voted more often for the Liberal Party while residents in the south, south-west and west of the city voted more for Labor (a pattern that persisted into the 1970s).[51]

This social division was also seen in patterns of educational opportunity. In 1959, the inner city and the outer western suburbs of Sydney had 29 percent of the enrolments in primary schools but only 16 percent of enrolments at the University of Sydney. In contrast, the mainly middle-class suburbs to the North of the central city area had 24 percent of the primary school population but 41 percent of enrolments at the University.

In 1961, the same year that the Education Act was passed establishing the Wyndham scheme, a committee appointed by the then Labor Minister of Education reported on higher education. Chaired by the Deputy Director General of Education in New South Wales (P. G. Price), the Committee had been appointed because of the growing educational and political problem that had emerged in higher education. For the first time in its history, the University of Sydney was considering a policy of quotas on enrolments because of the increasing demand from school leavers. Reviewing the pressure on admission to the three universities in the State, two of which were in Sydney, the Committee recommended the creation of another university in Sydney to meet the demand. Significantly, the Committee recommended the establishment of the third university in the northern suburbs, close to the main area of demand for university education.[52] The new Macquarie University opened in 1967—the first year of the new Higher School Certificate Examination. The institution was essentially a liberal arts university with a strong focus on interdisciplinary studies in the humanities and social sciences and preparation for the professions including teaching and later the law. Set in the heartland of the Northern Suburbs of

Sydney, but not near to a railway line as the Price Committee had hoped and thus less accessible to those living in the Inner West or the Outer West of the city, Macquarie University was designed essentially to meet increasing middle-class aspirations for higher education.[53]

Sydney in the 1960s and 1970s thus remained a city divided by social class, region, and opportunity. It was in these social contexts that comprehensive schools were established during the late 1960s and early 1970s. Different forms of the comprehensive school emerged in inner city working-class Sydney compared to the expanding middle-class districts and the new 'dormitory' suburbs for the working class on the western fringes of the city. The development of new university places responded to those patterns and pressures, but in a way that advantaged the growing middle-class suburbs.

The Secondary Reorganization of the Inner City

As has already been suggested, the new 'comprehensive school system' was often built out of the older differentiated public secondary schools. In particular, the establishment of comprehensive schools in the working-class suburbs south of Sydney Harbour and close to the inner city principally involved the reorganization of existing single sex schools rather than new foundations.

In the wake of the early twentieth-century reforms of Peter Board, a variety of junior technical schools for boys and domestic science schools for girls had been established in the suburbs of Ashfield, Marrickville, Newtown, Stanmore, Glebe, Leichhardt, Petersham, and Dulwich Hill. With the exception of Ashfield, which had a small enclave of middle-class suburban villas, all of these suburbs had status rankings as working-class suburbs. On the peninsula of Balmain, traditional home to waterside workers and their families, a 'Central School' similar to those in rural areas, was founded as late as 1945 offering upper primary education to early school leavers. Since the late nineteenth century the Catholic Church had also created its own network of single sex boys' high schools and girls' colleges in these or nearby suburbs. Despite the nomenclature, the curriculum in these Catholic schools was often similar to the junior technical and domestic science schools of the public sector.

By the 1960s, many of these inner-western suburbs in Sydney were undergoing a process of transformation. The Australian-born working class was moving out, or being moved out to the suburbs on the fringe of the city by the Housing Commission that managed 'public housing.' Replacing the old Australian working-class families of British and Irish extraction were the new immigrants from Europe. The Italian immigrants who arrived in Sydney in the period from about 1947 to 1961 tended to settle in suburbs such as Leichhardt, Ashfield, and Drummoyne while Greeks concentrated in other inner western suburbs such as Marrickville and Botany.[54] There was also a new generation of professionals attracted to the 'heritage' of these suburbs with their nineteenth-century and early twentieth-century housing, as well as their proximity to the central city of Sydney. At the same time, the growth of Sydney as an expanded and sprawling city of suburbs had changed the distribution of the population from when Board had first designed his system of differentiated secondary education. Overall, the proportion of those in the suburbs close to the inner city declined from almost one-quarter of the total Sydney population in 1921 to one-twentieth in 1971.[55]

This change in the composition, distribution, and size of the population complicated the comprehensive reorganization of Inner West schools. Usually, older buildings, formerly junior technical or domestic science or even older elementary public schools were given new names if not new buildings. And the single sex principle often still prevailed despite the introduction of the Wyndham scheme. Some schools, such as Stanmore Home Science School became Stanmore Girls' Junior High in 1962 only to 'close' in 1965, apparently supplanted by Petersham Girls' High in the next suburb. The previous Petersham Girls' Junior High had existed from 1944 to 1956. In the suburbs, almost next to Petersham, Newtown Junior Technical School became Newtown Junior High School in 1950 and then Newtown Boys' High School in 1960. Nearby, Enmore Boys' High School was established in 1955 only to become coeducational in 1977.

In the suburbs of Tempe and Arncliffe that still had heavy and light manufacturing industries in the 1960s and working-class status rankings of six and five, the older nomenclatures of 'junior technical' for boys and 'domestic science' for girls took longer to change. Tempe High School emerged in 1975 on the site of the former Tempe Boys' High School (1972–1974) which had previously been Tempe Boys' Junior High School (1962–1972), Tempe Boys' Junior Technical (1955–1962), Tempe Boys' Intermediate High (1949–1954) and originally Tempe Junior Technical High School (1913–1949). The new coeducational Tempe High had come about as result of a merger of the Boys' High with Arncliffe Girls' High (1965–1975) although there had previously been an Arncliffe Home Science (1913–1962) and Arncliffe Girls' Junior High School (1963–1964) on an old public school site.

Changing patterns of social class also had an influence in the Inner West. In Dulwich Hill, a suburb that was partly lower middle rather than working class, the former separate Dulwich Hill Junior Technical and Home Science schools were first briefly transformed into single sex junior high schools and then brought together in 1965 as the coeducational Dulwich High School. In Glebe, with a low status ranking, but a suburb which was being rapidly 'gentrified,' the Glebe Home Science School and Glebe Junior Technical Schools that were actually on the same site, 'closed' in 1956–1958 with the school becoming a primary school. A coeducational Glebe High School would open on a new site in 1979. In Balmain, where young middle-class professionals were slowly replacing working-class families, the former Central School and the nearby Rozelle Junior Technical became Rozelle Boys' Junior Technical High School only to be supplanted by the opening of a newly established coeducational Balmain High School in 1974. Nearby, Drummoyne Junior Boys' High School had already become Drummoyne Boys' High School in 1955. Similarly in the suburb of Ashfield, long part of the more 'gentrified' Inner West being on the railway line, and near to Trinity Grammar, an Anglican boys' corporate school, Ashfield Boys' Junior Technical High School became Ashfield Boys' High School in 1961.

The struggle to reorganize the Inner West schools as modern coeducational comprehensive highs was only partly complete in the late 1970s. By the late 1980s, continuing demographic changes, and the increased competition from the private sector led to further reorganization. This is discussed below in chapter 5.

Beachside Comprehensives

In contrast to the Inner West the suburbs on the northern peninsula of Sydney were generally middle class. Here established areas as well as former 'holiday retreats' and rural allotments were being transformed into car commuter suburbs.

One of the long-established settlements in the Northern Beaches area was the seaside suburb of Manly. The inhabitants of Manly in the 1960s were slightly more Anglo-Australian or British in background and less Roman Catholic than the New South Wales average. About one-third of the population was aged under twenty-one compared to the New South Wales average of 38 percent.[56] Initially, as in the Inner West, the single sex principle was maintained in Manly and surrounding suburbs as the older forms of 'post-primary' education were transformed into comprehensive high schools. Manly Home Science School for girls and Manly Junior High School for boys were both established in 1944. The girls' school later became Mackellar Junior High School in 1962 and a full High School in 1968. The Junior Boys' High School became Manly High School in 1949 with an enrolment of almost 1000; ten years later Manly Girls' High School opened.[57] By 1983, these two schools had merged into the newly named Freshwater High School. But the single sex 'comprehensive' model still remained at Mackellar Girls' and Balgowlah Boys' High schools that had opened in 1954.

Further up the peninsula and in the coastal hinterland, there was increasing suburbanization in Premier Askin's electorate of Collaroy. Narrabeen Girls' High (1954) and Narrabeen Boys' High (1959) were built hurriedly to meet the growing demographic pressures noted in the Wyndham Report. Not until 1976 did two new coeducational high schools—Narrabeen High and Cromer High—emerge out of these earlier single sex schools.

Perhaps the most significant development in this Northern peninsula was the design and construction of purpose-built comprehensive coeducational high schools in the new and expanding middle-class suburbs. By the 1960s, middle-class suburbia was taking over what had been previously been bushland. A number of comprehensive public high schools were established to meet the demographic pressures. Such schools were deliberately planned as community and neighborhood schools, built at the same time as the houses surrounding them. These were large schools built to accommodate between 1000 and 1200 pupils. Even in 2001, school principals could still reflect on the establishment of these comprehensive schools that included The Forest High (1961), Killarney Heights High (1967), and Davidson High (1973) as being organically based in the middle-class communities around them. In the 1960s and 1970s such groups as the local parents' and citizens' associations gave strong support to 'their' local schools.[58]

As one example, Davidson High carried images of both the past and the contemporary. The suburb of Davidson was named in honor of a former Governor of New South Wales a member of the Davidson Clan in Scotland. In keeping with the traditions of the corporate schools in the private sector, Davidson High was granted permission to use the crest, shield, and tartan of the Davidson Clan. Dressed in tartan uniforms the boys and girls of the new school had their own motto (soon changed from Latin to English)—"Sincerely if Wisely."[59] At the same time, the school architect had designed a school set amidst the Australian bush with provision for "subject-basing" allowing for both "ability grouping" and allocation of "groups of learning areas with facilities specially planned for the requirements of particular subjects."[60] Purpose-built and designed to meet the curriculum requirements of the Wyndham scheme, such schools had an aura of being both traditional and "modern." As such they had immediate appeal in the middle-class suburbs that surrounded them.

Comprehensives of the 'Hills' and the Outer West

In the 1960s, 'Western' Sydney represented about half the greater Sydney area and contained about one-third of the city's population. Much of the Outer West was still semirural. Parramatta High School on the then western outskirts had been established in 1913 as a coeducational school in accord with the pattern in 'rural areas' of New South Wales.[61] In 1945, a Cumberland County Council was established with the aim of controlling development and providing for a 'green belt' of open space but there was continuing pressure by local councils and developers for land for suburban estates.[62] In effect, the development of Western Sydney in the postwar period was soon marked by both new middle-class suburbs and working-class housing estates. By the 1950s, many middle-class families were moving for space and acreage to the 'Hills' district just north of Parramatta. In the 1960s, this area grew very quickly indeed, requiring a rapid increase in classrooms and staffing at primary school level and beyond.[63]

Prior to the 1950s, there had been no secondary schools in the Hills area. Carlingford District Rural School had been established in 1955. Of more significance was the opening of James Ruse Agricultural High School at Carlingford in 1959 on the ostensible grounds that the area was still semirural with many market gardens catering for the Sydney conurbation. The school had a selective form of entry that it retained. Originally a boys, school James Ruse became coeducational in 1977 catering for the aspirations of an expanding middle-class suburbia in the Hills. By the 1980s, it had a growing reputation for success at the Higher School Certificate Examination. The other coeducational comprehensive high schools in the area included Castle Hill High (1963), Carlingford High (1968), Baulkham Hills High (1971), Model Farms High (1975), and Muirfield High (1976). Crestwood High was opened in 1981.

The expansion of public education into the green fields of new middle-class suburbs was matched, but in a different way, in the creation of new schools in the further outer western suburbs. These were on the very fringes of the then greater Sydney area. Until World War II, the western areas beyond Parramatta had been dominated by farms and market gardens. With the postwar migration program, a number of migrant hostels were built as temporary accommodation for new arrivals. In the 1950s and 1960s, this outer western area became a place for new homes often built by the State Housing Commission that had embarked on a program of 'slum clearance' in the inner city. Public housing estates were first built in the 1950s with over 2000 individual dwellings in the suburbs of Dundas and

Villawood. By the 1960s there was an estate of 6,000 dwellings at 'Green Valley' followed by a housing estate of 9,000 homes at Mount Druitt.[64]

The major focus of this 'displacement' from the inner city was the suburb of Mount Druitt. By the early 1970s, the general Mount Druitt area had a population of 70,000. The average age was very young compared to older parts of Sydney. A majority of the population was living in the Housing Commission flats and houses.[65] To meet this population explosion in the Outer West of Sydney the Department of Education created a myriad of new schools. On the far western reaches of the area toward the Blue Mountains, which constituted a natural boundary to the growth of the metropolis, Penrith and St Marys high schools had already been opened in 1950. In 1959 separate boys' and girls' high schools on the same site opened at Blacktown that was east of Penrith. Between these two centers a process of building new comprehensive high schools across the Outer West now began with ten schools created over the following decade—Seven Hills High (1959), Riverstone High (1962), Rooty Hill High (1962), Nepean High (1963), Doonside High (1964), Mitchell High (1964), Grantham High (1966), Colyton High (1967), Mount Druitt High (1969) and Kingswood High (1969). The continuing population growth in the 1970s and 1980s brought into being a further eleven schools—Evans High (1972), Whalan High (1972), Dunheved High (1973), Shalvey High (1974), Cambridge Park High (1976), Plumpton High (1976), Bidwill High (1977), Braddock High (1981) renamed Cranebrook High in 1988, Jamison High (1982), St Clair High (1985), and Erskine Park High (1991).

First built in the middle of open fields, and even as the housing estates began to crowd in, these new schools seemed to promise spaces for new opportunities. They were all comprehensive and but for the Blacktown schools, coeducational. Some of that promise was soon blighted however. Many soon became identified as containing major social and educational problems. The area itself began to take on some of the social stigmas of poverty in the suburbs. The State Housing Commission was soon operating as an agency of both welfare and surveillance.[66] By the 1970s, there was a call for more remedial teachers and disadvantaged schools programs in the Outer West. A 1974 survey suggested that in schools such as Riverstone, Seven Hills, St Marys, Doonside, Rooty Hill, and Whalan more than one-third of the students had failed to meet a reading age of ten on entry to high school.[67] Here, a new version of the comprehensive high school was being created—a school of social and educational 'disadvantage' that struggled to deliver on the promise of the comprehensive ideal.

The actual introduction of the comprehensive school was not a pristine affair in terms of implementing an educational ideal or set of philosophical tenets.

The introduction was usually achieved with due regard to past practices—which included a number of the older 'sorting and selecting' technologies of student and curriculum management. They included the 'looking after' of students identified as oriented to academic work and possible university entrance. The new schools adapted, some reluctantly, to the social class character of their enrolments and their regional circumstances. As Conant had recognized in the United States, there were vast differences between the comprehensive schools in the slums compared to those in the suburbs of America. In England and Wales, 'comprehensivisation' in the 1960s and 1970s was achieved in different ways through the various Local Education Authorities. The old selective systems often remained in place with some comprehensive schools being essentially old secondary moderns without sixth forms attended by those from working-class backgrounds while middle-class students enrolled in the 'new' comprehensives geared for academic achievement and success.[68]

In New South Wales, a Liberal Government was responsible for much of the introduction of the comprehensive system even though the actual process of change remained in the hands of the central educational bureaucracy. Bedeviled by issues of staffing, resources, prior schooling organization, and the stresses associated with inner urban decline and gentrification, and outer suburban expansion, as well as the need to substantially increase the secondary schooling opportunities of rural students, the comprehensive school became a regionally diverse form. The major continuities were in rural districts where an Australian version of the comprehensive high school had long been found. The major changes occurred in Sydney. By the 1970s, the reorganization of inner city schools into comprehensives was only partly complete. Elsewhere in Sydney public comprehensive education took the form of a suburban neighborhood school albeit of different social composition depending on district and region.

In some respects, it could also be said that as in Britain the 'comprehensive revolution' of the 1960s in Australia served middle-class demands more than working-class interests. While all secondary schools under the Wyndham scheme offered six years of education the essential continuation of the academic curriculum was still associated with low rates of achievement for working-class students. On the other hand, comprehensive schools met the increasing middle-class demand for entry to higher education. By the early 1970s, about one-tenth of Australian school leavers were going on to university but there still remained major social class differences. More than one quarter of young males from professional backgrounds and more than one-fifth of females with fathers in the professions were going on to university. In contrast, only about 3 percent of males from unskilled working-class families and 2 percent of youth from working-class families were attending university. It seemed that over the 1960s the middle-class had continued to benefit from educational changes while for the working class there had been fewer improvements in educational opportunities from the introduction of comprehensive education.[69] For some working-class families, the loss of the junior technical high schools, with their emphasis on a practical curriculum and clearer vocational paths to working-class jobs was also an issue. The comprehensive high school involved losses as well as gains for some families.

Despite these qualifications, the impact of the 'public' ideal of the comprehensive school should not be underestimated. Even with the various compromises that were associated with its introduction, the period of the 1960s and 1970s can be considered as the high point of the development of centrally controlled and bureaucratically managed public education in Australia. During the 1960s nongovernment schools throughout Australia lost ground in terms of enrolments to public schools. In secondary education, numbers in Australian public secondary schools grew 273 percent between 1950 and 1968 compared to 173 percent in the nongovernment sector.[70] In New South Wales these years were associated with the establishment of the comprehensive high schools. In terms of the number of 'new' schools alone the effect was dramatic. The private sector had predominated in the nineteenth century and continued to grow in the early twentieth century with 47 corporate schools, all single sex, and representing all the major Christian religious denominations, being founded from the 1880s to the 1930s. Over the next four decades only another 11 corporate schools were established in New South Wales. In contrast, 38 public high schools had been opened in the half century after the Public Instruction Act of 1880 and a further 27 from 1930 to 1950. But in the two decades after 1950 more than 200 public comprehensive coeducational high schools, recruiting students from a local neighborhood, were established throughout New South Wales.[71] By 1975, more than three-quarters of students in New South Wales were in public schools, an increase of almost 5 percent since the release of the Wyndham Report.

Viewed from this perspective, the public comprehensive high school in New South Wales and most of the rest of Australia appeared not only well established but predominant at the end of the third quarter of the twentieth century. But by 1975 other events had intervened that would shape the long-term future of both public education and public comprehensive schools in particular. The chief among these events was the new and forceful interest of the national government in school education. The old constitutional barrier insisted on by the Menzies Liberal–Country coalition governments was reinterpreted and undermined. From the 1970s, federal governments, with all their financial resources, began to reshape both public and private schooling. Individual state control over the future of public education began to collapse in the process.

Chapter 4

In Retreat

The mid-1970s marked a high point of hopes for the public comprehensive high school. In Britain, a Labour Government returned to power in 1974 with a commitment to continuing comprehensive school reform. It seemed that the comprehensive secondary school was still the 'wave of the future' even though much remained to be achieved if the comprehensive school reform agenda was to be more than 'half way there.'[1] So it was in Australia. Writing in 1974, one commentator described the nature of the Australian comprehensive school in the following terms:

> A school which admits all children of appropriate age in a given area and provides a range of courses to suit their whole range of interests and abilities. In this sense, all States have a fully comprehensive system of primary schools, and all except Victoria and South Australia have a comprehensive secondary school system. South Australia and Victoria have a binary system, with separate technical and academic secondary schools, although only in Victoria are the systems also administratively distinct and South Australia is moving towards a fully comprehensive system.
>
> The true comprehensive school does not group or stream its students according to interests or abilities, but organizes them in heterogeneous groups which pursue a common core of studies together. More commonly, secondary schools stream their students either according to test performance or occupational interest, and provide separate courses for each stream. Such schools are properly called multi-lateral schools.
>
> In New South Wales the system of levels allows students to take different subjects at different levels, in either streamed or mixed classes in any particular subject, and a minority of schools is now upgrading even this arrangement in the early secondary forms. A similar situation obtains in South Australia and Western Australia.[2]

Even as these words were being written, the changing international situation was conspiring to threaten the pubic comprehensive school ideal. The oil crisis following the Arab–Israel conflict of 1973 brought to an end the long boom that had persisted in western economies since World War II. This had a marked impact on school leavers. Youth unemployment became entrenched. In Australia, the early 1970s marked the beginning of the era of the 'lost generation,' of young people leaving school and being unable to find work. By the mid-1970s, over one-sixth of young Australians aged 15 to 19 were looking for work; they were unemployed.[3] The specter of a generation out of work would become a continuing concern and a growing fear for not only working-class but also middle-class parents. Increasingly, the 'lost generation' became a generation remaining somewhat unwillingly at school placing new demands and expectations on school systems. By 1980 more than one-third of students in Australian schools were completing high school; by 1990 this had more than doubled to over 70 percent.[4] For New South Wales, the Wyndham scheme's concept of the final two years of high school as an academic 'top' became obsolete. With a fair part of whole student cohorts moving into Years 11 and 12, the senior school needed to develop comprehensive curriculum capacities, and very rapidly.

Within this new economic and educational climate, new thinking about managing change emerged. The postwar Keynesian settlements that supported a growing role for governments in national economies came under challenge. The 'New Right' preached that governments were the problem not the solution. Reliance on the 'market' was now urged as the solution to economic malaise. The rise of these neoliberal views had a major impact on all social policies but was associated with a particular approach toward education. Paralleling the view that ultimately only 'educational markets' could bring about change for the better was the continuing debate about 'educational standards.' Increasingly, there was a focus on the skills or lack of skills that young people brought to the workplace. There was also a backlash against the postwar moves toward public comprehensive schools. They were increasingly portrayed as leading to a decline in the 'basics' of education and even placing national economies in danger.[5]

By the 1980s the idea of the public comprehensive secondary school as a democratic institution of the postwar world seemed in retreat. In the United Kingdom and the United States the influence of the New Right on education policy was soon associated with new governmental policies. While the new political discourses appeared similar, the actual proposals for change sometimes took different directions. In the late 1960s and the early 1970s, those on the Tory Right associated with the *Black Papers* had railed against the 'comprehensive disaster.'[6] The election of the Thatcher Government in 1979 led to an end to the comprehensive reorganization that had continued during the 1970s. The new Conservative administration repealed the 1976 Act of the previous Labour Government that had virtually required Local Education Authorities to submit plans for introducing local comprehensive schools. The Thatcher Government now supported the re-emergence of selection and differentiation in secondary education, including more emphasis on vocational education and training for the majority of pupils.[7] In the United States, the presidency of Ronald Reagan was associated with the publication of *A Nation at Risk*. This seminal report of the National Commission on Excellence in Education drew a dire picture of American high schools. In international comparisons of educational tests in literacy and numeracy, American students were portrayed as falling behind their counterparts in such nations as Japan and Korea and even failing basic educational standards. The comprehensive high school was blamed for offering a 'cafeteria style' curriculum rather than ensuring that all students achieved basic standards in traditional academic subjects as well as the new basics such as computer science. The Report helped initiate an ongoing debate over the curriculum and educational outcomes in American high schools.[8]

Explanations for the overall decline of the comprehensive ideal in the 1970s and 1980s also related to different national and social contexts. It has been suggested that in Belgium it was often local practical considerations as much as ideology that had led to the rise and then decline of the comprehensive secondary school.[9] In Australia there was the emerging effect of the growing involvement of the Australian federal government in a national schools policy. While the Australian states continued to administer school systems, federal economic and now educational policy initially appeared to boost the social democratic status and goals of comprehensive public education, but would ultimately undermine them.

Federal Interventions and the Schools Commission

The major shift toward a new national schools policy occurred with the election of the reformist federal Labor Government under the leadership of Gough Whitlam in 1972. Education was at the forefront of the Whitlam agenda for change.[10] The new Government soon assumed full funding of universities and put an end to student tuition fees. After much heated discussion, Whitlam had also convinced his party to abandon its opposition to state aid for private schools. In government, he now proposed that all schools, government and nongovernment, be funded on the basis of 'need.'[11] On coming to office he quickly established an Interim Committee for a proposed Australian Schools Commission that would report on the financial needs of schools throughout Australia.

What became known as the Karmel Committee, after its chairman, the economist and academic Peter Karmel, laid down a blueprint for funding which continued to influence national educational policy for more than two decades.[12] The report of the Karmel Committee in 1973 occurred at the moment when the comprehensive school project in Australia appeared to be flowering. As the proponents of the comprehensive school recognized however, and as seen in the development of schools in the western suburbs of Sydney, the introduction of the comprehensive reorganization had not overcome social class and other differences. The supporters of the Karmel Committee then and now see its influence as focusing on issues of equity throughout all Australian schools, both public and private. Equity was to be achieved through increased financial resources to schools 'in need' whether they were in the public or private sector.

In pursuing this aim, the Karmel Committee introduced the concept of the 'disadvantaged school.' These were schools that "require greater than average resources if they are to be effective with the children they serve."[13] Illuminating this concept the Committee pointed out that it had visited an inner suburban high school where more than half the pupils had reading skills below the norm for their age. Less than half the students in the school were staying in school for four years of secondary education and only five percent remained to complete high school. Aware of the studies of James Coleman on equality of educational opportunity that had been published in the 1960s and the later compensatory programs of schooling introduced in the United States, the Karmel Committee hoped that increased financial resources would build relationships between 'disadvantaged' schools and their local communities. Essentially defined in terms of poverty, social and economic disadvantage was seen principally to lie in communities of migrant concentration and those with high Aboriginal populations. Significantly, the Committee reported that in certain States as a result of recent increased immigration, "larger proportions of enrolments are strongly disadvantaged in the Catholic systems than in the respective government ones."[14]

The Disadvantaged Schools Program (DSP) initiated by the newly created Australian Schools Commission on the recommendation of the Karmel Committee was one of the major educational legacies of the Whitlam Government of 1972–1975. Described later as one of the most extensive and experienced antipoverty programs in education anywhere in the world, the DSP funded 150,000 projects between 1974 and 1985 when it ceased. In 1977, four years after its introduction, the program was covering

400,000 students representing one-seventh of total school enrolments in Australia. Based principally on teacher involvement in projects the DSP supported new, often school-based curriculum development and work with local communities. With its overall focus on equity it could be seen as a continuation of the public comprehensive high school agenda even though the program was unable to cope with increasing levels of poverty. A review of the DSP in 1985 estimated that in 1973 there had been a quarter of a million students in poverty but with increasing unemployment in the 1970s this had risen to more than 600,000 which was 50 percent above the ceiling of support in the program.[15]

Apart from supporting such programs as the DSP, the new Australian Schools Commission that had been founded in 1973 as well as other federal agencies became a source of initiatives and curriculum ideas with obvious implication for the public comprehensive high school. One of the Commission's reports that would have great and continuing significance was *Girls, School and Society* (1975). This report legitimated a decade of criticisms arising from second-wave feminism that had identified schools as being key institutions for reproducing sex differences that led to inequality. There were significantly different school retention rates and different post-school opportunities for boys and girls, each of which disadvantaged girls. For the most part, the report advocated the development of antisex discrimination programs in all systems and schools. It generally regarded evidence concerning the impacts of coeducational as opposed to single sex schooling as inconclusive. The report and the state Education Department reports and programs proceeding from it certainly changed the practice of government comprehensive high schools but did not directly threaten them as schools appropriate for all youth. This developed later as evidence concerning the embeddedness of discriminatory practices and sex discriminatory school cultures became better known. In the 1980s, it became more possible for some lobbies either to advocate separate single sex teaching and programs within schools, or to advocate the retention and expansion of single sex schools, public and private.[16] The latter was a greater threat to the comprehensive coeducational high school.

By the 1980s, a number of research studies were confirming that increasing school retention rates as a result of high unemployment were doing little to improve the life chances of working-class youth. For many young people, staying in school to complete an academic curriculum seemed a waste of time, a 'ticket to nowhere,' merely prolonging the period before they left school to try and find a job.[17] During the 1970s, the federal government became more involved in supporting school to work transition programs. By the early 1980s, such programs constituted one-sixth of the total federal budget on manpower training.[18]

In 1980, the Schools Commission published a report on schooling for 15- and 16-year-olds suggesting that there was a need for a more 'adaptive' curriculum in order to sustain the interest of working-class youth.[19] One of the final reports of the Commission published in 1987 attempted to review secondary education as part of an overall youth policy for Australia, emphasizing the need for a continuing core curriculum but also practical skills that could relate to future employment. The Report also contained a strong defense of the comprehensive high school ideal and a rejection of all forms of selective secondary schooling:

> Just as schools should teach the values of a democracy, democracy needs to be informed about the forms of schooling it is nourishing. The local comprehensive high school is a reflection of the democratic aspirations of the society. It is open to all the children of a given area and does not differentiate amongst them on any characteristic. It seeks to ensure that their educational and occupational futures are kept open. Its comprehensiveness is frequently limited because the neighborhood it serves does not contain all social groups. Selective schools, of necessity, differentiate amongst children at an early age. Where selectivity, intentionally or unintentionally practised by schools, is an organized means of advantaging some children to the disadvantage of others by, for example, excluding the less able or the poor and bringing superior resources to the education of the already advantaged, then this means of organizing schooling, whilst very attractive to those who can gain its advantage, is antidemocratic.
>
> The Commission believes that public policy in a democracy should in no way assist the extension of selectivity in schooling designed for advantage but rather should, on democratic grounds, support the maintenance and further development of strong systems of comprehensive schools of the highest quality and the greatest measure of comprehensiveness in other schools that public policy can achieve.[20]

This was one of the last national statements on the democratic significance of the public comprehensive high school. Significantly, the Report that was intended to justify a new federally funded program, failed in that objective.

By the mid-1980s, there was already a changing emphasis in national education policy. The newly elected federal Hawke Labor Government was embarking on a program of economic reconstruction. After more than a decade of national funding of schools there was a call for account. Peter Karmel now chaired a new review emphasizing the need for tangible outputs rather than the increased financial inputs of recent years. As in other areas of government, the concepts of 'quality' and 'measurable outcomes' had begun to enter the policy discourse of education.[21]

In this new context, there were other pressures arising from Commonwealth involvement in education that would eventually help to undermine the overall Australian comprehensive high school project. Some of these were perhaps partly unintended consequences of the first Karmel Report of 1973. First, as well as a stress on 'equality' there was the new language and values associated with 'devolution,' 'diversity,' 'rights of parents,' 'choice,' and community involvement. These appeared in early chapters in the Karmel Report.[22] This was an implied if indirect criticism of the still highly centralized Australian public school systems. More specifically, the Karmel Committee paid particular attention to the needs of migrant communities so recognizing the growing cultural diversity in Australia. By the time of the Report in 1973, the effect of postwar migration was obvious in Australian schools. Approximately 40 percent of Australians were now migrants or the children of migrants. In the 1960s, the 'migrant problem' had been associated with the child migrant program and the devoting of resources to teaching English. The establishment of the Schools Commission led to a shift toward the concept of 'multicultural education' that not only recognized the ethnic diversity in many Australian schools but also emphasized the need to retain cultural diversity.[23]

The idea of 'multicultural education' was associated with the overall policy of 'multiculturalism' in Australian political life that developed out of a variety of influences including the move away from discriminatory policies on immigration. Even in its heyday in the 1970s 'multiculturalism' could have different meanings. For some it was simply a recognition of 'cultural pluralism'; for others it involved a commitment to change, either recognizing the 'rights' of ethnic communities or their welfare and educational needs.[24] The policies of multiculturalism in education now supported by the federal government and its agencies were supposedly designed to assure not only migrant parents but also the leaders of ethnic communities that it was possible for their children to integrate into the occupational structure while maintaining faith with the language and culture of former homelands. Increasingly, the governments in individual Australian states not only supported the teaching of community languages in public schools but even provided funds for part-time 'Saturday Schools' that had emerged within many ethnic communities.[25]

The policy of 'multiculturalism' seemed to be framed around the ethic of equity but it was also a challenge to the older assimilationist agenda of the public comprehensive high school. The policies of multiculturalism could go in several directions as far as public schooling was concerned. They might lead to a more diverse curriculum and a schooling culture more respectful of diversity within comprehensive high schools; they might also lead to degrees of separation. It was easy to argue that the languages, religions, and cultures of different ethnic groups were more satisfactorily supported in separate schools. This argument had increasingly been accepted for the Catholic schools of Australia and was soon adapted to other groups. In the process, a major argument for the Australian government comprehensive high school would be undermined; it would no longer be seen as the socially logical school for the children of all Australian citizens. The notion of a unitary Australian citizenship was simultaneously being reconceptualized under the impact of multiculturalism.

Of great significance, the original Karmel Report established the principle of government funding for all Australian schools. As such it put a virtual end to the debate over 'state aid' to private schools although coalitions of state aid opposers including government teachers' unions and government school parent organizations, including DOGS (the Council for the Defence of Government Schools) maintained their opposition.[26] The new approach of the Schools Commission and governments, Labor, and from 1975, a Liberal–National coalition under Prime Minister Malcolm Fraser created a new foundation for the growth of the private sector. Initially, the vast majority of the new federal funding for schools arising out of the Karmel Committee Report went to public schools. In the years 1974–1975, 69.8 percent of federal money for schools went to government schools and 27.2 percent to schools in the private sector with the remainder being in joint programs. With the exception of those who opposed all state aid to private schools there was a general view in the mid-1970s that the new system of federal funds was closely associated with educational equity.[27]

The election of the Fraser Government in 1975 is generally associated with the end to the postwar 'Keynesian settlement' in Australia. The new government was anxious to dampen expectations on what government could achieve. Federal funds for education and other social programs were reduced. This was the beginning of the sustained influence of the New Right in Australian national policy even though the Fraser Government often disappointed some of its conservative supporters. In a number of ways the federal Liberal–National Party coalition government of 1975–1982 continued the general education policies of its predecessors, particularly in the area of 'multiculturalism' with efforts to win the support of ethnic communities, many of which were close to the Labor side of politics. But the new government also shifted the balance of funds toward nongovernment schools. From 1975/76 to 1981/82, combined Commonwealth recurrent and capital funding of schools in the private sector rose some 70.0 percent. There was a decline of 11.9 percent for government schools.[28]

There is now general agreement that the adoption by government of the Karmel Report saved many Australian nongovernment schools from closure, particularly those in the Catholic sector that were under considerable financial difficulties in the 1960s with the necessity of employing and paying lay teachers.

Since the mid- to late-1970s, Federal Government policies have in the main continued to favor the private sector. The election of the Hawke federal Labor Government in 1983 brought a review of federal aid to schools. The needs formula of the Schools Commission that had been based on an index of school expenditure was replaced by a measure of a school's income, and schools were then grouped into funding categories. This was an effort to diminish funding to wealthier private schools. The new federal Government also initiated a 'new schools' policy in an effort to restrict the growth of the private sector and the resulting negative impact on enrolments in nearby public schools. Minimum enrolment levels were now imposed on prospective new private schools that were seeking federal aid. Despite these changes, during the late 1980s and early 1990s federal funding per student in private schools continued the steady increase that had begun in 1974.[29]

Effectively new federal funding arrangements in the 1970s and 1980s subsidized those who had chosen to send their children to nongovernment schools, none of which were comprehensive in a broad social sense, though many had developed broader curriculum offerings. The private costs of sending a student to a private school had been rising in the 1960s; by the 1980s this situation had been reversed. Over two-thirds of recurrent expenditure on nongovernment schools was now financed by governments. The private cost of nongovernment schooling in 1981–1982 was only about one-third of what it had been in 1968–1969.[30] The major beneficiaries of these new funding policies were Catholic parents and Catholic schools that still constituted almost four-fifths of the 'private' sector in Australia. But such funding arrangements had major implications for the future of public education and the comprehensive high school.

Writing almost two decades after the publication of the Karmel Report, one commentator pointed out that Australia had by then one of the strongest private educational sectors in the world. He suggested that four conditions favored the development of a large and influential nongovernment sector: "a mainly comprehensive public secondary system"; "powerful centrally directed educational administrations"; religious and ethnic heterogeneity; and substantial state aid to private schools. Of all the seven Anglo-American and Scandinavian countries studied only Australia stood high on all these four factors.[31]

In fact, a very strange phenomenon had developed in Australia. Variously and commonly described as the 'private,' 'non-government' or 'independent' sector, this sector was in fact increasingly funded publicly. As part of the process of receiving public funds, some, though limited controls were developed so that public funds were spent with some public accountability. In secondary education, public comprehensive schools were being competed with by mainly publicly funded secondary schools and systems that were not subject to the centralized and bureaucratic controls of the government systems.

Dilemmas of Selection, Examination, and Curriculum

Public comprehensive school systems in each of the Australian States were influenced by both the changing international contexts and the new politics of federal policy making during the 1970s and 1980s. Of all the Australian states, Victoria possibly moved furthest down the road of curriculum reform. With many older industries in such areas as clothing and footwear manufacturing and with large concentrations of postwar migrants, Victoria confronted a major issue of youth unemployment. In the 1980s the Labor Party won government in Victoria. There was growing attention to the problem of increasing and managing retention rates in the post-compulsory years of schooling. In early 1984, the Victorian Government released a discussion paper from the Ministerial Review of Post-Compulsory Schooling that was chaired by Jean Blackburn, one of the prime authors of the first Karmel Report in 1973. The final report of the Review in 1985 proposed that there be a 70 percent school retention rate to Year 12, a goal to be achieved by developing various 'pathways' including forms of further education and training, linked to schools.[32] Such an approach was clearly founded on very different ideas about the senior high school and who would enter it compared to those that had been developed in the Wyndham scheme in New South Wales some twenty years earlier.

In contrast, public education in New South Wales, which had been at the forefront of the moves toward comprehensive schools in the 1950s and 1960s, was constrained and uncertain in its approach to the continuing development of a comprehensive schools policy. As had become a common feature of educational reform in New South Wales, discussion tended to center on the issue of assessment and examination reform. There was also the continuing debate over the role of the surviving selective high schools. For a decade and a half these related issues dominated the debate over the future of the comprehensive high school.

In the early 1970s, optimistic prospects for the comprehensive high school seemed clearly established. The then ruling New South Wales Liberal Government was committed to continuing the development of the public comprehensive school model despite the changing politics of education and the new era of state aid for the private sector. Eric Willis, the Minister for

Education from 1972 to 1976, even indicated a rather lukewarm view of the private sector at the beginning of his tenure, seeing 'competition' as a feature of liberalism and informing the Parliament that "the independent school system should be retained to provide an alternative form of education, to give parents a choice and—to be realistic—to stave off a crisis in government schools. Our present level of assistance—federal and State—is not so great as to promote growth of private schools . . . but for this form of government assistance by this time most independent schools would have gone out of existence."[33] Drawing on the new public policy discourses of 'community' and administrative devolution, Willis proposed a new era in public education with elected school councils to share the responsibility for governing schools, although it is probable that a covert reason for the policy was the attempted reduction of the influence of the teachers' unions on education policy. Their opposition did in fact lead to the frustration of the scheme.[34]

More generally the Liberal–Country Party coalition government continued to rely on the Department of Education in the area of the curriculum, despite a number of Liberal backbenchers who now joined with the Liberal 'rebel' Douglas Darby in raising the issue of educational standards. Significantly, and despite the critics of educational standards within his party, Willis as Minister accepted the advice of his Departmental officials on the move to make all government secondary schools comprehensive. He thus supported the end to selective secondary education in the city of Newcastle as has been discussed in the previous chapter.

In October 1975, the Minister of Education appointed a committee to report on the surviving selective high schools. The new committee, composed principally of officials within the Department of Education, soon recommended that its terms of reference be altered to include "the identification and education of highly talented children in Years 7 to 12 in government schools" and "the organization of the education appropriate to these children."[35] This signified a change of emphasis, a reflection of the emerging shift toward differentiation even among those who supported comprehensive reorganization. By 1976–1977, with the federal Liberal–National government of Malcolm Fraser in power, the topic of special provision for the 'gifted and talented' had been taken up by the Australian Education Council, the body representing the Ministers and Directors of Education in each of the Australian states.[36] Using the new language that had been created by the Karmel Committee, the local New South Wales Committee even suggested that "The talented are possibly the most disadvantaged group in our schools for they generally have not received the stimulation to achieve their full potential."[37]

The New South Wales Labor Government elected in 1976 inherited this particular committee of enquiry. Under the leadership of Neville Wran (a barrister and an 'old boy' of Fort Street High) the new government was built on an alliance of interests that went beyond the traditional support of industrial trade unions. Premier Wran quickly established an Ethnic Affairs Commission to accommodate the interests of ethnic communities. 'Multicultural education' with a focus on community languages soon became official policy. By the end of the 1970s the Government was even proposing that the old assimilationist purposes of public schools would be replaced by a curriculum that provided multicultural perspectives and promoted intercultural understanding as well as supporting those learning English as a second language.[38]

The Labor Government was also closely associated with the New South Wales Teachers' Federation that was a strong and continuing supporter of the comprehensive ideal. Eric Bedford, a former teacher and now the Minister for Education, thus informed the Director of Education that the continuing existence of selective high schools was of "particular concern" to the Labor Government which believed that all public secondary schools should be comprehensive and coeducational. While not wishing to preempt the Report of the Committee if the abolition of selective schools was recommended, a "thoroughly conceived plan of action" should be implemented by 1978.[39]

The committee of enquiry lasted almost a year and a half receiving 250 submissions from teachers, parents, pupils and academics, as well as teacher unions and community organizations. In its report presented in 1977, the Committee reviewed the changes that had occurred since the Wyndham Report of two decades earlier. There was now a pattern of four years of universal secondary education. Universal provision thus raised the question as to whether there was adequate recognition of "highly talented students."[40] Much of the Report drew upon recent international literature that had attempted to define the 'talented.' While allowing for some definitions based on "creativity" much of the discussion sought ways to identify those who displayed "intellectual" abilities. On the issue of "special provision" the Committee argued against retaining the existing selective high schools because essentially they were failing to meet the needs of all the "gifted" and "talented." Only 13 of the then 419 state high schools were selective, containing a mere 3.2 percent of secondary pupils. The Committee had a number of reservations about the "educational relevance" of the selective high schools. Comparing the School Certificate results of students in selective high schools with those identified as "talented" in comprehensive high schools, the Committee found no major differences. The selective high schools did not have better teachers than those who taught in the comprehensives; and more problematically, their students came from restricted geographic areas. Many of the selective students were simply not "talented." It thus recommended that selective high schools be ended. Provision and support for the gifted and talented should be based on plans and programs developed within the Education Department regions of New South Wales and supported by a State Advisory Committee.[41]

When the Minister for Education called for public responses to the Report, of 430 submissions, 410 opposed the abolition of selective high schools. As in the early 1960s a campaign was mounted on the grounds that special schools were required for those of "special talents and interests." Moreover, it was suggested that comprehensive schools did not emphasize academic subjects sufficiently.[42] Only for Wollongong, the industrial city south of Sydney and a region with traditionally low school retention rates, did plans proceed to close the local selective high school and continue with comprehensive reorganization. The creation of three coeducational schools out of former single sex schools was envisaged.[43] Otherwise, the campaign to save the last small group of selective high schools was successful. As the Minister of Education later indicated:

> The inertia of the political system meant that the party would have to make a political issue out of throwing [selective schools] out. It is one thing for the Labor Party to allow the people dancing about on its left to pass resolutions at conference; it is another to let [the left determine] an issue at an election and invoke the ire of all those burgeoning middle class votes that increasingly you understand that you are going to have to attract as your old blue-collar support withers.[44]

This was probably the last occasion on which it was politically possible to close the New South Wales selective high schools. The limit of the Wyndham-inspired comprehensive reorganization plans had been reached. By the late 1970s, the growing uncertainties associated with youth unemployment seem to have strengthened the selective principle. Already Sydney Grammar School, one of the oldest corporate schools in New South Wales had begun to implement a policy of academic selection so as to assume the inheritance of the older state selective high schools. As the headmaster of Sydney Grammar later told a conference of 200 state high school principals, in his view comprehensive schools were not effective: "The current form of egalitarianism, whereby opportunities for groups of people rather than for individuals must be equal, seems to frustrate any attempt to provide quality education."[45] This was a view increasingly supported by sections of the media which, it has been suggested, acted as *The Black Papers* of Australia asserting that standards were in decline and calling for a return to both 'excellence' and the "basics."[46]

The report of the Committee on the Gifted and Talented and the decision not to close selective high schools in Sydney thus had a number of consequences. First, there was continuing pressure for programs for the 'gifted and talented' in comprehensive high schools, particularly those in middle-class areas but sometimes even as part of the 'disadvantaged schools' program.[47] Second, there was mounting criticism of the uneven regional distribution of the existing selective high schools and the zoning policy that restricted their enrolment. In 1983, the Liberal member for an electorate in the principally middle-class suburb of Earlwood in southwestern Sydney, pointed out that his electorate came within the intake of the boundaries of two selective high schools, St George Girls' High and Sydney Technical High. But the boundaries also crossed his electorate so that some pupils were qualified by residential address to attend the schools while others were not. As a result he said, parents were now giving false addresses to the Department or having their children live with relatives to qualify for entry. He posed the question: "If the justification for selective high schools is that they create a special educational environment for brighter students, the introduction of geographic boundaries defeats this purpose."[48] A similar complaint came from the Labor member for Bankstown in outer western Sydney who took exception to the fact that all the existing selective high schools were concentrated on the lower North Shore, the inner city, and southern Sydney. This produced an obvious discrimination against children from western Sydney and the rest of New South Wales. "I find it anathema that a child of the capabilities of an Einstein, living in a Sydney outer western suburb such as in the Penrith area, is automatically denied entry to a selective high school because of residential address." He argued that either the selective high schools be abolished or the residential intake qualification be ended.[49]

Allied to the issues of selection and standards was that of examination reform. Following the abolition of the external examination for the School Certificate in 1975 student results were based on school assessments with provision for state-wide moderation. By 1977, moderation was retained only in English and Mathematics. In the context of the debate over educational standards these changes attracted criticisms leading to the Secondary Schools Board issuing an invitation for comments and submissions on the School Certificate system. By the end of 1978, of the 900 submissions received, the majority indicated support for a partial externally assessed examination after four years of high school.[50]

At the end of 1979, the New South Wales Parliament established a select committee to examine the current procedures for the award of the School Certificate and whether they met the "concerns of the community regarding the education of students in the first four years of secondary school." The chair of the Committee was Brian McGowan, a Labor Member of Parliament. The other four members were drawn from the Labor Party and the Liberal–Country Party opposition. In contrast to the Wyndham

Committee this was a parliamentary enquiry, an indication of the growing politicization of educational issues.[51]

The McGowan Committee convened over eighteen months receiving submissions and interviewing witnesses. The report to the Parliament was a mixture of a continuing commitment to elements of educational progressivism as well as a recognition of new political realities. As with the earlier *Aims of Secondary Education* (1973), the Report began with a review of changes since the Wyndham Committee and the Education Act of 1961. As with the Wyndham Committee it sought to reconcile the interests of the academic elite with the needs of the majority of students. In some respects, it represented a call to past ideals at a time when increasing retention rates in school increasingly challenged old assumptions. The Committee argued that the guiding principles adopted by the Wyndham Committee remained relevant, and were "possibly timeless." It agreed that the primary purpose of secondary education was not to produce university matriculants, "but to give all adolescents the best possible preparation for adult life." Because most students in the junior secondary years had no university aspirations, it followed that there was no reason to orient the junior high school toward the Higher School Certificate. Nevertheless, the Committee argued that the students, for whom a Higher School Certificate was a prerequisite, were a significant minority whose interests must be considered. They argued that the junior secondary years had for too long been organized with the interests of the universities considered paramount, and that this had to change. It was a matter of ordering priorities correctly. They believed that any new curriculum reform must protect the rights of the university-bound student while raising to primacy the rights of the majority.[52]

The major recommendation of the McGowan Committee was a proposal to abolish the School Certificate and institute a Certificate of Secondary Education available to all students beyond the legal leaving age of fifteen. Individual schools would issue the Certificate under the guidelines of a central board with ultimate authority for secondary education being vested in the Minister for Education. As part of this reform schools could develop their own semester-length courses. Such a proposal appeared to be a continuation of the overall comprehensive ideal associated with progressive education: the new certificate was to be designed primarily as a 'record of achievement' for each individual student although courses would still be graded with provision for students to repeat a course. But there were also concessions toward supporting the 'gifted and talented' as well as meeting the concerns of the media over educational standards. The Committee thus favored 'ability grouping' across years and 'accelerated progression.' It also proposed an evaluation of 'basic skills' through a test that could be made available not only to school students but adults.

The last recommendation of the Committee was for the abolition of the current zoning arrangements whereby students had to attend the school designated for the area in which they lived.[53] This recommendation, when it was eventually given effect, and combined with the expansion of non-government schools, was as fated as any other reason to contribute to the decline of public comprehensive schooling.

The New South Wales Teachers' Federation, which still maintained close associations with the Labor Government, opposed the idea of de-zoning but also other recommendations of the McGowan Committee including the prospect of the new Certificate of Secondary Education that they argued would cause students to leave before the end of Year 10. The Federation was also concerned over the requirement to maintain detailed records of a pupil's school career as well as the loss of an individual school's control over assessments. One view suggested that: "In effect a struggle is underway between the Government and the Federation over the control of secondary education in New South Wales." The McGowan proposals were also undermined by the collapse of a prototype of the proposed assessment system that had been trialed in a local high school in McGowan's electorate.[54]

The pressing nature of anxieties around youth, youth unemployment, and a suitable secondary curriculum for young people saw continuing activity at the state level to clarify the purposes of secondary education and to produce effective reform. This activity occurred in the context of the pressures arising from an activist Schools Commission in Canberra with its power to recommend or withhold funding on a special purpose program basis.

In early 1983, at the request of a new Labor Minister of Education, Douglas Swann, the Director General of Education in association with Dr. Ken McKinnon, a former chair of the Schools Commission, issued a discussion paper on "Future Directions in Secondary Education" in New South Wales. Again reviewing the changes of the past two decades the discussion paper raised the question as to whether the conception of the Wyndham scheme providing for four years of general nonvocational education followed by two senior years directed toward tertiary studies still remained in operation. What had changed was not only the introduction of a greater range of courses and subjects in the junior years of secondary school but more significantly in the final two years, with the Board of Senior School Studies beginning to sanction 'Other Approved Studies' designed for those not proceeding to higher education. It was necessary therefore to go beyond even the McGowan Report in looking at the full six years of secondary schooling. The main proposal of the paper was to recommend a Board of Secondary Education to advise the Minister on secondary education from Years 7 to 12 with regard to catering for a diverse range of students while still providing a "core of learning." The Board would also develop policies and guidelines that would allow a school to choose an organizational pattern appropriate to local needs. There would also be provision for student accreditation and certificates for those who completed four, five, and six years of secondary schooling.[55]

The older Wyndham comprehensive scheme seemed to be coming apart. The new attention to the senior years of the high school raised new possibilities. One was that for the first time, the extension of a true 'comprehensive' curriculum organization to the final two years would complete the process begun by the Wyndham scheme. But there were other possibilities. The Minister of Education, Ron Mulock, indicated that in the light of the "Future Directions" paper he foresaw a number of new developments including a "pilot senior high school concept." He had asked the Director General of Education to report on the possibility of such a school for the western suburbs of Sydney. If such a proposal was launched he saw "no reason why high schools incorporating a special emphasis should not be developed." There was already the Conservatorium High School for music students so he asked: "Why could there not be developed a high school or a senior high school with a sports orientation?" Such an approach would be "an adjunct to the basic concept of our secondary system, providing neighborhood comprehensive coeducational high schools."[56]

By the mid-1980s public secondary education in New South Wales was undoubtedly at a watershed. One contemporary commentator suggested that there were now four influences operating: the new special 'interest' groups including the growing ethnically based organizations; the teachers unions; the effect of the economic recession and youth unemployment; and finally the educational bureaucracy that was struggling to maintain its traditional central control.[57] Complicating matters was the instability within the educational portfolio with five changes over the period 1976–1984.

The appointment of Rodney Cavalier as Minister of Education in early 1984 has been portrayed as an effort of the Labor Government to re-assert its control over public education. As a member of the left wing of the Labor Party, Cavalier has been seen as "the strongest Minister for Education since D. H. Drummond in the 1930," someone who believed "it possible to reconcile equality of opportunity with a solid academic grounding."[58] At the outset Cavalier supported the central Department of Education against the staffing demands of the New South Wales Teachers' Federation, determined to ensure that educational administrators would run the portfolio and not the Teachers' Federation with its assumed right of veto on policy.[59] While privately holding reservations regarding selective high schools he also made it clear early in his tenure of office that they would remain part of the educational landscape of public education. Having shelved the idea of a senior high school, Cavalier argued that the comprehensive coeducational neighborhood school remained the foundation of secondary education. He also suggested that the issue now emerging was about "specialities" with a number of the existing comprehensives developing reputations in such areas as music or catering for ethnic or Aboriginal communities. Finally, there was the need to cater to those with "special talents."[60] At the same time, the new Minister gave tacit approval to de-zoning later pointing out that by the end of the 1980s more than 40,000 students were attending schools outside their local school districts and almost three-quarters of applications for such enrolments were approved with the main refusals being based on the fact that many schools were already full.[61]

It was under Cavalier as Minister that the Swann–Mackinnon "Future Directions of Secondary Education" was issued in late 1984. Building on the earlier discussion paper the Report now introduced the principle of "six years of secondary education for all" or "at least the great majority of young people." The purpose of secondary education was that "every student acquires a well-consolidated general education encompassing skills of oral and written communication, quantitative reasoning and the other skills needed for successful participation in modern society."[62] Other principles advocated were a closer relationship between theoretical and applied studies, assessment and reporting of student achievement on the basis of "publicly understood statewide credentials," provision for new structures in the postcompulsory years including cooperation with Technical and Further Education colleges and involvement of the "community" in the curriculum, processes, and institutional forms of education. In terms of administrative arrangements a Board of Secondary Education would replace the two existing Boards of Studies. Under the chairmanship of the Director General of Education, the Board would oversee the general development and direction of the full six years of the secondary school curriculum. It would have a "core of learning" but with provision for mandatory options and opportunity for vocational subjects and interests in the final two years of schooling. Secondary education was now clearly conceived as a continuum stretching from the latter years of the primary school to the senior years of high school. A Certificate of Secondary Education, replacing the existing School Certificate would be available to any student leaving school prior to Year 12. The Higher School Certificate would remain as a public examination-based credential at the end of the six years of secondary education.[63]

Much of the Swann–Mackinnon Report formed the basis of the 1987 Education Act. Formally, the Act was an amendment to the Public Instruction Act of 1880 that had established the public school system of New South Wales. As such it carried both symbolic meaning as well as authorizing substantial reform. The actual objects of the Act were designed to "continue the system of public school education established by the Public Instruction Act of 1880," providing for continuing "registration of non-government schools" while also creating a new certificate of secondary education and a Board of Secondary Education. The arrangements for registration of private schools dated from the early twentieth century. Under the 1912 Bursary Endowment Act, schools had had to register with the statutory examination boards to allow their students to qualify for bursaries. The 1916 Public Instruction Act provided for private schools to be certified as offering "regular and efficient instruction." The 1961 Act that had established the Wyndham scheme allowed for the registration of schools to allow their students to sit for the School Certificate and Higher School Certificate. The 1987 Act required all schools enrolling students in the compulsory years of schooling to be registered. The overall aim was to ensure that all schools followed the curriculum now sanctioned by the new Board of Secondary Education. Both the Minister and the Board were able to close schools that were not registered and certified under the new arrangements for the school curriculum. With the new Board closely linked to the Department of Education, and the Director General as chair of the Board, this was an obvious effort to assert the role of both the educational bureaucracy and public education over a strengthening private school sector.[64] Commenting on the new legislation the now octogenarian Sir Harold Wyndham saw it simply as an extension of what he had instituted:

> I don't think that the fundamentals have changed. It doesn't seem to challenge the principles of the 1961 Act, it's a 1980s addendum to the Act. No education plan can be regarded as final; you are never finished in education.[65]

It could also be seen as a 'final' effort to maintain the old public education settlement that dated from the nineteenth century.

Market Liberalism?

In 1988, a new Liberal-National Party government came to power in New South Wales. In contrast to its state Liberal Party predecessor of the mid-1960s to the mid-1970s, this was a government of the 'New' or 'Neo-liberalism,' strongly convinced of the virtues of the 'market' and the effect it might have on developing new public policy. Even the new Liberal Premier was a marked departure from former Liberal leaders. Of Catholic Hungarian background, educated in an elite Jesuit corporate school, and with qualifications and experience in business management, Nicholas ('Nick') Greiner had been elected to the Parliament in 1980 becoming Opposition Leader in 1983 so ending a period of leadership instability in the state Liberal Party. Greiner soon identified his Party with a view of "Australian Liberalism in a Post-Ideological Age": "practical," "empirical" and "anti-ideological." "Modern Liberalism must be concerned with the re-design and reconstruction of any of our institutions that are outdated, out-moded or not working in the public interest."[66] In government this came to mean an agenda of administrative rationalization, to achieve economies and efficiencies; "post-bureaucratic" micro-reforms involved decentralization, to "let the managers manage"; "integrity in government" meant to govern in the "public interest" and so avoid corruption and catering to "special interests"; and finally a dose of "social-populism" often presented as "back to the basics."[67]

Education and schools were at the center of this agenda. The Minister for Education in the new government was initially a close confidant of the Premier. Educated at a public comprehensive high school and later a student radical of the 1960s, Terence ('Terry') Metherell had graduated with a doctorate in History. By the 1980s, he was attracted to elements of the market philosophy of the 'New Right' arguing in 1984 that the 'New Liberalism' should have five political principles: the supremacy of the individual, freedom of choice, equality of opportunity, commitment to care for the disadvantaged and a balance between economic growth and environmental protection.[68] He also learnt from changes already occurring overseas:

> We talked about the missing ingredients in education . . . more choice, more specialization, the question of better leadership in schools. We read and saw what was happening overseas and then we set about developing a framework of policies that gave effect and coherence to those principles.
>
> Into that we weaved the best of overseas practice . . . state of the art technology high schools, the creation of a level playing field between government and non-government schools so that the best qualities of one could be seen as the best qualities of the other and parents were given a real choice within the sectors and between the sectors.[69]

Part of this reform program could be achieved by administrative fiat in ways that would challenge the comprehensive high school ideal. By the end of 1988, public schools were finally and formally de-zoned, allowing parents to enroll their children outside their local school district.

At the same time, the new government moved quickly to establish eight new selective high schools in south and western Sydney as well as the

Newcastle and Wollongong regions. As the new Minister informed Department of Education officials it was no longer possible to close the existing selective high schools in Sydney. It was thus "inequitable" not to extend the principle of selection elsewhere and with de-zoning it should be possible to allow anyone in the State to apply for entry.[70] In public he informed the press ten days after the election of the new government that his "first aim" was:

> to stop the drift of students from government to non-government schools and to bring back the historic 75:25 ratio between the two respective sectors which would effectively mean a reduction in present non-government schools of up to three per cent. The way to achieve this, Dr Metherell believes, is to provide more choice within the government school sector by establishing more single sex high schools, more academically selective schools and more specialist schools in areas such as technology and the performing arts.[71]

By the end of 1988, despite the opposition of the Board of Secondary Education, the new Minister had announced that "a merit list" of the top 500 students in the Higher School Certificate examination would be published including the schools attended.[72] The new focus on 'school choice' also related to the appointment of Dr. Brian Scott, a business and educational consultant, to carry out a review of the education portfolio and the public school system. In tune with the 'post-bureaucracy' philosophy of the new Liberal Government the Scott review proposed a model of devolution and decentralization to provide "effective schools."

School principals were to be selected after due advertisement; once appointed they could recruit their own executive and eventually the teaching staff of a school. Each principal was to have a local budget and be able to allocate resources. School councils representing the local community would be appointed to assist in school management. To assist these changes new "clusters" of public schools would be created under "cluster directors." The central office of the Department of Education would be reduced in size and moved from its headquarters in the city that it had occupied since the early twentieth century.[73]

To accompany these proposed administrative changes, Metherell established a review of New South Wales schools with the prime aim of overturning the 1987 Public Instruction Act with its provisions for the registration of nongovernment schools (which the Liberals in Opposition had opposed) and the establishment of a Board of Secondary Education. The Review was also to examine ways to improve the "quality" of education in New South Wales.[74] As chair of the Review the new Minister appointed Sir John Carrick. Closely associated with the Liberal Party since its foundation in the 1940s, Carrick had been General Secretary of the State Liberal Party

(1948–1971) before being elected to the Federal Senate. From 1975 to 1979 he had been Federal Minister for Education in the Fraser Liberal Government overseeing a review of tertiary education. He had also been a mentor to Metherell who had worked for Carrick when he was Leader of the Government in the Australian Senate.[75] Educated in a selective high school Carrick was part of the old Liberal Party establishment that had once supported the encompassing civic purposes of public education. By the 1980s, his philosophy was more in accord with the New Liberalism suggesting that "Governments should be measured by the lightness with which they touch your purse."[76] The committee he chaired included representatives of the Department of Education and the New South Wales Teachers Federation as well as school principals and representatives of the private sector, business, and parent groups. The tension between the representatives of old and continuing interests and traditions and the era of 'New Liberalism' was in part reflected in the Review.

Of most significance, the Carrick-led review was concerned with all schools and not just public education. Much of the detail of the Report was devoted to curriculum issues in both primary and secondary schools but it also had significance for the future of the comprehensive school. As with the reviews of the 1980s it took as its reference point the earlier Wyndham Report and the changes since, but its interpretation of both the past and the future was quite different. Whereas the Wyndham Committee was essentially a statement contextualized by the evolving growth of public education and an almost inevitable emergence of the public comprehensive high school, the Carrick Committee emphasized the continuing strength of the private sector since the nineteenth century. It noted that by the 1980s one quarter of students in Australia remained outside public education, a much higher proportion internationally than in the United Kingdom and the United States and other Asia Pacific nations such as Japan and New Zealand. Of particular significance was the "strong Catholic tradition in schooling" and "a strong Catholic school system" that had to be taken into account in planning for the "improvement of the quality of schooling."[77] Equally, in the "provision of schooling" the Committee argued that any legislation must be based on five principles: the right of each child to education, the rights and responsibilities of parents, the duty of governments to prescribe and enforce basic standards, the provision of government schools of the highest possible standards, and the right of citizens to establish non-government schools.[78]

Within this philosophical context, the Review developed an uncertain view about the future of the public comprehensive high schools. It noted that since the Wyndham Report the comprehensive high school had been the "predominant organizational form" for secondary education even though recent initiatives of the new Liberal Government had led to more selective and specialist high schools. It then asserted:

> While commending these efforts to increase choice in schooling the Committee wishes to express its support for the retention of the comprehensive high school and its curriculum as the model for secondary schools. All students should have the opportunity to develop particular talents and interests and in some cases this opportunity can only be provided through specialist schools and arrangements. However, the local comprehensive school must continue to provide adequate opportunities for its students to develop their talents and interests.[79]

While accepting the new era of devolution preached by the earlier Scott Report, the Carrick Committee was still skeptical about the role of the 'market' and unfettered 'school choice.' A chapter in the Carrick Review on "Equity in Education" attempted to balance "freedom of choice" with needs of specific groups including Aboriginal and ethnic communities and the specific call for attention to gender equity. It was suggested that "market forces can be seen as ephemeral, following fads and fashions, and capable of creating a minority of less effective schools populated by less able children. Alternatively, market forces could be seen as the sensibility of the silent majority exercising its influence."[80] The Committee thus favored "restricted" choice in public education rather than total "free market dezoning," suggesting that "significant choice" could be achieved within individual comprehensive schools or through school clusters.[81] Overall, the Committee suggested that debate about freedom of choice and the strengths and weakness of government and nongovernment schools had to be seen in terms of the overall goals of education defined here as a mixture of individual and civic ends involving parental choice, pluralism, social unity, and quality education.[82]

The recommendations of the Carrick Committee formed the basis of the 1990 Education Reform Act. Based on the principles annunciated in the Review this legislation emphasized the rights of the child, the obligations of parents, the significance of 'quality education,' and the duty of the state particularly in the provision of public education. The Act provided for a new Board of Studies that would be independent of the Department of Education and would assume direct responsibility for a curriculum framework from kindergarten to Year 12 with a focus on Key Learning Areas. The new Board would develop and endorse courses that would be formally approved by the Minister of Education. The Board would have responsibility for the School Certificate (now reinstated and effectively replacing the Certificate of Secondary Education initiated under the 1987 Act) and the Higher School Certificate. On the contentious issue of the registration of the schools of the private sector, the Act separated out registration (the right to operate) from accreditation (the right to present candidates for the certificates of the new Board). Schools were also given the right on religious grounds to registration under the Act. Parents could also apply to educate their children in their own homes. In accord with one of the recommendations of the Carrick Committee there was even provision in the original legislation to register public schools but this was removed during the parliamentary debates.[83]

The Scott Report, the Carrick Review, and the 1990 Education Reform Act were all acted on within two years of the new Liberal government coming to power. Together they constituted the main agenda for reform. By the time that the 1990 Act was passed Metherell was no longer Minister of Education, having virtually been forced out of office by a public campaign opposing the 'cuts' he had introduced that had sought to reduce staffing and move resources in public schools from such areas as the North Shore to the expanding western suburbs of Sydney. By 1992, Premier Greiner had also resigned; a victim of his own campaign against corruption, leaving office with charges that he had tried to appoint Metherell to a senior position in the government executive service. From 1990 the 'politics of confrontation' was followed by the 'politics of review' and then the 'politics of accommodation' in the education portfolio. The Liberal Government was now more cautious in its reforms but much of the agenda remained. While not all the proposals of the Scott Report were implemented there was now a more decentralized Department and a commitment to devolution to the level of individual schools. In 1991, a new Director General of Education was appointed. Formerly Director General in South Australia, Dr. Ken Boston was one of the 'new managers' of public education who had his own agenda for change that in some ways went beyond the Scott Review. He instituted a program of 'quality assurance' involving local communities and business to assess the performance of local schools.[84]

Regional Responses

In particular localities in New South Wales, the various policy changes of the 1970s and 1980s played out differently. The Northern Beaches, the area of the peninsula north of Sydney, provides an example of how this could occur. Where parts of the Outer West of Sydney continued to experience urban expansion and population and infrastructure increase, in other parts of Sydney, and after the children of the 'baby boom' had passed through the secondary schools, new challenges for comprehensive high schooling occurred.

The highpoint of population and suburban expansion on the Northern Beaches was in the early 1970s. From the late 1970s the population began to age, with school-age youth numbers dropping quite dramatically, this in the context of new nongovernment school expansion, and the increasing wealth of households in the area to pay private school fees. There had been new coeducational comprehensive school openings in the 1970s. In 1980 in Manly, single sex schools were reorganized to reopen as coeducational schools, in the process hoping to stem enrolment loss. One of them, Manly High School became one of the Greiner government's new selective high schools. Its enrolment had sunk as low as 420 students in 1989. Under the circumstances of selectivity, by 2000 it had grown again to 728 students. The experience of this school was fortunate. Its growth probably exacerbated the decline of other public schools on the southern end of the peninsula.

In his analysis of the history of comprehensive schooling in this area John Hughes concluded that the two factors "beyond the control of the State government are regional demographic changes and the impact of a shift to private schools. The comprehensive school of the 1960s was the solution proposed to the massive surge in enrolments. The inevitable substantial decline arising from the ageing of the regional population would have required major reorganization of secondary school provision and inevitably some closures."[85] This reorganization came eventually, in 2003 as part of the multicampus collegiate solutions advocated by Director General Boston and discussed in more detail in the next chapter.

The major public education reforms of this period from the late 1960s were in secondary education. By the early 1990s, the reforms of the Metherell era had led to a general undermining of the public comprehensive school system despite the views of the Carrick Committee and others. Of particular effect was the de-zoning provisions and the creation of new selective and specialist high schools. The process Metherell began continued after he left as Minister. In 1988, there had been 12 secondary schools with some forms of restricted entry; by 1995 there were 63 specialist secondary schools: 19 academically selective, 28 new 'technology high schools,' four 'agricultural high schools,' four 'senior high schools,' two sports high schools and a rural technology high.[86] The New South Wales secondary school system now contained a variety of diverse schools. And, despite his professed aims, Metherell had not 'rescued' public education. When the Greiner government came to power 29.5 percent of secondary school students in New South Wales were educated in nongovernment schools. By 1995, when the Liberal Government was defeated 31.8 percent were in nongovernment schools, and the rate of loss had begun to increase.[87] The 'blame' for such a loss could not be laid at the door of state governments alone. The overriding significant fact of the 1970s through the 1980s had been the actions of the Australian federal government, whether Liberal–National, or Labor. The restoration of state aid to nongovernment schools encouraged at first a stabilization, then significant expansion of that sector. Where much of the oppositional rhetoric had concerned the allocation of tax-funded grants to the wealthier 'private' schools, in fact the greatest expansion occurred in the low-fee nongovernment school area. The Anglican Church, after a century's absence of interest in providing secondary schools for families of moderate or less than moderate means began building schools once more. Other churches, including some of the newer protestant denominations with pentecostalist and fundamentalist American origins were also significant starters.

Over the 1990s, the 'drift' to the private sector would continue as a 'market' in education was more firmly established. Changes in public policy in the two decades from 1970 to 1990 had led to the development of many thousands of new places in publicly funded nongovernment secondary schools. The great age of expansion for the public comprehensive school, and a fair acceptance of its mission to be the common secondary school for all Australian youth, let alone those of New South Wales, was over. The great age of post–World War II reconstruction and 'assimilation,' where common institutions were generally accepted as universally appropriate for all Australian youth was also over. Where social class and religion had once been the greatest of the discriminators in schooling, now there were ethnic and racial origins, and gender to consider as well as poverty, and in an educational context, concern for different kinds of abilities in students had made a strong comeback. The needs of the 'gifted and talented,' the non-English speaking background (NESB) and 'disabled' students, and those with poor literacy and numeracy skills for whatever reason, all needed to be met. The comprehensive high school was required to become ever more comprehensive in its capacity to accommodate the diverse needs. Policies of 'main-streaming' and separating into specialist schools could coexist. But the public education system was no longer expanding at the rates it had from the 1950s to the 1970s. The secondary students from the demographic hump of the baby-boom had passed through by the 1990s, and state aid decisions as well as new neoliberal public policy approaches also contributed to the declining capacities of public education. It was likely that many comprehensive government schools would lose students and consequent staffing and curriculum capacity in the process.

Chapter 5

The Market

In early 1997, one of Sydney's two daily newspapers, *The Daily Telegraph* devoted its front page to a school and its final year students, both of which had apparently 'failed.'[1] It appeared that not one student in Year 12 from the Mount Druitt High School, a state comprehensive, had achieved anything like the assessment scores required to achieve university entrance. Here was a prime example of the worst that could happen in the 1990s in the government comprehensive sector. The psychological impact of the headline, article, and the ensuing debate paralleled the English controversy surrounding the comments of Labour Minister for Education, Estelle Morris, that there were some inner city comprehensive schools that she would not touch with a "barge-pole."[2] Sydney it appeared also had its 'sink' and 'failing' secondary schools, all of which appeared to be in the government sector. It later appeared that none of the students, a photograph of whom had appeared in the story, had sought university entrance scores, but their public pillorying was insensitive to that fact. The event provided proof of the worst that the 'league tabling' of examination results and tertiary entrance indexes could do for the reputations of some students, some schools, and the government system of comprehensive secondary education in particular.

The New South Wales Department of Education and Training made its own enquiry into the incident. The subsequent report provided a useful analysis of the problems that some comprehensive high schools could develop by the end of the twentieth century.[3] The Mount Druitt High School was in Sydney's outer western suburbs, near Blacktown that the 2001 national census revealed as having one of the lowest median weekly individual income rates for metropolitan Sydney. It scored low on several other social indicators.[4] The report indicated these problems but also pointed to the demographic and school market issues:

> The slow decline in school enrolments at Mount Druitt High School is echoed in other government comprehensive high schools in this area. This overall decline can be attributed to growth in secondary provisions in the Catholic sector and to the impact of the development of St Marys Senior High School. . . . The Commonwealth Government's new policy on the funding of non-government schools is likely to contribute to this trend in future years.[5]

The senior high school, despite its name, was not a Catholic school, but a former comprehensive government school converted to a senior college in 1989 as part of the Metherell reforms. The problems of the Mount Druitt comprehensive school were induced not only by demographic problems, federal government policies that encouraged nongovernment schools in the area, but also state government policies that had left comprehensive schools in competition for senior students with a special purpose senior college. The report concluded that such developments had left a structure of secondary education in Mount Druitt that could only be described as "fragile." It argued that the numbers of senior students attending comprehensive schools in the area would continue to decline, severely limiting the curriculum options available.[6] In fact, schools such as these could hardly be classified 'comprehensive' in any broad curriculum sense. There were neither the students nor staff to sustain the promise of the comprehensive school in curriculum terms. These were schools that had become residualized in a social sense as well. Their enrolments included unrepresentatively high concentrations of students with unemployed parents, recently arrived non-English speaking migrant families, and in great part, as a result, high concentrations of students with significant learning difficulties.[7]

Diversity and the Comprehensive High Schools

The government secondary school system in New South Wales is one of the larger school systems in the world. There is no local government control in any substantial sense. Where there have been attempts to decentralize administration or devolve decision-making at various times in the late twentieth century, there was never any doubt that in the end, it was the state government through its Education Department that controlled public schooling, even if the directions of federal funding programs increasingly constrained many aspects of policy making. By 2001, the number of separate government secondary schools was 394, the number of students enrolled in postprimary education was 756,740 and the number of government secondary teachers was 69,681.[8] The regions of New South Wales include the broadest range of urban, suburban, country town, and rural districts. Under these circumstances, and despite the centralized control, it was inevitable that how schools operated in their different regions would develop rather differently. Some of the problems of schools such as Mount Druitt in the Outer West of Sydney could be quite absent from schools in other places, and in some cases schools only a few kilometers away.

Each region has its own peculiar mix of factors producing such diversity. The expectations of schools by different families and communities are strongly related to their social class characteristics, and the ever-changing relationships between families, youth labor markets, and higher education opportunities. The city of Sydney with a population of some four million in 2001 encompasses a variety of socially cohesive regions, partially dependent on differing real estate values and concentrations of certain ethnic groups and communities. It has mattered for many decades where one lived and where one was schooled, whether in the Eastern Suburbs or the Upper North Shore, or in the Inner or Outer West, and so on. The experienced character of secondary education, government and nongovernment has been very responsive to these differences, regardless of centralized controls and the provision of uniform school types across the government sector.[9] When we add the diversity of coastal regions north and south of Sydney, and the rural hinterland of New South Wales, with a further combined population of some 2.4 million, the reality of the diverse characteristics of comprehensive government schools is only increased. Crestwood High School for example is in the Hills District of Sydney. Established in 1981 on the frontier of new suburban development in the 1980s and 1990s, it is a relatively young school with plenty of students seeking to enroll within it. The end of zoning, that is the obligation of government schools to take students only from its allocated neighborhood, has meant that it can also select 'out of area' students as well as enroll those to whom it is obliged.[10] Real estate prices are moderately high, and though the parents of its students no doubt have mortgages large enough to keep them anxious when interest rates rise, the median individual income for the area is substantially larger than that for the Mount Druitt area.[11] In 2000, it had 1,054 students, 142 of whom were in Year 12, and despite competition from nearby government selective high schools, Baulkham Hills High and James Ruse Agricultural High, it did well enough in the public examination statistics that counted. It usually gained mention in the Higher School Certificate honors lists, and its students qualified for university entrance at reasonable rates.[12]

Glebe High School, founded only two years earlier than Crestwood in the Inner West of Sydney, also a comprehensive public high school had a very different history; so different that the school was closed in 2001. Its former buildings are now part of the multicampus Sydney Secondary College. The suburb of Glebe contained some public and working-class housing. Almost as old as Sydney itself and very close to the city center, by the 1970s it was beginning to gentrify quite rapidly. There was reason to believe that a new comprehensive high school would do quite well, but the new households of Glebe had few children. As the area became more middle class the schools of choice were often the nearby selective high schools such as Fort Street, as well as the Catholic and other nongovernment schools. By 2000, the school population was down to 314 students. It had had its fair share of critical incidents. Students with varying degrees of learning and social difficulties sought enrolment. Even though it had a small core of middle-class supporters ideologically committed to public comprehensive schooling, the school found it ever more difficult to stabilize around a broad curriculum, and to attract a school population socially representative of its neighborhood. Glebe High School, like its neighbor, Balmain High, were both schools that were unable to capitalize on the gentrification process; they became the residual schools of each area. Demography in the rapid decline of the school-age population had played its part in the process, but the peculiar history of the Inner West, with its wealth of government selective and nongovernment schools, low and high fee, had also played its part.[13]

In the Central West of New South Wales, over the Blue Mountains from Sydney lies one of Australia's wealthier agricultural regions. Country towns of substance exist across the landscape, and it is in some of these towns that comprehensive government high schools that fulfill many of their original objectives continue to thrive. Young High was established in 1946. The town had arisen from a mid-nineteenth-century gold rush. It had an associated anti-Chinese riot history. In the twentieth century it became known for its cherry growing and fruit processing as well as more general agricultural and pastoral activity. The school was far away enough from other substantial towns to survive as a well-supported district comprehensive. It is socially representative of its community in all but one respect. There is a local Catholic secondary school that until reasonably recently did not have a senior school. After Year 10 its students would often transfer to Young High. This school to a fair degree operates at the beginning of the twenty-first century under the conditions in which all government comprehensive schools were originally conceived, in some cases predating the Wyndham Report of the late 1950s. It would offer a unique set of educational opportunities to the youth of its district; it would be a coeducational district comprehensive school, operating without too much concern for competitors in a market.[14]

In other parts of regional and rural New South Wales, the patterns of success for the local comprehensive high school are more mixed. Two issues are of importance. One is the proximity of a large regional center (especially if less than 40 kilometers away) with bigger public high schools and low-fee Catholic and Anglican schools. The second and related issue is the provision of subsidized transport for students that may enable access to a larger school. Thus Bellingen High School in northern New South Wales suffers from the proximity of Coffs Harbour while Wingham High School suffers from the proximity of Taree. In this respect, there is competition for students even within the public sector across regional boundaries. This situation is also indicative of the wider trend: a concentration and centralization of resources and services within some parts of regional Australia. Under these circumstances, the smaller country comprehensive high schools are vulnerable to competition from larger regional centers. When critical incidents occur (e.g. incidents associated with drugs or violence, or antagonism between school decisions and the views of local parents), students may be lost quite rapidly. Such losses in already small schools can dramatically affect their teacher entitlements and breadth of curriculum offering, sometimes making them 'comprehensive' schools in name only.

At the same time, smaller country comprehensive high schools have access to resources that were not available until the 1980s. This has allowed more senior school subject choice in some circumstances. Thus where a TAFE (Technical and Further Education) facility exists in the same town or nearby, important vocational courses become available. The other 'distance' providers, often internet based, are more problematic in that considerable self-discipline and initiative are required by students to succeed with the public examination (Higher School Certificate) subjects studied apart from a teacher and class being provided within the school. There is evidence that small comprehensive high schools continue to need more staffing than their staffing allowances provide in order to deliver broad curriculum opportunities as required in fully comprehensive schools. Sometimes teachers are provided to small senior classes at the expense of large junior school classes. A common strategy, particularly in the elective subject area, is to join classes vertically (e.g., Years 10 and 11 will do subjects together): a practice that has existed in rural New South Wales schools for many years. Sometimes groups of schools can combine to offer a range of subjects, with students being bussed to take advantage of the opportunities.[15]

In the early twenty-first century, large regional centers, such as Coffs Harbour (Mid-north Coast) and Dubbo and Orange (Central West), and the cities of Newcastle and Wollongong, looked increasingly similar to parts of Sydney, with their range of public and private secondary schools. In this context for example, the effect of a public Senior College in Coffs Harbour sharing facilities with TAFE and a campus of the Southern Cross University appeared to have had both positive and negative effects on public education and comprehensive high schools in the district. The creation of the Senior College certainly hindered for a time the drift to the nongovernment sector expected with the growth of the local low-fee Anglican and Catholic schools, Bishop Druitt College and John Paul College. The Senior College was attractive to many senior secondary students from both the private and the public systems. Its existence may well have retarded the potential enrolment losses for public education in the Coffs Harbour region. On the other hand, it also placed some pressure on the 'traditional' Years 7–12 comprehensive high schools where 'choice' became possible and a school market was created within as well as beyond the government sector.

Nevertheless, in the Coffs Harbour region at least some local comprehensive high schools seem to be surviving well enough. The reasons for this are the same set of crucial factors that sustain some of the successful comprehensive high schools in Sydney. They include the following: relatively dynamic school leaderships skilled in both flexible student management and public relations, school histories not too weighed down for example by a tradition of having been a 'rough' boys' technical school, the lack of recent critical incidents (such as school yard stabbings or of pillorying in the press for poor HSC results), a fair representation of employed middle- and working-class parents with a commitment to public education and sufficient numbers of young people to go round.

The point of this discussion has been to show that in different parts of Sydney and the regions of New South Wales, in the 1990s and beyond, there has been no common history of secondary comprehensive school decline. In some places, urban, suburban, and rural comprehensive schooling continue to be successful. Nevertheless, there were mounting difficulties for some schools through the 1990s and into the twenty-first century, which required a public policy response. Such a response became especially urgent as the mass media, the daily newspapers, and the weekly news magazines in particular turned their gaze toward sites of difficulty.[16] One thing that nearly all the comprehensive government high schools had in common was an increasing difficulty in scoring well in the annual and most public of school success measures, ranking in the Higher School Certificate 'honor roll.' This was the surviving officially sanctioned and published 'league table' of schools following the Mount Druitt fiasco.[17]

Table 5.1 shows the declining fortunes of government secondary schools from 1990. In this table, the enrolments of comprehensive government

Table 5.1 Secondary students in government and nongovernment schools: New South Wales, 1990–2004 (%)

Year	Government	Nongovernment	% Shift to nongovernment
1990	69.3	30.7	+0.5
1991	69.0	31.0	+0.2
1992	69.2	30.8	−0.1
1993	69.0	31.0	+0.1
1994	68.7	31.3	+0.3
1995	68.2	31.8	+0.5
1996	67.9	32.1	+0.4
1997	67.4	32.6	+0.4
1998	66.9	33.1	+0.6
1999	66.1	33.9	+0.7
2000	65.3	34.7	+0.9
2001	64.5	35.5	+0.7
2002	64.0	36.0	+0.5
2003	63.4	36.6	+0.6
2004	62.9	37.1	+0.5

Source: Australian Bureau of Statistics, *Schools*, 4221.0 (1990–2005).

high schools are not differentiated from those of all government secondary schools, and in particular the academically selective schools. Because selective schools have been popular, enrolling many times fewer students than seek to enter them, the decline in enrolment share is higher for the comprehensives than public secondary education as a whole. The percentage decline in share for all government secondary schools from 1990 to 2004 was 6.4 percent; for the comprehensive school it was more. The high point for government secondary enrolments in the post World War II period was in the mid-1970s (76.0 percent in 1975 for example). The decline in the period since the strongest years for public comprehensive schools was well over 13 percent by 2005. The broad statistics disguise contrasting regional movements however. In some areas such as the eastern suburbs of Sydney, the loss of government secondary places was catastrophic.[18] In rapidly developing new suburbs in parts of outer suburban Sydney, the numbers of students and schools grew. For the whole of Sydney and the whole of New South Wales the general trend was clear enough. The decline of the public comprehensive high school as the dominant provider of secondary education was inexorable, and the rate of decline tended to increase over time.

Policy Responses to the Problems

Dr Ken Boston was appointed Director General of Education in New South Wales in 1992, in the last years of the Liberal–National coalition government. He was a notable survivor in the senior public service when the Labor government led by Bob Carr came to power in 1995, only resigning in 2002 to take up an educational post in England.[19] He embodied the policy continuity in public education that emerged in the post-Metherell period during the 1990s. In a series of significant and well-publicized statements during his period as Director General, Boston indicated that the era of the Wyndham-style comprehensive public school was over. If it was to survive at all, the comprehensive secondary school required radical adaptation.

In discussing the problems of the inner Sydney comprehensive schools, Boston argued in 1999 that:

> Whatever the factors that led to this decline a large number of schools in inner Sydney now have so few students and teachers that the existing educational infrastructure of the area is under-utilized. . . . In a contestable education market, the fewer curriculum choices schools are able to offer, the fewer students they are able to attract.[20]

Restructuring public education is always a fraught process as the 'rational' approaches of government meet the aspirations and loyalties of local school communities. In the 1990s and after, a series of radical schemes for restructure was promoted. Government turned toward the idea of promoting a comprehensive 'system' of public education. It was less prepared to adhere to the older Wyndham model of a comprehensive education being offered within one school. It was not only the fact of declining enrolments in many areas that led to this, but also imperatives associated with making links with TAFE and industry to promote VET (Vocational Education and Training), and to develop relationships with other organizations that in some cases could include the universities as well as business.

Boston argued the case forcefully, and in particular promoted collegiate, multicampus models of schooling.[21] If the expansion of the numbers of dedicated academically selective high schools, despite their popularity slowed in the first few years of the new century, the number of selective places did not. The provision of selective places in formerly comprehensive high schools was seen as a way of shoring up schools that were in danger of becoming impossibly small, and socially unrepresentative. What this meant for the idea of the comprehensive school was unclear to many. Some simply saw it as a means of making schools 'comprehensive' once more, in the sense of restoring lost middle-class enrolments to residualizing schools. It would give them a chance to re-establish academically oriented classes and curriculum offerings in their fragile senior schools.[22] Boston argued that an adaptive approach to the constituent institutions of a comprehensive 'system' was required. There could be junior and senior high schools, selective and nonselective, mixed selective and nonselective, and where local conditions allowed, older forms of comprehensive high schools might usefully survive as well.

Such an approach meant that the government of New South Wales continued its experiments begun in the 1980s, replacing standard comprehensive schools with a range of specialist schools.[23] The basis of specialization could continue to be a specific curriculum orientation, though without extensive additional resourcing some of those declared 'specialist' in the 1980s, such as the 'technology' high schools, had not met their promise and voluntarily or involuntarily lost their specialist designation. Increasingly, the basis of specialization became age and attainment. Junior and senior campuses made up new collegiates, clever students through attainment tests taken in their final year of primary school could be selected into academic high schools or selective streams in mixed high schools. In 2004, Year 6 students were invited to apply for places in selective schools and streams for 2005. There were seventeen fully selective schools advertised, and a further six with selective streams, and finally a further four agricultural high schools with selective entrance.[24] They were sufficient in number to negatively affect nearby comprehensive school enrolments.[25]

One of the most significant of the restructuring exercises was titled "Building the Future." After a period of conflict and consultation the public schools of inner Sydney were reconfigured, not quite as dramatically as the original draft report had proposed after strong campaigns by a number of schools, but especially Hunters Hill High (in a middle-class area), to remain open.[26] As well as the demographic reasons given for restructure, the report argued that "local co-educational high schools are not meeting the growing demand for single sex high schools, particularly for girls," nor were they "meeting the growing demand for selective high school classes."[27] Nevertheless, the changes for the Inner West were very substantial. In 2005, public secondary education was constituted by these schools:

- The Sydney Secondary College with coeducational junior and senior campuses, with mixed selective and nonselective enrolments, at Balmain, Glebe, and Leichhardt.
- Fort Street High School, an academically selective coeducational school, at Petersham.
- The Newtown School of the Performing Arts, a mixed selective and nonselective school with a curriculum specialization. Students

were selected into the performing arts stream in part by portfolio presentation.

- Dulwich Hill High and Marrickville High, two small and struggling comprehensive coeducational schools, one of which should have closed on the plans of the Education Department but was saved given an effective local campaign in the Deputy Premier's electorate.[28]
- Ashfield Boys' High, a single sex nonselective school.
- Tempe Languages High, a coeducational, curriculum specialist, nonselective school.

Like each of the regions of Sydney and New South Wales as a whole, the Inner West had its own peculiar history of secondary provision, but this provision in a highly populated area of Sydney clearly shows the decline of the comprehensive public school. There were only two such schools left in the coeducational, nonspecialist curriculum mode, and whether one of them would survive a future change of government was in doubt. In the Inner West, the public schools competed with a very strong set of Catholic secondary schools, most of which were constituents of a 'system' run by the Catholic Education Office in Sydney, and overwhelmingly funded by the federal government.

Elsewhere in Sydney there were other multicampus collegiates in the public system. In the Outer West was the Nirimba group (1999–) that included Wyndham College, a senior school and junior high schools. Also in the Outer West, the ill-fated Mount Druitt High was absorbed into the multicampus Chifley College (2000–). The Northern Beaches Secondary College (2003–) included separate boys' and girls' schools and a senior campus.[29] In the Central West of New South Wales there was the Dubbo College (2001–) incorporating three previously stand-alone comprehensive high schools.

Whether all these restructuring efforts actually made much difference to sustaining enrolments in the public education system is impossible to determine. That New South Wales continued to lose enrolment share to the nongovernment schools and school systems at roughly the same rate as other Australian states is clear enough. It is possible that the losses could have been faster without such policy approaches and restructures. Undoubtedly, the increased numbers of selective schools and selective places in a small number of schools could leave some comprehensive schools at greater risk of residualization, and consequent enrolment loss. For some families the only public school worth considering was a single sex or, more significantly, an academically selective school. If the child failed to achieve entrance there, the next step was often the seeking of a place in a nongovernment school.[30] Selective schooling was not necessarily the solution to shoring up the public system, because it tended to weaken a number of the standard comprehensive schools, especially if they were already under pressure as a result of demographic changes and the opening nearby of low-fee Catholic, Anglican, or other 'independent' schools. The religious denomination of a school was often less important to families than that it was a nonpublic school.[31]

As was the New South Wales tradition in secondary education reform, the major government-sponsored inquiry of the 1990s concentrated on changes to curriculum, assessment, and credentialing, particularly at the Higher School Certificate level. Barry McGaw from the ACER (Australian Council for Education Research) and later Deputy Director of Education for the OECD (Organization for Economic Cooperation and Development) led the inquiry, most of whose recommendations were eventually implemented. Published in 1997, the report, "Shaping the Future" made it quite clear that the HSC was for all students, and that it was required to "provide a curriculum structure which encourages students to complete secondary education."[32] In so doing it sought also to "elevate the intellectual demand of courses in the Higher School Certificate." A reduction of the range of English courses resulting from this aim for example eventually caused controversy, with some comprehensive high principals arguing that student retention, especially that of 'students at risk,' into Year 12 had consequently been harmed.[33] The Report validated the legitimate place of vocational training within the HSC and argued that vocational education should have stronger connections to the needs of industry, and a better organized system of crediting any training undertaken.[34] At the same time it argued for changed practices in terms of reporting achievement. The most significant was relevant to the Mount Druitt High School crisis. The Report recommended that the universities only be given HSC results for students who had applied for university admission; had such a system been in place in 1997, the Mount Druitt students would have been spared.[35]

The McGaw Report and its implementation came close to completing the slow process of overturning the vision that Harold Wyndham had held for the final two years of secondary schooling. The HSC could function at last as a credential of sufficient breadth to cater to the needs of a very great number of students in the comprehensive high school. At the same time, New South Wales firmly held to the principle that there should be public examinations and centralized control of the senior school curriculum where some other Australian states had moved from such a position. Retention to the end of high school is at least as responsive to the state of youth labor market as the structure of the curriculum, but the continuing fact of a universal credential in Year 12 attached to public examinations likely continued as a disincentive for some students to complete high school.

The HSC not only served the students of the comprehensive high schools of course. It also had to provide courses of study that the universities found acceptable. It had to satisfy the academic selective high schools and the non-government schools. Those schools in particular sought from the HSC results of their students evidence for the excellence of their educational programs and the 'distinction' of their schools. In turn, these were the facts that sold schools to parents in the education market. Where comprehensive schools occasionally wrenched such distinction they also did not hold back in the selling of their successes.[36]

The traditionally powerful New South Wales Teachers' Federation remains the union of public school teachers. Its commitment to public education is vigorous and well funded. It could not but view with alarm the decline of public education, the decline of the comprehensive high schools that remained the main vehicle for delivering educational opportunity to most of the youth of New South Wales, and the decline in the employment opportunities for public school teachers.[37] In a remarkably successful action, the Federation in 2001 decided to sponsor an "independent" enquiry into public education in New South Wales. Fortuitously, it chose Professor Tony Vinson whose background was in social and public policy development as the chief inquirer. Reports were released progressively. They were immediately accessible via the internet.[38] They not only did a great deal to validate the worth and necessary work of public education, but made cogent cases for reducing class sizes in public schools and paying teachers higher salaries. What was remarkable about the inquiry was that both the Labor government and the Opposition legitimated its reports by quoting and supporting many of the recommendations; it had an immediate effect on government policy, especially in the areas of class size reduction and substantial budget increases for teacher professional development. On the question of the future of comprehensive high schools however, the support was less forthcoming. Vinson's recommendation that of New South Wales' 28 selective schools, only 11 should remain, was swiftly rejected by the Labor government and the Liberal Opposition. The former Liberal minister, Metherell again argued that his additional selective schools had simply extended opportunities for a selective public education hitherto only accessible to students in the inner city.[39]

One of the reasons that the approach of Vinson was often acceptable, though not in the selective school area, was that it was able to make common cause with the state government against the bias of federal school funding toward the nongovernment, or as they were still popularly called, the 'private' schools. It was this funding bias that more than any other factor explained the accelerating decline of public comprehensive schools not only in New South Wales, but across Australia as a whole.

In previous chapters, we have traced the reasons for this bias in federal funding. With the accession of a new Liberal–National Party coalition government under Prime Minister John Howard in 1996, the expected swing toward greater levels of funding for the nongovernment sector quickly occurred. A new formula (SES) that remained to a degree 'needs based' established a new criterion for the funding of nongovernment schools. The addresses of enrolled students' homes were linked to a census-based index of income and parental education for their areas of residence. In the process, the government argued that there was no longer such a thing as funding a "wealthy school," but funding of schools on a fair index of the resources of the parents.[40] It was a politically astute move, because it raised the level of funding to nongovernment schools overall, it recognized the new constituency of the Liberal and National parties, that is, the so-called 'battler' families who did not necessarily live in wealthy areas but made great 'sacrifices' in order to educate their children advantageously. Simultaneously, the government intervened in the debate over what kinds of schools were likely to offer young people 'decent values' and discipline. They were more likely to be the nongovernment, church-based schools according to the Prime Minister.[41] These new funding initiatives were supported by a further initiative, that any nongovernment school that might have its funding reduced as a result of the new formula would not be subject to the new formula. The same could not be said of funding for government schools. The EBA (Enrolment Benchmark Adjustment) exercise that worked in tandem with the new SES (Socio-Economic Status) funding initiative led to reduced public education spending even if actual *numbers* in public schools rose, as opposed to the decline in the *proportion* of students in public schools.[42]

Given these circumstances the 'drift' away from public comprehensive schools gathered pace. New nongovernment school foundations were encouraged: Catholic, Anglican, other low-fee 'Christian' schools, and an increasing number of Muslim and other ethnic-religious community schools. In the decade to 2000, the number of Catholic schools had actually dropped from 593 to 589 as small institutions consolidated into larger ones, but those groups recording school numbers in excess of ten included 'Christian' (77), 'Independent' (66), Anglican (50), and Muslim (12).[43] Some started as primary schools, growing secondary enrolments as their students traveled upward through the school grades. The older church corporate schools, under some pressure in the 1970s to shore up declining enrolments with moves toward coeducation, experienced new stability and wealth. Many of these schools, with federal government income added to their yearly enrolment fees (which began to approach $20,000 per annum per student by 2005), were able to pay their teaching staffs substantially more than the public high schools.[44] New teaching and extracurricular facilities were expanded. The contrast between the physical plant and grounds of government and nongovernment schools in the early twenty-first century had never been greater. The nongovernment schools and systems became adept at defending their gains, immediately and effectively campaigning to head off any sign in election campaigns that national or state governments might wind back such gains.[45] The core argument was usually based around the comparative combined contribution of state and federal governments to the cost of educating a child in either system. It was true that governments usually spent more on educating the public school child. There were two assumptions demanded by the nongovernment school lobby pressing their 'justice' based argument. The first was that the additional income nongovernment schools gained from student fees should be left out of the comparative funding calculation, and second, that public taxation should by right support nonpublic schools and school systems.

By the late 1990s, federal government school policy encouraged parents to 'choose' schools that suited their family aspirations and the interests of their children. Nor was the state government immune from such thinking. The end of zoning for New South Wales public schools was in part predicated on such an approach. The state government also directly funded nongovernment schools, for example in schemes that subsidized interest payments on debt.[46] The way that government and nongovernment schools were funded often enabled the nongovernment schools to devote considerable resources, unavailable to government schools, to marketing, improving school plant and grounds, offering high teacher salaries, and recruiting teachers. As one of Australia's leading sociologists argued: under the circumstances of the developing markets of neoliberal social and economic policy, a great many middle-class Australians felt they were being forced from any abiding reliance on government or public institutions. The 'social contract' had been broken.[47] He could have gone further and added that they were being forced from the government comprehensive high schools in particular. The frustrations of many working-class families were of a different order. In the 'new' secondary education, many families were not market-oriented, and where school choice decisions were made, in the words of another sociologist, they tend to be defensive. The aim was to secure the new minimal credential for employment, the HSC, most often in government schools. They were a group who continue to be very dependent on the "bureaucratic machinery of state education to deliver a reasonable education for their children."[48] This was in a period in which the most common secondary school was under great pressure, and the dependence of youth on schooling for securing employment was never more crucial in Australian history.

Changing Social Composition of Enrolments

This discussion leads us toward a more systematic analysis of the social characteristics of the families who were using, and those who were leaving the comprehensive high schools. Since the 1970s the Australian census has regularly asked questions of the population about the schools in which their children were enrolled. Answers to these questions have been sorted with reference to a number of the social characteristics of the families involved.[49] In tracing these patterns through the census, we were especially interested in testing the idea that class, ethnicity, and regional issues and identifications were likely to be highly significant in explaining differences in such patterns. Before beginning the discussion however it is important to note that while 'class' and 'ethnicity' are material enough as tools in the analysis of patterns of school enrolment, they are also ideas that resist definition and easy categorization. Australian discussions on race, class, and ethnicity are different from those in the United Kingdom and the United States. Australia's immigration history is different and the issues surrounding its indigenous peoples are different. The class and ethnicity-related categories of the census are always composed with an eye to certainty in the counting of persons. They are never quite adequate in meeting any of the complex theoretical and historically contingent issues crucial to understanding the making and workings of class and ethnicity among populations. In this discussion, the census merely provides 'indicators' of the materiality of class and ethnicity in the social history of the public comprehensive school. Hence, the annual income of families, or the highest educational qualifications of parents, 'indicate' social class positioning, as do the 'country of birth' or a recent census category, the 'ancestry' of persons, 'indicate' ethnicity.

It needs to be said here also, that we were not uninterested in gender as producing different enrolment patterns in different schools. However, across systems and categories as large as 'government' and 'nongovernment,' gender is of little consequence. Where it is of real consequence is in the distribution of enrolments within different kinds of schools within the government and nongovernment systems, but that is not the immediate focus in this discussion.

Class

In the 1970s in New South Wales, the indicators of social class suggest middle and working classes were represented in the government high

Table 5.2 Type of secondary school attended by youth according to the highest educational qualifications of their fathers: New South Wales, 1976 and 2001 (%, *N*)

	1976					2001				
Highest qualification	**Gov't school**	**Catholic school**	**Other nongov't**	**Total**	**Total (*N*)**	**Gov't school**	**Catholic school**	**Other nongov't**	**Total**	**Total (*N*)**
University degree	57	21	21	100	15,009	49	25	27	100	66,830
Vocational/ other qualification	78	18	5	100	92,074	63	26	11	100	121,908
Non qualifications	80	18	3	100	136,933	64	24	12	100	18,982

Source: Australian Bureau of Statistics, Censuses 1976, 2001.

Table 5.3 Shift in participation in type of secondary school attended by youth according to the highest educational qualifications of their fathers: New South Wales, 1976–2001 (%)

	Percentage shift		
Highest qualification	**Government school**	**Catholic school**	**Other nongovernment**
University degree	−8	+4	+6
Vocational/other qualifications	−15	+8	+6
No qualifications	−16	+6	+9

Source: Australian Bureau of Statistics, Censuses 1976, 2001.

schools at not very different rates from their presence in society as a whole. By 2001 this had changed quite dramatically. The following tables (tables 5.2 and 5.3) indicate class shift; they are based on the occupations, labor force status, and highest educational qualifications of fathers who had their children in a New South Wales secondary school and the income of families as a whole.

While these tables 5.2 and 5.3 show that by 2001 less than half of the children of fathers with university degrees were in public schools, the rate of loss was less dramatic than for the other groups. The availability of government academically selective schools possibly slowed the rate of loss for this group. Nevertheless, at the high point of the comprehensive movement in the mid-1970s, children from this group were well represented in the comprehensive school. While in 2001 the other groups remained well represented in government secondary schools, the greater proportion of which were comprehensives, at 63 and 64 percent, the decline from representations of 78 and 80 percent was dramatic. These figures point to the fact that families from all social classes are moving from the government comprehensives. In 2001 however, children from the families most likely to be middle class, that is from families where the father had a university degree, were least likely to be in a government comprehensive high school. Tables 5.4 and 5.5 give a less equivocal message. The 'old' middle class of employers in this period radically reoriented their school loyalties to the nongovernment sector. The 'self-employed' and 'employee' are a mixed group spanning middle, working, and 'aspirational' classes. The 'aspirational class' is a relatively recent category often used by journalists and others to explain unexpected voting and other social behaviors of people in Australian cities. In Sydney the 'aspirationals' are typified as living in the outer suburbs, having high mortgages as they pursue home ownership. Into the 1980s they

Table 5.4 Type of secondary school attended by youth according to labor force status of their fathers: New South Wales, 1976 and 2001 (%, *N*)

	1976					2001				
Labor force status	**Gov't school**	**Catholic school**	**Other nongov't**	**Total**	**Total (*N*)**	**Gov't school**	**Catholic school**	**Other nongov't**	**Total**	**Total (*N*)**
Employer	67	21	12	100	26,142	44	30	26	100	46,949
Self-empl & employee	79	17	4	100	299,181	62	26	12	100	301,132
Unpaid wkr & unemployed	86	13	2	100	9,441	75	18	7	100	56,891

Source: Australian Bureau of Statistics, Censuses 1976, 2001.

Table 5.5 Shift in participation in type of secondary school attended by youth according to labor force status of their fathers: New South Wales, 1976–2001 (%)

	Percentage shift		
Labor force status	**Government school**	**Catholic school**	**Other nongovernment**
Employer	−23	+9	+14
Self-employed & employee	−17	+9	+8
Unpaid worker & unemployed	−11	+5	+5

Source: Australian Bureau of Statistics, Censuses 1976, 2001.

Table 5.6 Type of secondary school attended by youth according to family income per annum: New South Wales, 1996 (%, *N*)

Annual income (1996)	**Gov't school**	**Catholic school**	**Other nongov't**	**Total**	**Total (*N*)**
< \$25,999	79.9	14.8	5.4	100	69,691
\$26,000–\$41,599	75.3	19.0	5.7	100	68,950
\$41,600–\$62,399	69.6	22.9	7.5	100	77,387
\$62,400–\$103,999	62.3	26.4	11.3	100	69,970
> \$104,000	43.7	25.7	30.6	100	30,134

Source: Australian Bureau of Statistics, census 1996.

were considered reliable Labor voters. It is argued that their 'aspirations' in housing, consumer goods, and educational opportunities for their children make them vulnerable to non-Labor politics, nongovernment schooling and neoconservative campaigns about declining 'values' in society as a whole—but comprehensive government schools in some areas in particular. This is occasionally linked to the phenomenon of 'white flight' to the suburbs from the inner cities as it has occurred in the United States.[50] The comparison is specious given the gentrification of inner Sydney, and its very different ethnic and racial character. Nevertheless, families with some financial resources are also on the move from the comprehensive school. The residualizing effect for such schools may be seen in that the group with the lowest rate of drift are families who are likely to have the lowest levels of income. In all of these tables their gender bias needs to be taken into account. Fathers are not the sole producers of income for families.

If we turn to the less gender-biased indicator, 'family income,' we see the pattern of table 5.6. Given the difficulties of comparing income values over

Table 5.7 Type of secondary school attended by youth according to the occupation of their fathers: New South Wales, 1976 and 2001 (%, *N*)

	1976					2001				
Occupation of father	**Gov't school**	**Catholic school**	**Other nongov't**	**Total**	**Total (*N*)**	**Gov't school**	**Catholic school**	**Other nongov't**	**Total**	**Total (*N*)**
Professional	68	19	13	100	30,492	51	25	24	100	66,146
Managerial	68	21	11	100	38,397	51	28	22	100	57,868
All other employed	81	17	2	100	193,435	65	27	9	100	218,861

Source: Australian Bureau of Statistics, censuses 1976, 2001.

Table 5.8 Shift in participation in type of secondary school attended by youth according to occupation of their fathers: New South Wales, 1976–2001 (%)

	Percentage shift		
Occupation of father	**Government school**	**Catholic school**	**Other nongovernment**
Professional	−17	+6	+11
Managerial	−17	+7	+7
All other employed	−16	+10	+7

Source: Australian Bureau of Statistics, Censuses 1976, 2001.

Table 5.9 Type of secondary school attended by youth according to the occupation of their fathers, 'All other employed' only: New South Wales, 2001 (%)[51]

Occupation of father	**Government school**	**Catholic school**	**Other nongovernment**	**Total (*N*)**
Associate professionals	54	30	16	46,348
Skilled workers (trades)	65	27	8	62,377
Clerical/service (adv. & inter.)	61	29	10	28,190
Operators & related	71	24	5	44,415
Clerical/service (elem.)	67	24	9	12,623
Laborers & related	73	22	5	24,908

Source: Australian Bureau of Statistics, Census 2001.

the 25 years produced by inflation, we show the statistics for 1996 only. Though lacking fine differentiation, the connection between family income and the kind of school that children attended is quite direct. Wealthier families were far more likely to send their children to nongovernment secondary schools, but perhaps what is even more interesting is the continuing substantial presence of youth from very wealthy families in the public high schools—though not all of them. Family wealth is of course related to parental occupation. In tables 5.7 and 5.8, two occupational groups that are clearly middle class in orientation are contrasted with the rest. These patterns have some similarity to those above where fathers' qualifications were considered. Again the shift from government secondary schools is general. We get a finer tuned sense of class-related enrolments in table 5.9 that concentrates on the subprofessional/managerial group for 2001.

In these statistics, the pattern is clear enough. Families with fathers in traditional working-class occupations sustain higher enrolments in the government schools, but for all groups the Catholic schools provide a popular alternative. The children of white-collar workers, the 'associate professionals' and higher clerical groups were more likely than those of blue-collar workers to be in Catholic and other nongovernment schools.

Statistics such as the preceding provide great opportunities for more subtle analyses.[52] But the general patterns suggest that the middle class is considerably less attached to the government comprehensive high schools than it was even twenty-five years ago, but the drift is by no means confined to that group. The movement is general, and on the whole the statistics show a residualizing impact on the government secondary comprehensives. Some regions display the patterns in extreme of course. In the Inner West of Sydney, with its notable set of Catholic secondary schools, even in 1976 the government share of enrolments was only 69 percent. In the Outer West of Sydney, or rural areas such as the Central West, across the Blue Mountains, the government shares were much higher at 87 and 80 percent respectively (see table 5.13).

Ethnicity

After World War II there were massive waves of migration to Australia, considerably disrupting the domination of the British-Irish ethnic groups in Australia. That group, as has been discussed earlier was split by religion, and historically the public school system was far more likely to include Protestant youth than Catholic. In the postwar era, Europeans from the north, east, and south came to Australia in large numbers. Later there followed substantial groups from the Middle East, and eventually East and South East Asia. Their patterns of public school usage were dependent in part on their wealth and religion, especially in the early days of arrival. By the 1990s however, the patterns were far more complex as the second and third generations of migrants were often wealthier and better educated than the first, and their attachments to different schools and school systems developed as a result. By the 1990s, there were also increasing numbers of nongovernment schools based in communities defined by specific ethnic, national, and religious characteristics. Nor was the growing fragmentation of schooling along ethnic and religious lines restricted to the nongovernment sector. As the comprehensive government school remained in most places a 'neighborhood' school, the ethnic character of the neighborhood could define the ethnic character of the public school. The government selective schools were subject to these movements as well as the comprehensive. James Ruse High had very high proportions of

East Asians, mainly Chinese in origin. In other parts of Sydney, students of Vietnamese, Lebanese, or Pacific Islander origin made up considerable proportions of the enrolments in individual public high schools.

In some areas some schools attracted youth from particular ethnic groups beyond their immediate neighborhoods as it became known that there was a strong representation there, or that the school was responsive to the groups' needs and aspirations.[53] Ethnicity issues could play out negatively for schools, but most often for government comprehensives. In the 1990s and beyond there was considerable public anxiety about the activities of ethnic 'gangs' and some ethnic groups in different parts of Sydney, and in the comprehensive high schools. Newspaper headlines announced from time to time that violent ethnic youth gangs were disrupting schools. Of all the groups the Muslim Lebanese seemed to get the worst of it, but they were not the only ones.[54] Where incidents were thoroughly investigated, ethnicity as such was rarely an important issue, but of significance was the growing perception that it was. In some areas schools with reputations for high concentrations of specific ethnic groups, and rumored incidents of 'ethnic violence' became a reason for the withdrawal of middle class and other families.

Again, through the census it is possible to indicate the changes of loyalty of different ethnic groups to different kinds of schools. Religion is a major factor. With a strong alternative Catholic system of secondary schools in New South Wales, it is relatively easy to explain the behavior of Italian Catholic and Vietnamese Catholic families. But not all Vietnamese in New South Wales are Catholic, nor all Lebanese Muslim. So ethnic groups are divided not only by religion, but recency of arrival, and relative poverty or wealth. Some groups such as the Jewish have a growing number of faith-based schools available, others do not. This affects 'loyalty' to a system. The public comprehensive high school is a school that can be chosen, but it is also the school that is clearly available, and cheaply available, if desired alternatives are not. Except for Catholics and Jews, in 1976 the public high school system enrolled 85 to 96 percent of all other religious groups. Table 5.10 shows the dramatic changes by 2001 where those who identified in the census as having a religion had usually departed the public system by significant proportions. Visible also is the change in the use of the Catholic schools, where large numbers from other religious groups had made it an alternative to the public sector, presumably for reasons other than the schools' Catholicity.

Table 5.11 is based on the new census category for 2001, that is 'ancestry.' This category has its problems, but it is more likely than the old categories, such as 'country of birth' to indicate a sense of ethnic-national origins. Here, we clearly see different patterns of school use. The reasons why the groups used the schools differently are specific to each group. Nevertheless,

Table 5.10 Type of secondary school attended by youth according to their religion: New South Wales, 1976 and 2001 (%, *N*)

	1976					2001				
Religion	**Gov't school**	**Catholic school**	**Other nongov't**	**Total**	**Total (*N*)**	**Gov't school**	**Catholic school**	**Other nongov't**	**Total (%)**	**Total (*N*)**
Catholic	50	50	0	96,037	100	41	54	5	100	141,954
Anglican	92	1	7	94,592	100	74	8	18	100	91,081
Uniting	93	0	6	39,752	100	78	7	15	100	26,364
Orthodox*	92	5	3	9,319	100	61	23	16	100	12,021
Other Christian	90	2	8	17,009	100	66	8	26	100	44,004
Judaism	64	0	36	1,301	100	29	1	70	100	2,482
Islam	96	2	2	992	100	86	5	9	100	12,939
Other religion	85	7	8	454	100	81	10	9	100	15,793
No religion**	89	6	5	36,949	100	80	8	12	100	82,590
Total	78	18	5	296,404	100	64	23	13	100	429,228

* In 1976, Greek Orthodox; in 2001 all Orthodox **No religion and 'no religion stated' and 'indeterminate' combined.

Source: Australian Bureau of Statistics, Censuses 1976, 2001.

Table 5.11 Type of secondary school attended by youth according to ancestry: New South Wales, 2001 (%, *N*)

Ancestry	Government school	Catholic school	Other nongovernment	Total (%)	Total (*N*)
Australian peoples	66	21	13	100	158,465
British	65	20	15	100	125,965
Irish	49	40	11	100	13,912
North & Western European	62	21	17	100	7,256
Southern European	38	55	7	100	15,171
Other European	60	24	16	100	15,873
Arab	51	41	8	100	13,289
Jewish	37	4	59	100	305
Pacific Islander	76	18	6	100	2,850
South East Asian	60	34	5	100	12,572
Chinese	70	16	14	100	20,986
Southern Asian	70	18	12	100	8,173
Other Asian	65	16	19	100	4,903
South & Central American	51	40	9	100	2,034
SubSaharan African	43	24	33	100	2,081
Other	74	15	11	100	7,056
Not stated & unclearly stated (combined)	67	22	10	100	18,345

Source: Australian Bureau of Statistics, Census 2001.

they give the different sets and systems of schools a specific ethnic character. Multiculturalism in Australian schools has not simply been about reducing the British-Australian dominated and assimilationist character of school curricula and practices. It has also allowed the encouragement of ethnic-based nongovernment schools that are not in the least ethnically diverse. While the government comprehensive schools are likely the most ethnically diverse, they are still over- and under-representative of some ethnic groups. When specific regions and individual schools are examined particular ethnic concentrations are often quite pronounced.

Geographical Location

So in this discussion of the social character of the government comprehensive high school we turn to the final major producer of difference. Geographical location is important. School markets can only be produced in reasonably dense population areas. Real estate prices and histories of settlement produce different class and ethnic-based neighborhoods supporting different mixes of government and nongovernment schools. Australia's openness to immigration has led to different communities settling in some places rather than others. The employment opportunities available attract migrants, making Sydney the most ethnically diverse region of New South Wales. Much of the rural hinterland remains overwhelmingly mono-ethnic, British/Irish-Australian with smaller groups of indigenous peoples.

To show these differences dependent on region, four Sydney (urban and suburban) regions, a coastal-rural, and one central New South Wales rural region (Table 5.12) have been chosen for the discussion. In table 5.13, the different proportions of the population in 1976 and 2001, in the different schools and systems, show the strength of the government comprehensive high schools in the rural areas in particular.

Table 5.12 Regions of New South Wales chosen for analysis: 1976–2004

Urban (Sydney)	
Northern Beaches	Mainly suburban with little industry. Mainly Anglo-Australian middle-class population. Some areas suburban, some very wealthy indeed. Manly-Warringah area of Sydney.
Inner West	Old area of Sydney with significant though declining industry. Originally, a large working-class population with strong gentrification. Large non-British/Irish origin population. Includes Balmain, Glebe, Marrickville, Newtown, and Ashfield.
Outer West	Mainly suburban with considerable industry. Large population center with working and middle class; but includes significant areas of poverty. Mixed ethnically. Includes Blacktown and Penrith.
Hills District	Rapidly growing suburban area with high proportions of families with children. British/Irish-origin Australians predominate. Includes Baulkham Hills, Kellyville, and Carlingford.
Rural (New South Wales)	
Central West	Large country towns include Bathurst, Orange, Parkes, and Young. Significant agriculture and grazing. Mainly British/Irish-origin Australian.
Mid-North Coast	Some large country towns including Coffs Harbour and Taree. Significant agriculture, dairy, fishing, and tourist industries. Mainly British/Irish-origin Australian.

Table 5.13 Type of secondary school attended by youth according to region of residence: New South Wales, 1976 and 2001 (%, *N*)

	1976					2001				
Region	**Gov't school**	**Catholic school**	**Other nongov't**	**Total (%)**	**Total (*N*)**	**Gov't school**	**Catholic school**	**Other nongov't**	**Total (%)**	**Total (*N*)**
Northern Beaches	76	17	7	100	13,533	53	26	21	100	12,633
Inner West	69	29	2	100	9,395	49	33	18	100	8,341
Outer West	87	12	1	100	16,692	60	31	9	100	31,669
Hills	76	17	7	100	5,556	46	29	26	100	12,554
Central West	80	18	2	100	14,129	66	23	11	100	17,675
Mid-North Coast	93	7	0	100	7,149	73	19	8	100	17,241
New South Wales	78	18	5	100	296,419	64	23	13	100	429,242

Source: Australian Bureau of Statistics, censuses 1976, 2001.

The social and economic character of the regions has changed over the twenty-five years. Nevertheless, there remain distinctive patterns of school allegiance. In 1976, the two rural areas had very high proportions of students in comprehensive government high schools. In the Mid-North Coast in particular there was little alternative to the government sector. Since then new 'Christian' and low-fee Anglican schools have been established and Catholic schools expanded. In the Central West there were long-established Catholic and a few other nongovernment schools. Clearly, the provision of state secondary schools provided an essential means of education to the great majority of families in these rural areas. Much the same may be said for the Outer Western suburbs of Sydney, which in 1976 were very working class. They were 'high mortgage' areas also. By 1996 however, this high level of support for government schooling had dropped dramatically (27 percent), almost as dramatically as in the Hills District (30 percent), also another high mortgage, though much more middle-class area.

Though the two rural regions retained secondary enrolments in government comprehensive schools at higher levels than New South Wales as a whole, and certainly the areas of Sydney reported here, the rate of enrolment loss was still considerable. In terms of the way that some of the social characteristics we have discussed above played out differently in the regions, we restrict ourselves to a brief discussion of the ethnic character of the school enrolments in the Outer West of Sydney compared with the Inner West. Table 5.14 provides an indication of differing patterns of ethnic enrolment for 1996. It has already been shown that for ethnicity-related enrolments that religious affiliation and the provision of church-run schools have been a major feature of regional diversity. The Inner West of Sydney with its strong Catholic school system and attendance is the obvious example. For families from Italy and the Philippines, both predominantly Catholic countries, the Catholic schools of the Inner and Outer West are the majority provider, but at very high rates in the Inner West. The government system with its few remaining comprehensive schools only enrolls youth with Italian-born fathers at 21 percent. For the group most likely to be recently arrived, the Chinese in the Inner and Outer West, the government high schools are better used than for most other ethnic groups.

Each of the regions has peculiar patterns of ethnically based secondary school attendance. The rural regions were strongly monocultural on this measure. The Northern Beaches and the Hills District were also British/Irish-Australian, though by 1996, significant numbers of children of Italian-born parents were present in each of these suburban regions. They similarly favored Catholic secondary schools, though not quite to the same levels in the Inner West. The other urban region in this study that had considerable ethnic diversity was the Outer West. The diversity did not necessarily produce

Table 5.14 Type of secondary school attended by youth according to birthplace of father, Inner West & Outer West: Sydney, 1996 (%, *N*)

	Inner West					Outer West				
Birthplace	**Gov't school**	**Catholic school**	**Other nongov't**	**Total (%)**	**Total (*N*)**	**Gov't school**	**Catholic school**	**Other nongov't**	**Total (%)**	**Total (*N*)**
Australia	49	29	23	100	2,065	69	23	8	100	12,891
China	70	25	5	100	305	73	23	3	100	172
Greece	62	27	11	100	356	73	24	3	100	202
Italy	21	76	3	100	590	44	52	4	100	454
Lebanon	47	50	3	100	415	61	35	4	100	404
Philippines	41	57	2	100	132	39	57	4	100	1,602
U.K.	57	16	27	100	349	74	18	8	100	2,255
Vietnam	75	23	2	100	416	67	31	2	100	139

Source: Australian Bureau of Statistics, Census 1996.

similar patterns of secondary school enrolment. For example, there, the 'Australians' were 20 percent more likely to be in a state school.

In looking at Aboriginal and Torres Strait Islanders, we find a huge discrepancy between those willing to identify as such in 1976 (217 persons for example in the Central West of the State) as opposed to 3,182 in 1996. This is clearly the product of the revolution of attitude and respect attending indigenous peoples in Australia since the mid-1970s. In all the regions in 1976, for those willing to identify, between 95 and 100 percent sent their children to government schools. It was a very different situation in the 1996 census as table 5.15 shows. In fact in 1996, patterns of attendance closely resembled those of the population as a whole, though the tendency is for state secondary schools to take a slightly higher proportion of indigenous students. What this table does not tell us, as for all these tables, is the kind of other nongovernment schools being attended. The growing Aboriginal middle class does not necessarily have a commitment to the government comprehensive high school.[55]

In this section, having looked at the regions we can see that school provision policies play out differently, despite the centralized policy making and administration exercised by federal and state governments. This diversity is not only indicated by social factors, and the agency of families in using schools and school systems differently, but the local histories of secondary school provision also. For inner city areas, the government comprehensive high school was of relatively short duration in comparison with rural districts and outer suburban areas. The Inner West had a complex mix of boys' and girls,' technical, domestic science, and junior secondary schools lasting well into the 1970s, a decade after the apparent introduction of comprehensive government schooling to New South Wales. The era then of genuine comprehensive schools is quite short. The advent of the selective Newtown Performing Arts High in 1990 began the period of change, which became dramatic with the incorporation of Leichhardt, Glebe, and Balmain high schools into the Sydney Secondary College in 2002. The era of the comprehensive coeducational high school in the Inner West lasted a mere twenty to twenty-five years.

The contrast with the Outer West, the suburbs that mainly developed post–World War II is striking. In this area, all the government high schools except one were coeducational, multilateral and then comprehensive either from the 1960s or their foundation. They were the schools for the people, and by contrast with the Inner West there were very few nongovernment schools until the late 1970s. The Catholic share of the nongovernment sector was much less visible. In these areas of new suburban developments there are now a large number of 'Christian' schools, begun by a variety of churches and sects, Protestant, some fundamentalist and pentecostal. This is the group of schools, with the Catholic group that provide

Table 5.15 Aboriginal and Torres Strait Islander (A & TSI) secondary enrolments by school type and region compared with total enrolments of youth: New South Wales, 1996 (%)

	Government school			Catholic school			Other nongovernment		
Region	**A & TSI**	**Total**	**% Difference**	**A & TSI**	**Total**	**% Difference**	**A & TSI**	**Total**	**% Difference**
Northern Beaches	62	60	+2	22	23	−1	16	16	0
Inner West	55	50	+5	33	36	−3	12	14	−2
Outer West	67	64	+3	26	28	−2	7	7	0
Hills District	51	50	+1	29	30	−1	20	20	0
Central West	74	71	+3	20	22	−2	7	7	0
Mid North Coast	79	78	+1	16	17	−1	5	5	0

Source: Australian Bureau of Statistics, Census 1996.

a clear alternative to the government comprehensives. St. Marys Senior College lost its comprehensive status in 1989, but in this district it was not until the end of the 1990s that a large number of comprehensives were reorganized as junior and senior campuses of multicampus colleges.

Across the Blue Mountains in the Central West, the history of comprehensive schooling was different again. By the 1950s, most towns of substance had at the least either a full or intermediate high school. The period of the Wyndham scheme saw the transformation of many of the intermediate schools into comprehensive high schools, though there would always have been problems with providing a 'comprehensive' curriculum for senior students, especially in the smaller towns. Nevertheless, these schools, especially those that began as 'central' and 'district' schools were genuine community schools. These schools have been least affected by the changes of policy from the late 1980s. There has been continuity of community and comprehensive schooling for the previous fifty years. The town of Dubbo was the first to see the multicampus solution to government secondary education provision. In 2001, the three high schools of Dubbo were rearranged into a multicampus of senior and junior schools. Like the Inner West, the dominant nongovernment provider was the Catholic schools, every fair-sized town having at the least a Catholic school that could take students through to Year 10. With increased funding from federal and state governments it has been possible for some to achieve full secondary school status in more recent times. Also, in some of the larger towns, the 'Christian' schools have taken advantage of new funding, with several start-ups from the early 1980s.

To conclude this discussion of regional diversity in Sydney and New South Wales, especially in the last twenty years or so, a major point has been to demonstrate the ways in which policies generated from centralized governments operate differently in the regions. This is important for understanding the history of comprehensive schooling. In the inner city areas of Sydney, the comprehensive high school has a fleeting history. In the outer suburban areas, and in the rural districts, the comprehensive government high school was historically stronger, indeed the dominant system for up to half a century. But as this discussion has also shown, the levels of participation are in decline regardless of region. The outer suburban and rural comprehensive high schools remain stronger because they originally enrolled a much higher proportion of the school population. In many rural areas it remains difficult to establish a market enabling genuine school choice.[56]

At the beginning of the twenty-first century, the system of government comprehensive high schools remained a very large system. Nevertheless, it was under threat in a number of different areas. The state Labor government elected in 1995 experimented with alternatives, especially the multi-campus schools. It also experimented with shoring up the comprehensive schools with increased numbers of programs for 'gifted and talented' students.[57] Even though there were expressions of confidence in the future of the comprehensives from time to time, including the Vinson inquiry, the decisions to sustain the selective schools, and to increase the number of selective places in mixed schools signified a reduced role and status. In many areas, the schools were in fair difficulty for reasons that were only partly explained by the existence of rival government and nongovernment schools. For demographic and other reasons related to gentrification, transport corridors, new suburban developments, and real estate price movements, many comprehensive high schools found their enrolments diminishing, and their ability to offer a broad curriculum reduced. The interest of the mass media in who went to which schools, which schools were successful or failing, and the intense interest in any possible links between youth and ethnic-related violence and schooling usually affected the government comprehensives worse than other schools.

Although the period of neoliberal influenced school policies began earlier than the period covered by this chapter, this was the period in which the social and educational consequences of those policies began to be seen most clearly. Government comprehensives in many areas became residualized as schools of the 'safety net,' specializing in the students with significant learning and social disadvantages. A former Director General of Education, Fenton Sharpe, reflected on the trajectory of the comprehensives in 2000. His focus was on the division of the public schools into the academically selective and comprehensive, and on arguing that school success should not only be measured by academic outcomes through public examination results:

> Of course, comprehensive schools have suffered as a result of the success of selective schools. The title 'comprehensive' has become a misnomer in the metropolitan areas of NSW. A comprehensive school, by definition, suggests both girls and boys, the full range of academic and other educational capacities represented in the local community and, in a multicultural society such as ours, a variety of backgrounds, cultures and religions. Such schools have been at the forefront of forging the cohesiveness and vigor of contemporary Australian society.
>
> Yet, in competition with the selectives that have creamed off the academically most gifted, the teachers and students in these schools have to fight a constant battle to counter the perception that they are second best.[58]

The reasons for the vulnerability of the public comprehensive high school are complex, but are clearly related to the operation of both a market in schooling as well as a market ideology. This market and its associated ideology are also related to the concerns of the Australian middle class.

There is no doubt that an anxiety exists among the Australian middle class in respect to the future of their children.[59] This is particularly so in a society and economy where there remains relatively high youth unemployment and where ever greater sections of the labor market are responsive to credentialism. Even if some social theorists argue that cultural and social capital are primarily reproduced in the family and that schooling does not make a substantial difference to educational and social outcomes, it would seem that many in the middle class feel that they cannot afford any level of risk potentially involved in the matter of choosing a good school.[60] This anxiety, which is not confined to the middle class, is also sustained by the current ideology of the 'good citizen' parent who exercises discrimination and choice in the matter of the schooling of his or her child. Within this ideology, the market in education, no matter how artificially maintained by state funding, is responded to in terms of perceived private interest and the apparent quality of the commodity offered. If parents detect a failure in the quality of schooling offered then it is obviously in the interests of their children to exercise choice if it is available.

In these circumstances, the importance of funding arrangements can not be denied. The re-introduction of 'state aid,' but more importantly the generosity of federal funding, never more so than from the 1990s crucially affected the comprehensive schools. This funding helped not only its original targets, the 'disadvantaged' nongovernment schools, but all nongovernment schools. It also encouraged new, low-fee schools. There is no doubt that the impact of federal funding in particular allowed nongovernment schools to appear more attractive in a number of ways, and not only through the provision and display of physical facilities. The nongovernment sector was required to commit to fewer 'public' responsibilities in respect to either a broad curriculum or the nature of its student enrolment, retaining strong powers over both student selection and expulsion. The nongovernment school also enjoyed easier control over the hiring and firing of teachers. The government comprehensive high school was part of a system, and very few staffing decisions were determined locally.

In the 1990s, the strange interaction of neoconservative pressures with neoliberalism also added to the difficulties of the government comprehensive high school. Where once its ideals were perceived as supporting common civic and citizenship values, egalitarianism, and inclusivity, by the end of the 1990s the neoconservatives were arguing that such schools lacked values in general.[61] Apparently indiscipline was common, the work ethic was in doubt, and the schools lacked clear philosophic and religious/spiritual foundations. Apparently the unionized public school teacher was wedded to self-interest, substantiated according to the neoconservatives by their pursuit of wage rises at the expense of students through the use of stop-work action. Most of this argument was both ignorant and vicious, especially as its progenitors were notoriously silent when nongovernment schools were troubled for one reason or another. Elements of the Catholic Church had attacked public education for its 'godlessness' for more than a century, but the rise of a new conservatism in both the Anglican and Catholic churches, especially in Sydney toward the end of the 1990s, and the willingness of the federal government in particular to succor these lobbies meant that the most powerful and wealthiest level of government was no friend to the public school.[62]

Despite these difficulties, there is also plenty of evidence that the public comprehensive high school has survived well in some areas, and has also adapted to meet changing conditions. Two aspects of this stand out. The stories from regional New South Wales certainly show that it is easier for a public comprehensive high school to prosper where the market is controlled or restricted in some way. Here, the idealized local public comprehensive high school can exist comfortably even if the future for all its students may be restrained by local economic conditions. Second, in the large regional centers, and particularly in Sydney, the future for public comprehensive high schools seems to be dependant upon them becoming more diverse institutions. Sometimes this diversity can occur in partnership with other schools or with other parts of the public education system. In this respect, the current articulation with TAFE and emphasis on vocational education may well be meeting the interests of many students in ways that were not possible under previous curriculum arrangements. Some comprehensive high schools have become more comprehensive. Some smaller schools have become more comprehensive also not only through the use of cooperative arrangements but through their use and support of new distance education information technologies.

Nevertheless, at the beginning of the twenty-first century the government comprehensive high school was under threat. New ways needed to be found to relate to the social and cultural diversity that existed, particularly in many parts of Sydney. With the success of both market-based neoliberal and neoconservative contexts for schooling, substantial reinvention of comprehensive schooling was required if more than mere survival as a base or 'residual' system was not to be the primary aim.

Conclusion

In 1999, the Director General of Education and Training, Ken Boston summarized the case for the retreat from the comprehensive secondary school in New South Wales. He told his audience that it was difficult for many to imagine an educational landscape without the comprehensive high, but he argued that "the reality is that the origins of the comprehensive high school are deeply rooted in another time and in an Australia far different from the country we now know."[1] He argued that the immediate post–World War II years that produced the schools were marked by the necessity to cope with the demographic pressures producing radically expanded secondary school populations. Coinciding with the expansion was a belief "that in the formative years of adolescence there should be a substantial commonality of learning experiences for students before they started the individual journeys of adulthood."[2]

Boston then argued that the cultural, social, and economic changes had been so great since the 1950s and 1960s that the stand-alone comprehensive high school was no longer an adequate institution capable of containing them. First, the notion of adolescence had changed. The old fixed boundaries of adolescence had been extended and fragmented. Youth culture was now substantially experienced outside the secondary school. The technological and knowledge revolutions had also breached the old fixed walls of the school. While the comprehensive high school had certainly been a step forward in delivering "education for all," the new question had become "what our young people, at an individual level, are able to do with that provision." In particular, the standard comprehensive school had delivered poorly in the area of vocational education. Boston also implied that the old notions of adolescence and the comprehensive high school were dependent on a much more accessible youth labor market than existed in recent times. Now that successful transition to adulthood was so closely linked to successful entry into a difficult employment market, failure to significantly assist young people in that area by comprehensive high schools could no longer be tolerated.

He went on to argue that retention to Year 12 was more crucial than ever, and that it was increasingly clear that without relevant and extended education and training, the consequence was a very great "risk of unemployment, incidental or casual employment, social marginalization, poverty and dependence on social security throughout their lives." He argued that retention rate improvement in the late 1990s had stalled and even retreated. The consequence for the 15 percent of youth not completing secondary school would be disastrous. To deal with all youth the comprehensive school had to radically reconceptualize itself, not so much as a universal provider of education, but as a "partner in a student's learning, perhaps together with a technical college or university or a private training provider or perhaps an employer through a traineeship arrangement. It will almost certainly mean less focus on the school as the defining boundary of place and time."[3]

The consequence of this thinking was that there would be no single form of comprehensive secondary schooling in Australia for the future. The future required a much greater diversity of institutions than had been tolerated in the past. There would still be "a common framework" but the challenge would be to give youth "access to learning and training packages which are integrated into post-school options and life long learning opportunities." He concluded that some comprehensive high schools were meeting the challenge, but too many regarded the change required as mere "experimentation on the fringe." While Boston stopped well short of assigning the comprehensive government high school to antiquity he demanded that change was required in order "to stay the same."[4] The 'same' had been expressed earlier in the lecture; it was the "universal beliefs" about what was required from an educational system, that is:

1. a belief that all young people have a right to quality education, irrespective of family income or individual ability
2. a belief that this education should equip them with the knowledge and skills for worthwhile and rewarding lives
3. a belief that education is a powerful tool for creating a fairer, more just society—giving everyone a 'fair go'
4. a belief that education is essential for an ordered, civic society.[5]

These were 'beliefs' that would have been subscribed to by most attendees of the New Education Fellowship conference in 1937, but at that time the comprehensive high school was in the process of being imagined as the solution to the problem. In the 1990s, it was being imagined as one of the sources of the problem.

Boston's discussion of what was required in terms of reform was partly encompassed by the definition of a comprehensive secondary school used by the Department of Education and Training to inform parents about public education in New South Wales:

> The foundation of government secondary education in NSW is the comprehensive high school. Most high schools are comprehensive enrolling boys and girls from Years 7 to 12. They provide quality education in a broad range of subjects focusing on the needs of their local community.
>
> Innovative multi-campus comprehensive schools are also being introduced in a range of locations. These provide enhanced links with local TAFE colleges and universities. They often involve both junior and senior campuses designed for the specific needs of students.[6]

Where the first paragraph of this definition would have been recognizable to the writers of the Wyndham Report, the second would not. The second paragraph shows the adaptive nature of comprehensive education in New South Wales since the 1970s. The original model of a comprehensive secondary education occurring in a school 'under one roof' was departed from first in Tasmania and the Australian Capital Territory. The links with other providers, especially TAFE, were also new from the 1950s idea of comprehensive secondary education, though not likely to have been contradictory to its spirit. Less compatible was the development of junior and senior campuses in comprehensive collegiate institutions.

There are substantial but understandable deficiencies in this Boston and Education Department-led discussion of adaptive comprehensive schooling and education. It lacks a sense of the sociological contexts and potential impacts of the changes. It lacks positioning within the politics of public education as they have developed in Australia. The consequence of these absences is to play down the possibility that many of the new institutions and relationships of education were as likely to further disadvantage some users of public education as to assist them. It is some of these issues that we come back to in our conclusion.

The idea that secondary education should be provided universally in most Western countries, including Australia is still barely a century old. It stands to reason that there should have been fair difficulty in most countries in determining the best means of providing such education. Before World War II in Australia there were many reasons why a highly differentiated model of secondary schooling should have been the most acceptable solution to the problem. There was well-entrenched segmentation and well-supported beliefs and practices that deliberately excluded most youth from full secondary schooling. Many secondary school providers did not believe that all 'adolescents' required a 'secondary' education; at best a year or two of 'post-primary' training might be useful. (Much of Australia's working-class population would have agreed at the time.) Most providers believed that male and female, middle and working class, Aboriginal and non-Aboriginal youth required very different educations. The educational theories and technologies associated with 'ability' and 'intelligence' that came into prominence from the 1920s reinforced the idea that different schools and different curricula were required for different children. It was usually believed that only a minority could benefit from full secondary education. Then there were the exclusions based on religion as well as social class. The best-established secondary schools were corporate and private, often belonging to powerful churches. Their schooling cultures were adapted versions of Arnoldianism. Such secondary schooling provided educational and cultural experiences that were suitable for the preparation of leaders in society.[7] The universities were complicit in such aims. Secondary education remained an education for the middle and ruling classes, those classes that would form the professions, would own substantial businesses and property, those who would assume key positions in the public service, industry, and business.

The development of the public high school in New South Wales remained constrained by such considerations until the period of World War I when new demands associated with national efficiency and educational opportunity saw the elevation of academic merit as a reason for opening new public high schools to new groups of students, but these were not community schools for all adolescents. Nor were the rural high schools that were opened in the 1920s, but they edged closer to the idea that universal secondary schooling could be met by single coeducational institutions that had a particular responsibility for all youth in geographically defined neighborhoods or districts.

As the rural high school began its movement toward becoming a community secondary school, albeit multilateral in its curriculum organization and with very few students in the senior years, many of the ideas of educational progressivism that supported inclusive educational institutions and practices became better known. The intellectual movements that helped established the ACER (Australian Council for Education Research) also provided the motivation for Harold Wyndham to work on turning the ideal of comprehensive secondary education into a reality in New South Wales. In doing so the comprehensive secondary school became a late addition to the public institutions and programs constituting the postwar reconstruction period. Not only would the comprehensive schools planned by the Wyndham Report of 1957 contribute better educated citizens to Australia, citizens who would enjoy unprecedented educational 'opportunities,' but also solve the rapidly developing crisis of producing enough schools for the demographic and immigration-induced bulge of children and youth requiring an extended school education in the 1960s and 1970s.

The demand by many middle-class families for an academically oriented education could be met in the new comprehensive schools. With expanding enrolments and a strict system of school zoning, sufficient curriculum options could be directed toward meeting their needs, and in any case, the final two years of the New South Wales version of the comprehensive high school would constitute an 'academic top' to the four years of a 'comprehensive bottom.'

The emergence of the comprehensive government high school in the 1960s constituted an apotheosis for the public education system whose history the Whig historians had always been inclined to describe as a narrative of disinterested and inspired progress from the Public Instruction Act of 1880.[8] The distressing era of denominational rivalry, ill-trained teachers, disorganized and patchy school coverage would all be left behind. In its place would be a centralized, well-resourced, efficient system of public schools organized along bureaucratic lines. Left out of this narrative for the most part were the excluded communities, Catholic-Irish and Aboriginal, the women who were absorbed into subordinated teaching roles in schools, and the rigidities of discipline, routine, pedagogy, and curriculum that alienated many of the children of families who were compelled to school for the first time in the history of the colony. From this litany of problems Francis Anderson and Peter Board had plenty to criticize from the turn of the century, and much to improve in the first great reform era from then to World War I. In time, however, they were absorbed into the narrative of progress that culminated afresh with the Wyndham scheme.

The decline from the period of apotheosis to that of pressure, criticism, and difficulty was relatively swift. From the 1970s, public education was forced once more to compete with a newly resourced and invigorated 'private' or nongovernment school sector as a result of the restoration of state aid to church, corporate, and other 'private' schools. Demography provided another blow as a previously expanding public school system lost enrolments or stagnated in old and the now growing-old 'new suburbs' of the postwar period. The rise of neoliberalism to major influence in government undermined all public institutions and their purposes, not only public schools.[9] The systems of public transport, public health, social welfare, as well as public education could all be seen as harboring inefficiencies and anticompetitive practices. If public systems of provision were to survive they had to be subject to the disciplines of competition in the market, and the practices of the new managerialism that involved the devolution of many responsibilities that had previously been assumed by the central bureaucracy.[10] Many school managers (as school principals began to be known under the new theories of public administration) saw their job as difficult, managing in fact a declining system in a period of declining resources and government commitment, state and federal, to public education. The new challenges for comprehensive government schools were severe enough without an apparent retreat in support from the center.[11]

So it was that the idea that the government comprehensive high school would become the dominant, even hegemonic secondary school in New South Wales (and Australia) began to disappear. These schools, still the majority of secondary schools educating the majority of youth, became one of a number of different schools not only in the nongovernment sector, but in the public sector also, that could be chosen. Where families did not choose actively, the local comprehensive usually remained the natural next post-primary school.

The reasons for this contracted status of the government comprehensive high schools in the scheme of educational provision in New South Wales and Australia are both historical and many in number. First, there was the survival of alternatives in both the government and nongovernment sector. Surviving nongovernment schools from the period before restored state aid, and surviving selective public secondary schools despite the Wyndham scheme provided a constituency and a base for renewed efforts to diversify and differentiate schools. Second, the introduction of federally funded state aid allowed the restoration and expansion of the Catholic system of low-fee secondary schools. This expansion of the nongovernment sector was extended to new groups of low-fee Anglican, Lutheran, Uniting and mainstream and new 'Christian' churches, as well as non-Christian and ethnic community schools. Third, is the economic and youth labor market characteristics of the last decades of the twentieth century and the first of the twenty-first. As the youth labor market contracted, and as the Australian economy developed postindustrial characteristics, in which much better technological skills, and higher credential levels were required for employment, schooling became more important for youth and their families. Less could be left to chance. The families of 'middle Australia' felt the pressure to exercise far greater discrimination in the choice of a school. The government comprehensive tended to become the base, or fall-back option where active choice could not be made.[12] Fourth was the rise of 'economic rationalism,' an Australian variant of the global triumphs of neoliberalism. These movements legitimated criticism of public institutions, and reinvigorated trust in competition, markets, and private institutions as the way forward for economic and social development. The comprehensive government high school increasingly looked like a 'safety-net' school for the youth of citizens who could not use or compete in the developing markets that were particularly active in secondary schooling. Fifth was a rising criticism, often from groups identifying as neoconservative, that the quality of teaching and learning in government schools in particular was substandard. New regimes of standardized testing, concentration on achieving certain 'competencies,' and mounting criticism of the HSC results, but more generally the values, discipline, and professionalism of schools, their students, and teaching staffs impacted severely on government comprehensive high schools. The defense of 'public education' became an important issue in the politics of New South Wales.

Undoubtedly, such a list could be added to. But there are other issues that have contributed to the weakening of the comprehensive high school ideal, which are of more 'internal' derivation as opposed to the external pressures.

Of these, a major one was always the problematic of the comprehensive high school being a neighborhood school. If the neighborhood was middle class, the chances of the school being successful in many different ways was and remains significantly higher than if the neighborhood had very high levels of unemployed and generally poor families. Zoning could sometimes mediate these influences, but in a period of de-zoning, some schools were socially residualized and began to fail quite rapidly. If they survived as small schools, the likelihood that they would offer a 'comprehensive' curriculum was limited.

The second issue related to the comprehensive high as a school with 'assimilation' at the heart of its original project. It would provide a common curriculum core to all Australian youth; it had a firm sense of what was required to produce Australian citizens. It residually retained some Protestant biases deriving from the history of public education in Australia. In the beginning these had provided public schools with their firm set of values, but the comprehensive school was initially at least, ill-prepared for the rapid growth of different ethnicities among the school population and then multiculturalism as a set of policies that displaced assimilation as a core public school project. Different constituencies grew within the comprehensive high school that required the recognition of needs associated with particular ethnic and religious communities. The same could be said for the issues arising from gender, though the balance of concern changed from an early concentration on the inequities experienced by girls to the developing 'boy problem.'[13] Similarly, though in very different ways, the claims of the 'gifted and talented,' sexual orientation minorities, and other groups all demanded an ever more comprehensive school able to accommodate wide diversity. Neither Australia nor its public schools fragmented into warring 'tribes,' but nor did older dominant views of what constituted acceptable subordination of individual differences to collective values and purposes work the same way. It was easier for academically selective, or single-sex, or church, or ethnic, or wealthy schools, government or non-government to present as cohesive organizations with a set of coherent purposes. In the new school market place, such schools were easier to sell than the comprehensives.

Deprived of its uncontested place as the hegemonic Australian secondary school, the comprehensive high school has had to develop an adapted set of purposes. Some of these are produced in common with the expectations of all Australian schools, in terms of meeting the needs of youth in rapidly changing economic, technological, and youth labor market circumstances. Some purposes are produced very differently in different comprehensive schools as an identifiable niche in an educational market is sought out. Specialities such as sports or gifted and talented, or vocational education and training programs are made much of. They become the commodities with which a school can tempt an identifiable market segment. As important as these are in defining modern comprehensive schools, there is still the further role that these schools play in terms of very basic access issues in secondary schooling. For rural, new suburban, poorer, and recently arrived immigrant families the government comprehensive high school is often the only school within easy reach, perhaps geographically as well as financially. The recognition of the importance of this role is a problem of course, because it may mean that the comprehensive school is socially comprehensive no longer. The effect of 'specializing' in such enrolments can lead to residualization if important resources are not made available to such schools, or, if public policy is capable of imagining it, the development of a specialist school of a new type. Under such circumstances, the old expectations of the comprehensive high school, of welding a geographic 'neighborhood' together and the delivery of a very broad curriculum are displaced.

This great tendency toward specialization, and meeting the individual needs of families and children in the context of the new educational markets has exercised many policy analysts. The debates in the United States have led to the development of publicly funded charter schools in many states and a great deal of energy devoted to discussing how voucher-based funding of public education might work. In Australia, Brian Caldwell and colleagues have argued for a de-bureaucratization of Australian public schooling. They retain no particular commitment to the public comprehensive high school. They advocate an Australian version of charter schooling. They also imply that the old public and private divide in Australian education is increasingly obsolete.[14] In one sense this is true enough, given the fact that virtually all schools in Australia are now substantially funded from public and tax-raised revenue. Most Catholic schools have a strong social justice element incorporated in their statements of purpose as well as their practice. The difference, it could be argued is that some publicly funded schools are maintained by the federal government with substantial degrees of autonomy. Other publicly funded schools are maintained by state governments, but they are part of a system, with very limited autonomy.

Such an analysis is flawed however. There is no secondary school but the government comprehensive that is completely open to all youth regardless of social, ethnic, religious, or other origin—or indeed the wealth of their families. It is the only school that remains very substantially a 'free' school. While it is routinely possible and predictable that schools within the public system should be used for private purposes, the comprehensive schools are less deliberately structured in ways that enable that to occur.

Despite its inadequacies at various times in its fifty-year history the government comprehensive high school has been able to adapt to new circumstances. Few such schools now operate as 'stand-alone' facilities. Much greater curriculum diversity exists than was thought possible a half century previous. Schools' relationships with local communities, including the various ethnic and religious minorities have often developed in unimagined and positive ways. The government comprehensive high school is a school that is adaptable, and refuses to capitulate to the idea that separate schools are required for youth arbitrarily fragmented according to the wealth, social status, religion, or the ethnic origins of their parents. The cost of this refusal in terms of the neoliberal marketization of schooling, is the relative disadvantage of such schools in the market. The government comprehensive high schools remain the schools that educate most Australian youth—but possibly not for much longer.

The government comprehensive high school is the one secondary school in Australia that appears to be suffering the most as a result of neoliberal policy inspired changes in school funding policies. These schools, originally serving a broad cross-section of Australian families are becoming less representative. There is strong evidence of middle-class 'flight' from a number of these schools. Similarly, there is evidence that some ethnic groups are more likely to use some schools and systems rather than others, but the pattern varies according to region. Government funding policies are not particularly responsive to the new pressures on government comprehensive high schools as their school populations are increasingly drawn from populations that are subject to high unemployment, or are relatively poor and disempowered. The problems of such schools in the parts of Australian cities that have undergone deindustrialization have been eloquently described and analyzed in Pat Thomson's *Schooling the Rustbelt Kid*.[15]

In the Western world, Australia has one of the largest nongovernment school sectors. Despite nongovernment schools receiving public funding they have reasonably few limitations placed on them with regard to curriculum obligations or student acceptance or expulsion procedures. This fact produces a potentially explosive politics concerning social justice issues as substantially free but poorly funded government comprehensive schools find it more difficult to retain students from wealthier and academically advantaged backgrounds. Government comprehensive schools rarely have the ability to choose their student bodies, nor should they. As governments search for policy solutions to the problems, their commitment to public schooling is undermined by an increasingly numerous and powerful electorate committed to neoliberal versions of school choice only made possible by federal funding of nongovernment schools in the first place.

The Australian sociologist Richard Teese convincingly argues that many nongovernment schools and some selective government schools, are able to manage their market advantages to the point that "school failure" may be "exported." "Private schools, operating on an assured platform of public grants, drain secondary education of the cultural resources represented by family education, life-style and know-how and pump these into the most profitable locations of the curriculum. The school system becomes polarized."[16] Teese is pessimistic concerning the future for comprehensive state high schooling.

> In comprehensive high schools, residential segregation brings together many students with multiple disadvantages—low self-esteem, poor basic learning, language handicaps, poverty and family breakdown. Instead of a mass of cultural and economic resources being concentrated on one advantageous site and applied to the high end of the curriculum—as happens in private schools—there is an accumulation of liabilities at the one site. This weakens the instructional effort and risks severe retribution against those students who stray into the more academic subjects.[17]

In all this process, new definitions of the state and its responsibilities and relationships to its citizen populations are being forged. Indeed a new definition of the good citizen is also being forged. The good citizen becomes one who contributes to the welfare of all by pursuing somewhat relentlessly his or her private interests.[18] The demands of such a citizen on schools are transformed in the process. With financial assistance from government, parents choose the 'best' school for their children. Pressure is brought to bear on rejected schools to reform themselves. In the process, schools that specialize in some areas of the curriculum with high value in a credentials or labor market, or even schools that through high fee structures can advertise social exclusivity, are increasingly seen as the only successful schools.

The consequence of this for state comprehensive high schools, whose ideal purpose is not to specialize, but to provide social inclusivity, is to place them at a severe disadvantage in the competition for enrolments and resources in an educational market. The ideal citizen whom the state comprehensive high school was meant to serve was not conceived as having a social class or ethnic background. The Schools Commission period in the 1970s and 1980s disabused public school systems of that notion. Nevertheless comprehensive high schools were meant to be 'neighborhood' or community schools, offering roughly equal opportunity to all. In the policy context of neoliberalism and the pressures of renewed globalization, the postmodern citizen and the postmodern school tend no longer to situate themselves primarily in a particular, geographically based, community. They are meant to, and in an increasing number of cases, seek advantage in a wider market. Under these circumstances, there is a real social justice question. Some families are manifestly more able to access and manipulate the resources available in such a market than others. Some comprehensive public secondary schools have adapted remarkably well to the new circumstances. Others, however, are faced with insurmountable problems as they attempt to provide a good secondary education to their students. In the end, the policy context of neoliberalism does not provide a favorable context for these schools or their students. Often they are punished further for the disadvantages from which they suffer.

Continual reform in education has become a characteristic of recent modern history. Despite the real differences in the circumstances of the rise of the comprehensive ideal in the United States, Britain, and Australia, this study has shown that there are elements of a shared history as well. They certainly share in varying degrees the current problems. Whether the comprehensive government high school will retain a secure place in the educational arrangements of the future in such countries is by no means certain.

Epilogue

Craig Campbell

In the period 2005–2012, seven years since the writing of the first edition of this book, the comprehensive high school in Australia has benefitted little from continuing educational reform. In New South Wales, the main focus of this study, there was a period of relative policy quiescence. The institutions, public and nongovernmental, that organize secondary schooling remained much the same. Nevertheless if state government policies affecting the public comprehensive high school remained stable, then the same cannot be said for the interventions of the Australian federal government. Much of this epilogue discusses federal policy and its effects on the continuing history of the public comprehensive high school.

Nor do there appear to have been remarkable policy shifts internationally, or at least in those countries that Australia compares itself with educationally through the Organisation for Economic Cooperation and Development (OECD). Intensification of existing policy directions is probably the most accurate characterization of international and Australian educational reform. The OECD regularly produces comparative statistics concerning national efforts in improving levels of literacy and numeracy. The regular publication of the Program for International Student Assessment (PISA) statistics are important for educational policy making in each of the OECD countries. Their impacts are usually more significant than the policy arguments, now often regarded as tired, and likely not "evidence-based," that sought to support comprehensive public school systems in a range of countries through the twentieth century.

In 2007 an international study of the comprehensive high school was published.[1] Significantly it was titled *The Death of the Comprehensive High School?* The majority of its separately authored chapters confirmed the precarious state of comprehensive schools in countries such as the United Kingdom, the United States, New Zealand, and Australia.

We know that the attempts by governments to invent common secondary schools for all youth was a twentieth-century project. It was in the 1950s and 1960s that the comprehensive high school appeared most likely to succeed across the English-speaking world. Pioneered in Scandinavia and the United States such a school promised to solve a number of problems.[2]

First was the newly discovered adolescent. A new institution was required to protect youth from premature entry into dangerous adult worlds. The school also promised greater social cohesion, especially where new migrants were required to assimilate rapidly, and where old and new ethnic, racial, religious, class. and other social divisions were endemic. It promised better informed citizens for democracies. It promised a great leveling up of average educational standards. No longer would too many young people be trapped in schools—central, junior technical, secondary modern, and similar—that routinely reduced opportunities for higher education and careers. Such a high school also promised a common curriculum, at least in the junior years, that would meet modern labor market requirements. Young people would be better "adjusted" for employment and living in modern societies.

The essays in *The Death of the Comprehensive High School?* tend to suggest that these expectations were too heavy a burden for any single institution to meet.

Two essays make specific populations their focus. Thomas Pedroni and Pavla Miller contrast individual and group private purposes, with the public policy intentions of comprehensive schooling.[3] Pedroni writes about Black American voucher-using families. Miller looks at Italian-Australian families. Such families become rational actors in the schooling circumstances of the cities within which they live. They are not selfish users of neoliberal-inspired reforms to public schooling. Instead they make the best of the schooling opportunities presented to them, within the contexts of their family histories, cultural circumstances, and, in some cases, long-standing historical discriminations. Comprehensive public schools may or may not form part of such families' educational projects. These essays demonstrate the potential explanatory power that attention to the stories of real families can bring to the debate.

This approach contrasts dramatically with the essay by Rene Gonzalez and Anthony De Jesus.[4] Latino and Latina youth in the United States are constructed as certain victims of uncaring, alienating, overlarge comprehensive high schools. The authors' advocacy of segregated schooling is problematic, failing to overcome crude portrayals of both comprehensive and segregated community schooling. Their demand for the "death" of the comprehensive school is nevertheless significant, representing as it does the hostility of various groups who have felt marginalized within such schools. Their conclusion aligns with that of Jose Rosario who interprets contrasting documentary films on American secondary schools.[5] He concludes that "soul-making," especially in large comprehensive schools, did not occur well. The systems and authoritarianism of the large comprehensive high schools produced multiple problems for students and teachers.

David Crook's essay on England and Wales introduces a significant distinction between *comprehensive schooling* and *comprehensive education.* Comprehensive schools may be in deep trouble, but the curriculum that young people experience in the wide variety of alternative or successor schools is likely to be comprehensive in character. This is rightly seen as an achievement of the comprehensive schooling movement. For New South Wales, a variation of this argument was used by the Director General of Education, Ken Boston, in 1999 when he argued that a comprehensive public school *system* was a more sensible goal than that every school attempt to be comprehensive (see p. 124).

Franklin and McCulloch argued that the main question for the comprehensive school is that of whom such a school should serve.[6] This looks like a simple question—the answer is: "All young people in a society"—but as the different essays point out, there is contested ground between the theory, policy, and practice. *The Death of the Comprehensive High School?* covers much of the contest. Nevertheless there is room for further research and discussion. For example, the enemies of comprehensive schooling and their interests need systematic analysis. We can ask other questions such as whether very small schools with strong pastoral ethos are always the superior alternative. Recent school choice policies have their problems. Parents may choose a school, but schools may not choose to enroll their children. Do we know enough about how comprehensive schools operate in different urban, suburban, and rural contexts? And if comprehensive schools make way for specialist schools, how likely is it that such schools will not turn into hierarchies of schools, differentiated not only in terms of their curriculum specializations but also in supporting increased levels of social selection and exclusivity?

Such comment hardly exhausts the recent international literature on comprehensive secondary schooling, but it does indicate the continuing significance of the debate, both national and international.

Commissioned in 2010, the then Labor federal minister for education in Australia, Julia Gillard, initiated a review of national funding arrangements for all schools, public and nongovernment. Recommendations were to be "financially sustainable and effective in promoting excellent educational outcomes for all Australian students."[7] Potentially the most significant review of Australian education in 20 years, the Gonski Report produced evidence that the schools most likely to be in trouble or failing, were public schools that were being forced into enrolling unrepresentatively large numbers of students in poverty, with learning difficulties, and poor command of

English. The Report recommended a substantial reinvestment in "disadvantaged" schools and "disadvantaged" students.

The Gonski Report also used OECD and other data arising from literacy and numeracy testing to argue that nations that had diverse and hierarchical systems of schools were more likely to have large gaps between higher and lower performing students and schools, and that national average scores in literacy and numeracy would consequently decline. Australia was clearly such a nation. The Report identified 18 coexisting school systems in Australia. One of the paradoxes of the Report's conclusions was that, even though this source of decline was identified, Gonski was asked to support the choices parents might make among a diverse range of schools, public and nongovernment. There was little in the report to suggest that comprehensive public high schools would be much better off as a result of funding reform in the long term. Such schools are almost always the most disadvantaged where school markets are encouraged.[8]

In New South Wales, the secondary school enrolment trends we identified from 1990 to 2004 (p. 123) showed the decline in the proportion of students enrolled in public high schools. This decline continued through the following decade as Table E1 shows. In 2011 the enrolment in public high schools was down another one percent.

As was true in Table 5.1 (p. 123), the percentage of secondary students in all public secondary schools is not the same as the percentage in public comprehensive schools. The existence of some 17 fully selective schools, and 23 partially selective, as well as a variety of special schools reduces the proportion. Some 4,150 places are made available each year in academically selective streams or schools. Counting these reduces the proportion of New South Wales secondary students in comprehensive schools as no more than 57 percent of all enrolments.

Table E1 Secondary students, full and part-time, in government and nongovernment schools: New South Wales, 2011 (%)

School sector	% of NSW enrolment
Government/public	62
Nongovernment	38
Catholic 24	
Other nongovernment 15	
Total (%)	100
Total enrolment (N)	503,171

Note: There are rounding effects in percentage totals.
Source: Australian Bureau of Statistics, *Schools Australia 2012*, 4221.0.

Public debate on the mix of schools in New South Wales, their relative effectiveness, the instruments they use to include and exclude students only increases over time. We have argued elsewhere that parental anxiety about the future of their children intensified in the post-Global Financial Crisis world.[9] This is not the only factor however. Since writing this book, the federal government, using its usual means of persuasion against the states, that is making major grants for school funding conditional on the implementation of its school reform policies, has opened to public scrutiny, on a school-by-school basis, the results of its literacy and numeracy basic skills testing. These tests are known by the acronym NAPLAN, the National Assessment Program on Literacy and Numeracy. To disseminate the results, the Australian Curriculum, Assessment and Reporting Authority (ACARA) has produced for the national government the My School website (http://www.myschool.edu.au/). Professor Barry McGaw, sometime Education Director for the OECD and chair of the enquiry that reformed public examinations in New South Wales in the late 1990s, supervised the development of the site.

My School is a remarkable national achievement. Nearly every primary and secondary school in Australia is represented. There is a general description of each school, but more important, a vigorous attempt to contextualize the NAPLAN results for each school in relation to the social character of its enrolling families, and the wealth of the school, with attention paid to school income derived from a variety of sources, and converted into a figure that suggests how much is spent on each child. ACARA has been sensitive to the critics of school "league tabling," and refused to publish state or nationwide tables revealing the "best" and "worst" schools. Comparisons are essential to the project however, so schools are routinely compared with those that enroll students of roughly equal socioeconomic characteristics (an Index of Community Socio-Economic Advantage—ICSEA—is the instrument used). As a consequence readers of individual schools' webpages can easily discover whether progress has been made since the last year on NAPLAN scores, and whether the school is doing better or worse than schools with comparable enrolments according to the ICSEA.

Regardless of the safeguards, it is relatively easy to produce the state and nationwide school league tables that newspapers publish with great fanfare. The My School site is very popular. It provides a wealth of information informing parents entering the school market; it supplies data that tell schools of their success, or otherwise. Public schools are compared not only with like, but nongovernment schools also. Nevertheless, the responsibility of most comprehensive public high schools for an undifferentiated enrolment, various programs for students with learning difficulties, and their lack of local control over teacher staffing and enrolment are barely signaled.

The schools that are usually worse off as a result of public comparison are the comprehensive public high schools.

In early 2012 the league tables constructed from 2011 NAPLAN data were published by Sydney's morning broadsheet newspaper.[10] The most successful schools, the top ten in each category were as follows in Table E2.

The public, academically selective schools in urban Sydney, were predictably the most successful schools in terms of the numeracy and literacy tests. They remain among the most desirable schools, in terms of the competition involved in order to achieve entrance. In 2012, for example, more than 13,500 students sat the entry tests for 4,158 places.[11] As our research has shown, the effort put in by parents in order to achieve these places for their children is considerable. An increasing proportion of the places are taken by young people from ambitious non-English speaking background (NESB) families. The degree to which coaching colleges and tutors may be used to achieve advantage in the selective entrance tests is a dividing issue among the middle-classes of Sydney.[12] In 2010 an analysis of selective school results showed that 42 percent of NESB students sitting the test were successful, in comparison with some 23 percent of English-speaking background families.[13]

The ethnicity issues exposed also revealed that some of the non-south and non-east Asian background students, in particular Arab speaking families, were strongly underrepresented even in applying to sit the tests.[14] These sorts of issues have been controversial for some time, but the My School statistics added a further virulent component to the debate. Occasionally there were other moral panics in the media, that there was "white flight" or "white middle class flight" from public comprehensive high schools in various regions of the state.[15]

Because the enrolments of each school were categorized by the My School website in terms of socioeconomic advantage, a measure that

Table E2 League table of most successful secondary schools in New South Wales: My School, 2011 (N)

NAPLAN test	**Public comprehensive**	**Public selective**	**Catholic**	**Other nongovernment**
Grammar	0	9	0	1
Numeracy	0	10	0	0
Reading	0	10	0	0
Spelling	0	10	0	0
Writing	0	8	0	2

Source: *Sydney Morning Herald*, 27 February 2012, Supplement.

included the educational background of parents as well as indications of their wealth, it was discovered that almost universally, the selective public high school attracted the highest ICSEA rankings—they were the most socially exclusive of nearly all schools, whether public or nongovernment. This produced a politics that included intensive criticism from nongovernment schools and their supporters, demanding that exclusive educational opportunities for wealthier, usually highly educated professional parents in public schools should attract school fees, perhaps means-tested. It is a fair hypothesis that elite nongovernment, or in the more popular parlance of Australian educational discourse, that "top private" schools were disturbed that their market promises of relative social exclusivity and excellence in education were inferior to those of the public selective schools. The debate often had populist characteristics. In one formulation, elements of the professional and wealthy middle class were "hijacking" the best public schools for their own purposes, leaving the rest of the population dependent on the declining comprehensive public schools.[16]

Earlier in this book we pointed to the problem of residualizing public comprehensive high schools. We looked at the trouble that the outer western suburban comprehensive high school, Mount Druitt, got into during the late 1990s. From 2000 it was incorporated as a junior school (Years 7 to 10) within the multicampus Chifley College. Nevertheless My School published the NAPLAN results of the successor school, the Mount Druitt campus. They were very far from the top 10, in fact, at 753, it was among the lowest ranked schools in the state (the schools lowest in the league tables for average rank were in the 760s). The diversity of circumstances among public schools is considerable. In Table E3 we contrast two of the highest NAPLAN achieving public selective schools, with a comprehensive high in a middle class area of Sydney whose history we consider below, and the Mount Druitt campus in its working class area with its high levels of unemployment. We add in the only two "top 10" nongovernment schools, Abbotsleigh, an Anglican girls' school, and Sydney Grammar School, a secular boys' school.

The table indicates one of the enduring problems with measuring "school success" with tests restricted to literacy and numeracy. Some public comprehensive high schools, catering as they often have for populations that have rarely achieved major benefit from schooling, will be permanently entrenched in positions below those schools that control their enrolments by charging high fees and select their students on the grounds of prior, and significant academic achievement.

As pointed out in earlier chapters, the regional circumstances of public comprehensive high schools have been a major issue. It is impossible here to update the developments in each of the six regions that we selected for

Table E3 My School data on select schools in Sydney, New South Wales, 2011

School name & category	ICSEA	NAPLAN average rank	Income per student ($)	CAPEX ($)
James Ruse Agricultural High School *Public, selective*	1,181	1	12,248	686,359
North Sydney Girls High School *Public, selective*	1,187	2	11,630	454,635
Abbotsleigh *High fee, nongovernment, Anglican*	1,196	23	22,748	6,458,428
Sydney Grammar School *High fee, nongovernment, secular*	1,222	9	29,670	11,780,152
Pennant Hills High School *Public comprehensive*	1,117	142	10,866	1,010,737
Mount Druitt Campus (Chifley Coll.) *Public junior comprehensive*	883	753	13,332	946,257

Notes: ICSEA, Index of Community Socio-Economic Advantage, national average, 1,000; NAPLAN ave. rank is the mean of ranks for grammar, numeracy, reading, spelling & writing; Income, a school's yearly income per student in 2010, national average $13,583; CAPEX, a school's capital expenditure, the national average, $1.3 million.

Source: *Sydney Morning Herald*, 27 February 2012, Supplement, calculated from My School web-site, http://www.myschool.edu.au/, accessed 20 March 2012.

analysis (see p. 142). If we take one of the regional cities, Coffs Harbour on the Pacific coast, in northern New South Wales, and look at the My School data associated with the schools that are in that city, or are close by, we can draw the conclusion that it is probable that where school markets can be constructed, then, as in Sydney, the comprehensives are likely to do less well than the specialized public and nongovernment secondary schools.

This is certainly the case for Coffs Harbour and district, where according to Table E4, the public comprehensive high schools enroll students from families below the state average in terms of the ICSEA index. Each of the nongovernment schools specialize in families above the state average. There is a strong correlation between ICSEA index, average NAPLAN rank, and whether a school is a government comprehensive or not.

A large number of the families who were interviewed for our study on school choice and the middle class in Sydney defended public comprehensive

Table E4 My School data on Coffs Harbour schools, north coast, New South Wales, 2011

School name and category	ICSEA	NAPLAN average rank	Income per student ($)	CAPEX ($)
Bishop Druitt College *Anglican, nongovernment*	1,122	190	13,790	1,511,309
John Paul College *Catholic, nongovernment*	1,034	200	12,996	1,807,584
Coffs Harbour Christian Community *Low fee, nongovernment*	1,033	317	11,085	2,371,401
Coffs Harbour High School *Public comprehensive*	974	495	11,055	2,915,627
Orara High School *Public comprehensive*	917	605	14,207	1,363,813
Toormina High School *Public comprehensive*	936	581	12,358	516,493

Source: *Sydney Morning Herald*, 27 February 2012, Supplement, calculated from My School web-site, http://www.myschool.edu.au/, accessed 20 March 2012.

high schools. This was especially true in middle class suburbs where the enrollments in the comprehensive public school remained broadly representative of the local population. On the whole, however, the criticisms were strong. Comprehensive schools tended to be portrayed as the places that had difficulty in producing orderly and disciplined young people, where teachers were subject to unreasonable pressures as they sought to do their work, and as places where school principals had insufficient control over student entry or the appointment of teaching staff. The critical discourse surrounding such commentary included the idea of "values," with government comprehensives often being portrayed as deficient.[17]

Those parents interviewed, who were coming to grips with being active in the school market as they sought advantage for their children, often believed that "ordinary" schools were no longer good enough. Many no longer relied on family traditions in schooling. This affected those with long histories in nongovernment as well as public education. The availability of NAPLAN data through the My School website intensified awareness of the market, and the process by which the comprehensive high schools were perceived as ordinary, and sometimes second-rate.

Pennant Hills High in the mainly middle-class Hills area of Sydney is one of the comprehensive public high schools that has retained substantial support from its parental community through the 1970s to the 2010s. Its history is instructive for the retention of confidence in comprehensive schools in an increasingly difficult policy climate.[18] Although this story concentrates on the school leadership and its responses to the changing contexts of schools policy, the importance of the school's geographical site, in the middle of an area well above the state average in terms of employment, household wealth, and real estate value, must not be lost sight of. These characteristics are in part revealed by My School data. See table E3 above.

The school's long-term late twentieth-century principal (1975–1995) embraced the idea of Pennant Hills High as a comprehensive school, but primarily serving as a school that would offer a curriculum encouraging university entrance. He was an enthusiast for foreign languages in the curriculum. He publicly opposed the reforms of the Greiner government, referred to earlier in this book, which were seen as harmful to comprehensive schools. He viewed with concern the increase in the number of selective public high schools that had the potential to affect the academic performance of the school. In 1992 the school was publicising its Higher School Certificate (HSC) Year 12 results. Five of its students were in the top one percent of the state. As a strategy to shore up the school against the coming threat of the selective schools, the principal refused the introduction of Vocational Education and Training (VET) subjects and courses. They would lower the middle-class enrolment by attracting more working class students into the vocational track. The school would remain a successful comprehensive high school by resisting a more comprehensive, potentially stratified, curriculum.

The threat of the academically selective and specialist schools could not be avoided however. James Ruse Agricultural, Cherrybrook Technology, Baulkham Hills, Normanhurst Boys, and Hornsby Girls public high schools each gained market advantage, often at the expense of the area's comprehensive schools. For a time these newly selective and specialist schools appeared to make little difference, but the district surrounding Pennant Hills was also a prime area for new nongovernment school startups. In the late 1990s there was a period in which academic successes for the school were reduced. Later principals, after 1995, were less likely to resist state government education policies. VET subjects were introduced at this time, and Pennant Hills High became more comprehensive in the curriculum that it offered, but in the measure that the media took notice of, HSC results, the school farewelled its glory days of a decade previous.

The school remained advantaged in that its closeness to public transport, its general reputation and history, and the regard with which it was held in its community generally held, even if the "top" students were mainly going elsewhere. There were still lists of out-of-area students waiting to be enrolled, likely avoiding comprehensive high schools close to where they actually lived. Early in the twenty-first century a new principal concentrated on building relationships with community, and overhauling the school's welfare, behavior management, and other policies. Arson attacks on the school inspired remarkable outbursts of community support. The subsequent rebuilding of the school plant allowed an opportunity to increase the role that new information technologies would play in the curriculum.

The impression was given that the school leadership and its curriculum reform effort were dynamic, but attempting to prosper while surrounded by selective and specialist public, as well as nongovernment schools, was the continuing challenge, and problem. Slippage out of the top 200 schools in terms of Year 12 HSC results had immediate consequences. Year 7 enrolments dropped. Policy responses included working harder with potential student families from "feeder" primary schools, introducing a new set of Gifted and Talented Students (GATS) classes. Selling the school required subtle strategies. "Comprehensive," coeducational, and "community-based" schooling could be argued as advantageous—as long as the NAPLAN and HSC results held up reasonably well. Parents and potential parents interested in the school were alert, and watching.

This brief history of Pennant Hills High is representative of many comprehensive public high schools that continue not only to survive, but do reasonably well in circumstances that are, on the whole, hostile.

As has been signaled earlier, the New South Wales state governments in the last decade or so have produced little in the way of change to the circumstances of comprehensive high schools in that state.[19]

With the departure of Labor Premier Bob Carr, avowedly an "education premier," and after Ken Boston resigned as Director General of Education in 2002, and with the appointment of senior public servants as directors of education who had no particular expertise in the education field, new policy initiatives became thin on the ground. Increasing political instability led to three premiers in six years. The education portfolio also changed rapidly with the ministers: Carmel Tebutt (2005–2007), John Della Bosca (2007–2008), and Verity Firth (2008–2011). With growing pressure on the state budget, financial management overshadowed the administration of public education. The government was increasingly subject at best to charges of tiredness, and at worst, cronyism and corruption. It was overwhelmingly defeated at the election in 2011.

But there were a few initiatives late in the Labor government's last term of office, the final effects of which remain to be determined. Under its last minister of education, Verity Firth, the Labor government decided to raise the school leaving age to 16. From 2010, all students had to complete Year 10, and until they turned 17 they had to be in school or in education and training or full-time employment. This promised to extend the ambit of education to include more lower socioeconomic groups, thereby attempting to tackle the related issues of social disadvantage, lack of skills, and the unemployment that had plagued many youth from poorer backgrounds since the unemployment crises of the 1970s. There was virtually no discussion as to how this might relate to the future of the surviving local comprehensive high schools. There was the chance that they would have to provide programs for ever more students resentful of the custodial role schools assumed despite the policy intention, to improve student employability through further education and training. Raising the school leaving and training ages was hardly an issue for those public and nongovernment schools that already boasted strong retention rates.

In 2009, the Labor government also increased the number of selective places, especially through increasing the number of selective enrolments for formerly comprehensive schools. This was a popular policy given the pressure on the places. Its likely effect on the remaining comprehensive schools was little discussed.

Also late in its term of government, Labor allowed the introduction of "ethics" classes as an alternative for families who did not wish to have their children participate in religious instruction, or "scripture" classes in public schools. This unleashed a bitter public debate, especially critical from those who held that public schools were suspect in terms of their "values" and "values education." On the whole the defenders of secular ethics classes held their own, and the incoming conservative, Liberal-National Coalition government appeared prepared to tolerate their existence, for the time being at least. This debate was likely to have confirmed a variety of community perceptions about the relative characters of public and nongovernment schools. Most nongovernment schools in Australia are owned by churches and their trusts. In the early twenty-first century they have usually found it easier to assert a stronger values foundation than the public schools.[20]

And then a policy process initiated by the Labor government came to completion at the end of the first year of the incoming government of Premier Barry O'Farrell. The Coalition's Minister of Education, Adrian Piccoli, and the premier announced that it would implement policy devolving considerable power over school finances and teacher staffing to public school principals.[21] It was argued that this devolution strategy would allow the people who knew their local communities best, identified primarily as school principals, control over the resources, human and financial, required to meet local needs. Changes to principal salaries and classification, teacher salaries, more local control over teacher appointments—the linking of school budgets to "student learning outcomes"—were all part of the reform. Problems with the program piloting such policies were largely ignored.

Responses to the devolution policy were somewhat predictable.[22] Public school principal associations were mainly in favor, the New South Wales Teachers Federation was critical, as was at least one comprehensive high school principal who bravely spoke out against his employer. Gary Joannides argued that responsibility, and therefore accountability, for public education was being shifted from the central Education Department to school principals. He also feared that devolution would see eventual reductions in public school resourcing.[23] A few months later in 2012, the New South Wales state budget did in fact substantially reduce funding for public schools.

As a program yet to be implemented, it is difficult to say how devolution will affect public comprehensive high schools. Research on such devolutionary programs elsewhere in Australia, the United Kingdom, and the United States suggests that the effects will likely be variable. Some schools and their communities will use the increased controls to advantage. In those comprehensive high schools already advantaged by substantial resources, experienced teachers, and student populations from middle-class neighborhoods, the chances are that they will improve their positions in the school market. Schools in difficulty may be less able to benefit from devolution. Those that have advantages, that seize the opportunities, may become less "comprehensive."[24] Martin Forsey's ethnographic study of Como High School in Western Australia showed how, under devolved circumstances, a public school principal attempted to take her comprehensive high school up-market. She unilaterally changed the name of the school to that of a "college." She recruited fee-paying students without education department authorization. She discouraged working-class enrolments. She began the first stages of reorganizing the management positions in the school and recruited corporate sponsors for new initiatives not traditionally part of the work of public schools. She fostered a curriculum that would increase the middle-class intake of the school. Eventually this principal was suspended and demoted—not necessarily for her policies, but because of her misuse of school funds.[25]

An initiative in 2011 of the newly elected Liberal-National government was to remove one of the remaining elements of the original Wyndham Scheme that had introduced public comprehensive high schools to New South Wales. It abolished once and for all the School Certificate, the old Year 10 completion credential introduced in the 1960s. Critics in recent times had argued that the certificate was responsible for New South Wales' poor retention of students to Year 12, relative to other Australian states that is.[26]

In Australia, in 2012, there is a federal Labor government. Like the New South Wales Labor government in recent times it has experienced leadership turmoil. It seems rather unlikely to win the 2013 federal election. It is this government that published the Gonski Report. It argued that the schools most in need of additional funding were the public schools enrolling most children from families where poverty, unemployment, and "disadvantage" were highest. These were the students and schools at most risk of losing out, even in a country like Australia whose wealth had given it membership of the G20 economic forum composed of the 20 wealthiest nations in the world. Comprehensive government high schools, but also some Catholic systemic schools, especially those enrolling high proportions of the disadvantaged, stood to gain considerable additional resources if the recommendations of the Gonski Report were implemented.

It is by no means certain however that the recommendations will be implemented either by a returned Labor, or future Liberal-National Coalition government. The arguments for reduced taxation, balanced budgets, and further encouragement of school markets remain strong, and under such circumstances, prospects for the comprehensive government high school in both New South Wales and Australia look bleak. At the same time there are possibilities. In inner Sydney in recent times there has been a campaign for an increased number of comprehensive high schools. Some parts of Sydney have lost too many such schools, as a new baby boom and continuing immigration occurs.[27]

In March 2012 the issue of comprehensive government schools once more occupied writers of the *Sydney Morning Herald*. An editorial was devoted to the subject. Its readers were told that:

> An all-comprehensive system has . . . been tried—as far that is as possible—under the Wyndham scheme from 1962. Before Wyndham, schools separated students into academic and vocational streams, though that division was becoming blurred. Wyndham confirmed the trend, making the comprehensive high school the standard. It worked, for a while. But it assumed a minimum school leaving age of 14 or 15. Those who were unsuited to high school could leave. In 1971 it was accepted that about three-quarters would.
>
> But as jobs for young people have dried up, governments have encouraged and, since 2010, required, all students regardless of inclination to stay at school until 17. The consequence of that has undermined the previous appeal of comprehensive government schools. There are many exceptions but bit by bit some comprehensives have gained reputations as schools for those who do not want to be at school. Their decline has tainted the reputation of an entire sector.
>
> The result has been the return of de facto streaming: a middle-class flight to private schools in search of an educational environment conducive to academic achievement, and free of the need to cater to a significant population of unmotivated students. Parents who attended Wyndham's comprehensives can be heard lamenting that these days they have to send their children to

> private schools to obtain the sort of education they received. The trend prompted NSW governments to beef up the selective system as a way to tempt middle-class students back. The popularity of the selective school test (13,500 candidates for 4,100 places) shows the ploy has worked but it has also transformed the education system.
>
> The choice of school clearly causes problems for the comprehensive system. But something has to give way if comprehensives are to return to the respected place they once held.[28]

Despite a couple of minor inaccuracies, the editorial identifies several of the continuing problems for comprehensive secondary schools in the modern era. They are subject to residualization, enrolling students of disadvantage. They appear inadequate to the task of educating the very ambitious, the seekers of distinction. They appear inferior to too many nongovernment and selective public schools . . . and so it goes on. This kind of school actually remains an essential school, especially for families who cannot or will not participate in the school market, but such schools remain an intractable policy problem as well.

Notes

Introduction

1. David L. Angus and Jeffrey Mirel, *The Failed Promise of the American High School, 1890–1995* (New York: Teachers College Press, 1999).
2. Simon Marginson, *Educating Australia: Government, Economy and Citizen since 1960* (Cambridge: Cambridge University Press, 1997), Geoff Whitty, "Creating Quasi-Markets in Education," *Review of Research in Education* 22 (1997).
3. Bob Lingard, John Knight, and Paige Porter, eds, *Schooling Reform in Hard Times* (London: Falmer, 1993), Simon Marginson, *Education and Public Policy in Australia* (Cambridge: Cambridge University Press, 1993), Simon Marginson, *Markets in Education* (Sydney: Allen & Unwin, 1997).
4. James Bryant Conant, *Slums and Suburbs* (New York: McGraw-Hill, 1961), pp. 81–82.
5. For England, see Alan C. Kerkhoff et al., *Going Comprehensive in England and Wales: A Study of Uneven Change* (London: Woburn Press, 1996), Chris Taylor, *Geography of the 'New' Education Market: Secondary School Choice in England and Wales* (Aldershot (UK): Ashgate, 2002).
6. I. L. Kandel, "Impressions of Australian Education," in *Education for Complete Living: The Challenge of To-Day*, ed. K. S. Cunningham (Melbourne: Melbourne University Press, 1938), p. 659; R. Freeman Butts, *Assumptions Underlying Australian Education* (Melbourne: Australian Council for Educational Research, 1957).
7. Martin Johnson, *Failing School, Failing City: The Reality of Inner City Education* (Charlbury (UK): Jon Carpenter, 1999).
8. See Richard Teese, *Academic Success and Social Power: Examinations and Inequity* (Melbourne: Melbourne University Press, 2000), p. 189.
9. David F. Labaree, *How to Succeed in School without Really Learning: The Credentials Race in American Education* (New Haven: Yale University Press, 1997).
10. John McLaren, *A Dictionary of Australian Education* (Brisbane: University of Queensland Press, 1974), p. 66.
11. See Angus and Mirel, *The Failed Promise of the American High School, 1890–1995*, Gerald Grant, *The World We Created at Hamilton High*

(Cambridge: Harvard University Press, 1988), Arthur G. Powell, Eleanor Farrar, and David K. Cohen, *The Shopping Mall High School: Winners and Losers in the Educational Marketplace* (Boston: Houghton Mifflin, 1985).

12. Two key texts are C. B. Cox and A. E. Dyson, eds., *Fight for Education: A Black Paper* (London: The Critical Quarterly Society, 1969) and David Rubinstein and Colin Stoneman, eds, *Education for Democracy* (Harmondsworth: Penguin Books, 1970).
13. On Hall, adolescence and the high school: Joseph Kett, *Rites of Passage: Adolescence in America 1790 to the Present* (New York: Basic Books, 1977), Craig Campbell, "Modern Adolescence and Secondary Schooling: An Historiographical Review," *Forum of Education (Australia)* 50, no. 1 (1995), Dorothy Ross, *G. Stanley Hall: The Psychologist as Prophet* (Chicago: University of Chicago Press, 1972).
14. See David Labaree, *The Making of an American High School: The Credentials Market and the Central High School of Philadelphia, 1838–1939* (New Haven: Yale University Press, 1988), Craig Campbell, "Secondary Schooling, Modern Adolescence and the Reconstitution of the Middle Class," *History of Education Review* 24, no. 1 (1995), Reed Ueda, *Avenues to Adulthood: The Origins of the High School and Social Mobility in an American Suburb* (Cambridge: Cambridge University Press, 1987).
15. See Stephen Ball and Carol Vincent, "New Class Relations in Education: The Strategies of the 'Fearful' Middle Classes," in *Sociology of Education Today*, ed. Jack Demaine (Houndsmills (UK): Palgrave, 2001), Craig Campbell, "Changing School Loyalties and the Middle Class: A Reflection on the Developing Fate of State Comprehensive High Schooling," *The Australian Educational Researcher* 31, no. 1 (2005), Sally Power et al., *Education and the Middle Class* (Buckingham: Open University Press, 2003); and an example from the Australian media, Catharine Lumby, "Class Distinction," *The Bulletin*, August 22, 2000.
16. Pat Thomson, *Schooling the Rustbelt Kids: Making the Difference in Changing Times* (Sydney: Allen & Unwin, 2002); and for example, R. Connell and others, *Making the Difference: Schools, Families and Social Division* (Sydney: George Allen & Unwin, 1982), Christine Griffin, *Representations of Youth: The Study of Youth and Adolescence in Britain and America* (Cambridge: Polity Press, 1993), J. C. Walker, *Louts and Legends: Male Youth Culture in an Inner City School* (Sydney: Allen & Unwin, 1988), Paul E. Willis, *Learning to Labour: How Working Class Kids Get Working Class Jobs* (Farnborough (U.K.): Saxon House, 1977).
17. H. S. Wyndham (Chair), "Report of the Committee Appointed to Survey Secondary Education in New South Wales" (Sydney: Government of New South Wales, 1957).
18. John P. Hughes, "Harold Wyndham and Educational Reform in Australia," *Education Research and Perspectives* 29, no. 1 (2002).
19. Jill Duffield, "The Making of the Wyndham Scheme in New South Wales," *History of Education Review* 19, no. 1 (1990), p. 37.
20. Kerkhoff et al., *Going Comprehensive in England and Wales.*

21. See Gary McCulloch, *Failing the Ordinary Child? The Theory and Practice of Working-Class Secondary Education* (Buckingham: Open University Press, 1998), pp. 133–46.
22. See Caroline Benn and Clyde Chitty, *Thirty Years On: Is Comprehensive Education Alive and Well or Struggling to Survive?*, 2nd ed. (London: Penguin Books, 1997), Clyde Chitty and John Dunford, "The Comprehensive Ideal," in *State Schools: New Labour and the Conservative Legacy*, ed. Clyde Chitty and John Dunford (London: Woburn Press, 1999), Clyde Chitty and Brian Simon, eds, *Promoting Comprehensive Education in the 21st Century* (Stoke on Trent: Trentham Books, 2001).
23. See David Tyack, *The One Best System: A History of American Urban Education* (Cambridge: Harvard University Press, 1974).
24. Duffield, "The Making of the Wyndham Scheme in New South Wales."
25. William G. Wraga, "A Progressive Legacy Squandered: *The Cardinal Principles* Report Reconsidered," *History of Education Quarterly* 41, no. 4 (2001).
26. Geoffrey Riordan and Sam Weller, *The Reformation of Education in N.S.W.: The 1990 Education Reform Act* [Web-site] (AARE, 2000, available from http://www.aare.edu.au/00pap/rio00358.htm), Geoffrey Sherington, "Education Policy," in *Reform and Reversal: Lessons from the Coalition Government in New South Wales 1988–1995*, ed. Martin Laffin and Martin Painter (Melbourne: Macmillan, 1995).
27. Judith Brett, *Australian Liberals and the Moral Middle Class: From Alfred Deakin to John Howard* (Cambridge: Cambridge University Press, 2003), Marian Sawer, *The Ethical State? Social Liberalism in Australia* (Melbourne: Melbourne University Press, 2003).

1 Origins

1. John Roach, *A History of Secondary Education in England, 1800–1870* (London: Longman, 1986), p. 4. See also June Purvis, *A History of Women's Education in England* (Milton Keynes: Open University Press, 1991), pp. 65–95.
2. Key references in the literature include: David Allsobrook, *Schools for the Shires: The Reform of Middle-Class Education in Mid-Victorian England* (Manchester: Manchester University Press, 1986), John Chandos, *Boys Together: English Public Schools 1800–1864* (New Haven: Yale University Press, 1984), Sheila Fletcher, *Feminists and Bureaucrats: A Study in the Development of Girls' Education in the Nineteenth Century* (Cambridge: Cambridge University Press, 1980), Jonathan Gathorne-Hardy, *The Public School Phenomenon, 597–1977* (London: Hodder & Stoughton, 1977), J. R. de S. Honey, *Tom Brown's Universe: The Development of the Victorian Public School* (London: Millington, 1977), J. A. Mangan, *Athleticism in the Victorian and Edwardian Public School* (Cambridge: Cambridge University Press, 1981), David Newsome, *Godliness and Good Learning: Four Studies on a Victorian Ideal* (London: John Murray, 1961).
3. For example, August Heckscher, *St Paul's: The Life of a New England School* (New York: Charles Scribener, 1980). See also Peter W. Cookson and Caroline

Hodges Persell, *Preparing for Power: America's Elite Boarding Schools* (New York: Basic Books, 1985), Arthur G. Powell, *Lessons from Privilege: The American Prep School Tradition* (Cambridge (Mass.): Harvard University Press, 1996).

4. Nancy Beadie and Kim Tolley, eds, *Chartered Schools: Two Hundred Years of Independent Academies in the United States, 1727–1925* (New York: Routledge Falmer, 2002).
5. David Labaree, *The Making of an American High School: The Credentials Market and the Central High School of Philadelphia, 1838–1939* (New Haven: Yale University Press, 1988), William J. Reese, *The Origins of the American High School* (New Haven: Yale University Press, 1995).
6. Cited in William J. Reese, "Changing Conceptions of Public and Private in American Educational History," in *Public or Private Education? Lessons from History*, ed. Richard Aldrich (London: Woburn Press, 2004), p. 151.
7. David Tyack and Elisabeth Hansot, *Learning Together: A History of Coeducation in American Schools* (New Haven: Yale University Press, 1990).
8. Christopher Mooney, "Securing a Private Classical Education in and around Sydney: 1830–1850," *History of Education Review* 25, no. 1 (1996), Elizabeth Windschuttle, "Educating the Daughters of the Ruling Class in Colonial New South Wales, 1788–1850," *Melbourne Studies in Education* (1980).
9. D. W. A. Baker, *Preacher, Politician, Patriot: A Life of John Dunmore Lang* (Melbourne: Melbourne University Press, 1998), C. Turney, "Henry Carmichael: His Advanced Educational Thought and Practice," in *Pioneers of Australian Education: A Study of the Development of Education in New South Wales in the Nineteenth Century*, ed. C. Turney (Sydney: Sydney University Press, 1969).
10. E. W. Dunlop, "The Public High Schools of New South Wales, 1883–1912," *Journal of the Royal Australian Historical Society* 51, no. 1 (1965). For Scottish secondary education see R. D. Anderson, *Education and Opportunity in Victorian Scotland: Schools and Universities* (Oxford: Clarendon Press, 1983).
11. Marjorie Theobald, *Knowing Women: Origins of Women's Education in Nineteenth-Century Australia* (Cambridge: Cambridge University Press, 1996), Marjorie Theobald, "The PLC Mystique: Reflections on the Reform of Female Education in Nineteenth Century Australia," *Australian Historical Studies* 23, no. 92 (1989).
12. Geoffrey Sherington, R. C. Petersen, and Ian Brice, *Learning to Lead: A History of Girls' and Boys' Corporate Secondary Schools in Australia* (Sydney: Allen & Unwin, 1987), C. E. W. Bean, *Here, My Son: An Account of the Independent and Other Corporate Boys' Schools of Australia* (Sydney: Angus & Robertson, 1950).
13. Geoffrey Sherington, "Athleticism in the Antipodes," *History of Education Review* 12, no. 2 (1983), Honey, *Tom Brown's Universe*, John Honey, "The Sinews of Society: The Public Schools as a 'System,' " in *The Rise of the Modern Educational System: Structural Change and Social Reproduction 1870–1920*, ed. Detlef K. Muller, Fritz Ringer, and Brian Simon (Cambridge: Cambridge University Press, 1987).
14. Martin Crotty, *Making the Australian Male: Middle-Class Masculinity 1870–1920* (Melbourne: Melbourne University Press, 2001), Geoffrey Sherington and Mark Connellan, "Socialisation, Imperialism and War: Ideology and Ethnicity in

Australian Corporate Schools 1880–1918," in *'Benefits Bestowed'? Education and British Imperialism*, ed. J. A. Mangan (Manchester: Manchester University Press, 1988).

15. Kathleen Fitzpatrick, *PLC Melbourne: The First Century, 1875–1975* (Melbourne: Presbyterian Ladies' College, 1975), Noeleen Kyle, *Her Natural Destiny: The Education of Women in New South Wales* (Sydney: NSWU Press, 1986), Theobald, *Knowing Women*, Thomas A. O'Donoghue, *Upholding the Faith: The Process of Education in Catholic Schools in Australia, 1922–1965* (New York: Peter Lang, 2001).
16. Clifford Turney, *Grammar: A History of Sydney Grammar School 1819–1988* (Sydney: Allen & Unwin, 1989).
17. David Adams, "Frederick Charles Faulkner: A Classicist in the Antipodes," in *Pioneers of Education in Western Australia*, ed. Laadan Fletcher (Perth: University of Western Australia Press, 1982), Rupert Goodman, *Secondary Education in Queensland, 1860–1960* (Canberra: Australian National University Press, 1968), Martin Sullivan, "Fifty Years of Opposition to Queensland's Grammar Schools," *Melbourne Studies in Education* (1974).
18. Andy Green, *Education and State Formation: The Rise of Education Systems in England, France and the USA* (London: Macmillan, 1990), J. A. Mangan, ed., *A Significant Social Revolution: Cross-Cultural Aspects of the Evolution of Compulsory Education* (London: Woburn Press, 1994).
19. See A. G. Austin and R. J. W. Selleck, *The Australian Government School 1830–1914* (Melbourne: Pitman, 1975).
20. Malcolm Vick, "Class, Gender and Administration: The 1851 Education Act in South Australia," *History of Education Review* 17, no. 1 (1988), Malcolm Vick, "Schooling and the Production of Local Communities in Mid-Nineteenth-Century Australia," *Historical Studies in Education* 6, no. 3 (1994).
21. Austin and Selleck, *The Australian Government School 1830–1914.*
22. Alison Mackinnon, *One Foot on the Ladder: Origins and Outcomes of Girls' Secondary Schooling in South Australia* (Brisbane: University of Queensland Press, 1984). See also Helen Jones, *Nothing Seemed Impossible: Women's Education and Social Change in South Australia 1875–1915* (Brisbane: University of Queensland Press, 1985).
23. See Sherington, "Athleticism in the Antipodes."
24. Kyle, *Her Natural Destiny*, p. 111, Theobald, *Knowing Women*, pp. 123–24.
25. Dunlop, "The Public High Schools of New South Wales, 1883–1912."
26. See Bob Bessant, "The Influence of the 'Public Schools' on the Early High Schools of Victoria," *History of Education Review* 13, no. 1 (1984), Geoffrey Sherington, "Public Commitment and Private Choice in Australian Secondary Education," in *Public or Private Education? Lessons from History*, ed. Richard Aldrich (London: Woburn Press, 2004).
27. See Richard Davis, *Open to Talent: The Centenary History of the University of Tasmania, 1890–1990* (Hobart: University of Tasmania, 1990).
28. Clifford Turney, Ursula Bygott, and Peter Chippendale, *Australia's First: A History of the University of Sydney 1850–1939* (Sydney: University of Sydney, 1991), pp. 291–95.

29. Ursula Bygott and K. J. Cable, *Pioneer Women Graduates of the University of Sydney 1881–1921* (Sydney: University of Sydney, 1985).
30. Meriel Vlaeminke, *The English Higher Grade Schools: A Lost Opportunity* (London: Woburn Press, 2000).
31. Carole Hooper, "Opposition Triumphant: Against State Secondary Schooling in Victoria, 1850–1911," in *Toward the State High School in Australia: Social Histories of State Secondary Schooling in Victoria, Tasmania and South Australia, 1850–1925*, ed. Craig Campbell, Carole Hooper, and Mary Fearnley-Sander (Sydney: ANZHES, 1999). On early support for academic studies in elementary education, see Denis Grundy, "The Formation of a Disordered Teaching Service in Victoria, 1851–1871," *History of Education Review* 18, no. 2 (1989).
32. Geoffrey Sherington, "Families and State Schooling in the Illawarra, 1840–1940," in *Family, School and State in Australian History*, ed. Marjorie R. Theobald and R. J. W. Selleck (Sydney: Allen and Unwin, 1990).
33. Ronald S. Horan, *Fort Street: The School* (Sydney: Honeysett, 1989).
34. See Craig Campbell, "Secondary Schooling, Modern Adolescence and the Reconstitution of the Middle Class," *History of Education Review* 24, no. 1 (1995), J. R. Gillis, *Youth and History: Tradition and Change in European Age Relations 1770–Present*, 2nd ed. (New York: Academic Press, 1981), Selwyn K. Troen, "The Discovery of the Adolescent by American Educational Reformers, 1900–1920: An Economic Perspective," in *Schooling and Society: Studies in the History of Education*, ed. Lawrence Stone (Baltimore: Johns Hopkins University Press, 1976).
35. David McCallum, *The Social Production of Merit: Education, Psychology and Politics in Australia 1900–1950* (London: Falmer Press, 1990), Gillian Sutherland, *Ability, Merit, and Measurement: Mental Testing and English Education, 1880–1940* (Oxford: Clarendon Press, 1984), Adrian Wooldridge, *Measuring the Mind: Education and Psychology in England, c. 1860–1990* (Cambridge: Cambridge University Press, 1994).
36. Theodore R. Sizer, *Secondary Schools at the Turn of the Century* (New Haven: Yale University Press, 1964).
37. Raymond E. Callahan, *Education and the Cult of Efficiency* (Chicago: University of Chicago Press, 1962), Edward A. Krug, *The Shaping of the American High School 1880–1920* (Madison: University of Wisconsin Press, 1969).
38. William G. Wraga, "A Progressive Legacy Squandered: *The Cardinal Principles* Report Reconsidered," *History of Education Quarterly* 41, no. 4 (2001).
39. See David John Hogan, *Class and Reform: School and Society in Chicago, 1880–1930* (Philadelphia: University of Pennsylvania Press, 1985), Labaree, *The Making of an American High School*, Joel Perlmann, *Ethnic Differences: Schooling and Social Structure among the Irish, Italians, Jews and Blacks in an American City, 1880–1935* (Cambridge: Cambridge University Press, 1988).
40. A. B. Hollingshead, *Elmtown's Youth: The Impact of Social Classes on Adolescents* (New York: John Wiley, 1961).
41. David L. Angus and Jeffrey Mirel, *The Failed Promise of the American High School, 1890–1995* (New York: Teachers College Press, 1999).
42. Eric Ashby and Mary Anderson, *Portrait of Haldane at Work on Education* (London: Macmillan, 1974), G. R. Searle, *The Quest for National Efficiency: A*

Study in British Politics and Political Thought, 1899–1914 (Oxford: Blackwell, 1971).

43. David Reeder, "The Reconstruction of Secondary Education in England, 1869–1920," in *The Rise of the Modern Educational System: Structural Change and Social Reproduction 1870–1920*, ed. Detlef K. Muller, Fritz Ringer, and Brian Simon (Cambridge: Cambridge University Press, 1987).
44. Vlaeminke, *The English Higher Grade Schools*. For an earlier critique see Brian Simon, *Education and the Labour Movement 1870–1920* (London: Lawrence & Wishart, 1965).
45. Wooldridge, *Measuring the Mind*, pp. 220–252.
46. Henry Hadow (Chair), "The Education of the Adolescent" (London: The Consultative Committee on Secondary Education (HMSO), 1926), Brian Simon, *The Politics of Educational Reform 1920–1940* (London: Lawrence & Wishart, 1974).
47. Craig Campbell, "The Social Origins of Australian State High Schools: An Historiographical Review," in *Toward the State High School in Australia*, ed. Craig Campbell, Carole Hooper, and Mary Fearnley-Sander (Sydney: ANZHES, 1999).
48. See Bob Bessant, "The Emergence of State Secondary Education," in *Australian Education in the Twentieth Century: Studies in the Development of State Education*, ed. J. Cleverley and J. Lawry (Melbourne: Longman, 1972), pp. 124–25.
49. For example, W. Pember Reeves, *State Experiments in Australia and New Zealand*, 2 vols. (Melbourne: Macmillan, 1969).
50. On Peter Board in the Australian liberal tradition see Gregory Melleuish, *Cultural Liberalism in Australia: A Study in Intellectual and Cultural History* (Cambridge: Cambridge University Press, 1995), pp. 72–75. On this significant group of directors of education see A. R. Crane and W. G. Walker, *Peter Board: His Contribution to the Development of Education in New South Wales* (Melbourne: ACER, 1957), Elizabeth Kwan, "Williams, Alfred," in *Australian Dictionary of Biography*, ed. John Ritchie (Melbourne: Melbourne University Press, 1990), R. J. W. Selleck, *Frank Tate: A Biography* (Melbourne: Melbourne University Press, 1982).
51. See Francis Anderson, *The Public School System of New South Wales* (Sydney: Angus & Robertson, 1901).
52. Ibid., p. 10.
53. Ibid., pp. 22–28.
54. Ibid., p. 8. Italics in the original.
55. Ibid., p. 6.
56. Ibid., pp. 19–20.
57. Ibid., p. 28.
58. Ibid., p. 31.
59. Ibid., p. 16.
60. Ibid., pp. 14–15.
61. New South Wales, "Report of the Commissioners, Mainly on Secondary Education, Containing the Summarized Reports . . . (Chair: G. H. Knibbs &

J. W. Turner)" (Sydney: Royal Commission on Primary, Secondary, Technical and Other Branches of Education, 1904), p. 3.

62. New South Wales, "Report of the Commissioners," pp. 3 and 10.
63. Ibid., p. 6.
64. Ibid., pp. 8–9.
65. Ibid., pp. 55 and 58.
66. On the thrust of the Committee of Ten, and its significance for American secondary education see Jurgen Herbst, *The Once and Future School: Three Hundred and Fifty Years of American Secondary Education* (New York: Routledge, 1996), pp. 117–130.
67. New South Wales, "Knibbs-Turner Report," p. 72.
68. Ibid., p. 10.
69. See Alfred Williams, "Preliminary Report of the Director of Education Upon Observations Made During an Official Visit to Europe and America 1907 . . ." (Adelaide: Education Department, South Australia, 1908).
70. New South Wales, "Knibbs-Turner Report," pp. 52 and 54.
71. P. Board, "A Report Following Upon Observations of American Education," (Sydney: New South Wales. Department of Education, 1909), pp. 10 and 20.
72. Ibid., p. 26.
73. Ibid., p. 24.
74. Ibid., p. 21.
75. Ibid., p. 20.
76. Francis Anderson, "Educational Policy and Development," in *Federal Handbook Prepared in Connection with the Eighty-Fourth Meeting of the British Association for the Advancement of Science Held in Australia* . . . ed. G. H. Knibbs (Melbourne: Commonwealth of Australia, 1914), p. 519.
77. Ibid., p. 523.
78. Ibid., p. 532.
79. Ibid., p. 535.
80. Alexander Mackie, "Education in Australia," in *Australia: Economic and Political Studies*, ed. Meredith Atkinson (Melbourne: Macmillan, 1920), pp. 252–53.
81. Ibid., pp. 262–64.
82. S. H. Smith and G. T. Spaull, *History of Education in New South Wales (1788–1925)* (Sydney: George B. Philip & Son, 1925), p. 255.
83. See Percival R. Cole, "New South Wales," in *Education in Australia: A Comparative Study of the Educational Systems of the Australian States*, ed. G. S. Browne (London: Macmillan, 1927) for a contemporary description of much of this activity in New South Wales.
84. See David Tyack, *The One Best System: A History of American Urban Education* (Cambridge: Harvard University Press, 1974).
85. For key works in the Australian historiography on such reform at this time in history, see McCallum, *The Social Production of Merit*, Pavla Miller, *Long Division: State Schooling in South Australian Society* (Adelaide: Wakefield Press, 1986).
86. Frank Tate, "Introduction," in *Education for Complete Living: The Challenge of To-Day*, ed. K. S. Cunningham (Melbourne: Melbourne University Press, 1938), p. xiii.

87. See B. K. Hyams and B. Bessant, *Schools for the People? An Introduction to the History of State Education in Australia* (Melbourne: Longman, 1972), pp. 127–130.
88. The subcommittees are listed on p. 1 of the report. New South Wales, "Inquiry into Certain Educational Questions (R. S. Wallace, Chairman)," (Sydney: Legislative Assembly, 1934).
89. Ibid., p. 3.
90. Ibid.
91. Peter Board, "The Development of Secondary Education in Australia," in *The Education of the Adolescent in Australia*, ed. Percival R. Cole (Melbourne: Melbourne University Press, 1935), esp. p. 9.
92. See W. F. Connell, *The Australian Council for Educational Research, 1930–80* (Melbourne: Australian Council for Educational Research, 1980), Michael White, "Carnegie Philanthropy in Australia in the Nineteen Thirties—a Reassessment," *History of Education Review* 26, no. 1 (1997), Brian Williams, "Cunningham, Kenneth Stewart," in *Australian Dictionary of Biography*, ed. John Ritchie (Melbourne: Melbourne University Press, 1993). Cunningham coauthored an early study of an attempt to introduce comprehensive education to a corporate girls' school: K. S. Cunningham and Dorothy J. Ross, *An Australian School at Work* (Melbourne: ACER, 1967).
93. William C. Radford, *The Educational Needs of a Rural Community* (Melbourne: Melbourne University Press, 1939), p. 161.
94. J. A. La Nauze, "Some Aspects of Educational Opportunity in South Australia," in *Australian Educational Studies*, ed. J. D. G. Medley (Melbourne: Melbourne University Press, 1940). For the debate on issues of access and equality in the 1940s, see McCallum, *The Social Production of Merit*, pp. 101–124.
95. John Godfrey, " 'Perhaps the Most Important, and Certainly the Most Exciting Event in the Whole History of Education in Australia': The 1937 New Education Fellowship Conference and New South Wales Examination Reform," *History of Education Review* 33, no. 2 (2004).
96. Beatrice Ensor, "A New World in the Making," in *Education for Complete Living: The Challenge of To-Day*, ed. K. S. Cunningham (Melbourne: Melbourne University Press, 1938), Harold Rugg, "Education and Social Progress in the New Industrial-Democratic Countries," in *Education for Complete Living*, p. 96
97. Edmund de S. Brunner, "The Place of the School in Modern Society," in *Education for Complete Living*, p. 61; Harold Rugg, "Democracy, Indoctrination, and Controversial Issues in the Schools," in *Education for Complete Living*, p. 170.
98. Brunner, "The Place of the School in Modern Society," p. 3.
99. Ibid., p. 63; Edmund de S. Brunner, "The School and the Rural Community," in *Education for Complete Living*, p. 241, F. W. Hart, "Criticisms of Education in Australia," in *Education for Complete Living*, p. 661.
100. Brunner, "The Place of the School in Modern Society" p. 65, Laurin Zilliacus, "Examinations," in *Education for Complete Living*, p. 319; A. Lismer, "Education

through Art," in *Education for Complete Living*, p. 390, E. G. Malherbe, "Delinquency as an Educational Problem," in *Education for Complete Living*, p. 580, Hart, "Criticisms of Education in Australia," p. 663.

101. Ensor, "A New World in the Making," p. 94.
102. Ibid., pp. 95–96, F. C. Happold, "Education as a Training for Real Life," in *Education for Complete Living*, pp. 183, 189, William Boyd, "The Education of the Adolescent," in *Education for Complete Living*,
103. I. L. Kandel, "School and Society," in *Education for Complete Living*, p. 102, E. G. Malherbe, "Adapting Education to Modern Needs," in *Education for Complete Living*, p. 115; E. Salter Davies, "Values: Or the Old Learning and the New Spirit," in *Education for Complete Living*, p. 131; H. R. Hamley, "Education and the Art of Living," in *Education for Complete Living*, Happold, "Education as a Training for Real Life."
104. Cyril Norwood, "Coming Changes," in *Education for Complete Living*, pp. 151–52, William Boyd, "Education and Citizenship," in *Education for Complete Living*, p. 192.
105. Rugg, "Democracy, Indoctrination, and Controversial Issues in the Schools."
106. Beatrice Ensor, "Pupil Activity in Modern Education," in *Education for Complete Living*, Harold Rugg, "The Curriculum in the Child-Centred School," in *Education for Complete Living*, esp. p. 341.
107. Boyd, "The Education of the Adolescent," Susan Isaacs, "The Importance of the Child's Emotional Life," in *Education for Complete Living*.
108. Malherbe, "Delinquency as an Educational Problem," p. 580, Isaacs, "The Importance of the Child's Emotional Life," p. 621.
109. I. L. Kandel, "Impressions of Australian Education," in *Education for Complete Living*, p. 659.
110. Ensor, "A New World in the Making" and Kandel, "Impressions of Australian Education," pp. 654–55.
111. See Gary McCulloch, *Educational Reconstruction: The 1944 Education Act and the Twenty-First Century* (Ilford: Woburn Press, 1994), Brian Simon, *Education and the Social Order, 1940–1990* (London: Lawrence & Wishart, 1991).
112. B. Bessant and A. D. Spaull, *Politics of Schooling* (Melbourne: Pitman, 1976).
113. J. D. G. Medley, *Education for Democracy, The Future of Education* (Melbourne: ACER, 1943).
114. Ibid., p. 16
115. John Hughes, "Harold Wyndham and Educational Reform in Australia 1925–1968," *Education Research and Perspectives* 29, no. 1, (2002), pp. 107–108.
116. Don Smart, "The Pattern of Post-War Federal Intervention in Education," in *Federal Intervention in Australian Education*, ed. Grant Harman and Don Smart (Melbourne: Georgian House, 1982).
117. Australian Council for Educational Research, *A Plan for Australia, The Future of Education* (Melbourne: ACER, 1953), p. 21.
118. Robert Anderson, "The Idea of the Secondary School in Nineteenth-Century Europe," *Paedagogica Historica* 40, no. 1 and 2 (2004), pp. 93–106. This view

challenges the earlier claims that secondary education in Europe was highly systematized and segmented in the nineteenth century. See Detlef K. Muller, Fritz Ringer, and Brian Simon, eds, *The Rise of the Modern Educational System: Structural Change and Social Reproduction 1870–1920* (Cambridge: Cambridge University Press, 1987).

119. See Lawrence A. Cremin, *The Transformation of the School: Progressivism in American Education, 1876–1957* (New York: Random House, 1961), Richard Hofstadter, *Anti-Intellectualism in American Life* (New York: Vintage, 1963).
120. Campbell, Hooper, and Fearnley-Sander, eds, *Toward the State High School in Australia.*
121. Mark Peel and Janet McCalman, *Who Went Where in 'Who's Who 1988?': The Schooling of the Australian Elite* (Melbourne: University of Melbourne, 1992). See also Campbell, "Secondary Schooling, Modern Adolescence and the Reconstitution of the Middle Class," Peter Gronn, "Schooling for Ruling: The Social Composition of Admissions to Geelong Grammar School 1930–1939," *Australian Historical Studies* 25, no. 98 (1992), G. Sherington, "The Headmasters—E. N. McQueen, L. C. Robson and J. R. Darling," in *Pioneers of Australian Education: Studies of the Development of Education in Australia 1900–50*, ed. C. Turney (Sydney: Sydney University Press, 1983).

2 Postwar Planning

1. James Bryant Conant, *The American High School Today: A First Report to Interested Citizens* (New York: McGraw-Hill, 1959). See also Robert L. Hampel, *The Last Little Citadel: American High Schools since 1940* (Boston: Houghton Mifflin, 1986), John L. Rury, "Democracy's High School? Social Change and American Secondary Education in the Post-Conant Era," *American Educational Research Journal* 39, no. 2 (2002), and Floyd M. Hammack, ed, *The Comprehensive High School Today* (New York: Teachers College Press, 2004).
2. Conant, *The American High School Today*, p. 17.
3. Ibid., p. 15.
4. Ibid., p. 37.
5. Ibid, pp. 46–49.
6. Sherman Dorn, *Creating the Dropout: An Institutional and Social History of School Failure* (Westport (Conn.): Praeger, 1996).
7. John L. Rury, "The Problems of Educating Urban Youth: James B. Conant and the Changing Context of Metropolitan America, 1945–1995," in Hammack, ed. *The Comprehensive High School Today.*
8. Conant, *The American High School Today*, pp. 77–96.
9. James Bryant Conant, *Slums and Suburbs* (New York: McGraw-Hill, 1961).
10. James B. Conant, *The Comprehensive High School: A Second Report to Interested Citizens* (New York: McGraw-Hill, 1967).
11. For a general discussion of the views of Conant see Hammack, ed., *The Comprehensive High School Today.*

12. Geoffrey Crowther (Chair), "15 to 18: A report of the Central Advisory Council for Education (England)" (London: Ministry of Education, 1959), vol. 1, pp. 3–10. (Henceforth *The Crowther Report.*)
13. Ibid., pp. 16–23.
14. Ibid., pp. 45–53, 72–73.
15. Brian Simon, *Intelligence Testing and the Comprehensive School* (London: Lawrence & Wishart, 1953). See also Brian Simon, *The Common Secondary School* (London: Lawrence & Wishart, 1955).
16. *The Crowther Report*, vol 2. See also J. E. Floud, A. H. Halsey, and F. M. Martin, eds, *Social Class and Educational Opportunity* (London: William Heinemann, 1956).
17. David Rubinstein and Brian Simon, *The Evolution of the Comprehensive School, 1926–1972*, 2nd ed. (London: Routledge & Kegan Paul, 1973), pp. 52–85.
18. *The Crowther Report*, vol. 1, pp. 447–74.
19. Alan C. Kerkhoff et al., *Going Comprehensive in England and Wales: A Study of Uneven Change* (London: Woburn Press, 1996).
20. Rubinstein and Simon, *The Evolution of the Comprehensive School, 1926–1972*, pp. 83–85. For the influence of Pedley see David Crook, "The Disputed Origins of the Leicestershire Two-Tier Comprehensive Schools Plan," *History of Education Society Bulletin*, no. 50 (1992), Robin Pedley, *Comprehensive Education: A New Approach* (London: Victor Gollancz, 1956).
21. Brian Simon, "The Tory Government and Education 1951–60: Background to Breakout," *History of Education* 14, no. 4 (1985). See also Brian Simon, *Education and the Social Order, 1940–1990* (London: Lawrence & Wishart, 1991), pp. 150–220.
22. *The Crowther Report*, vol. 1, pp. 54–60.
23. Geoffrey Sherington, *Australia's Immigrants 1788–1988* (Sydney: Allen & Unwin, 1990).
24. Lionel Frost and Tony Dingle, "Sustaining Suburbia: An Historical Perspective on Australia's Urban Growth," in *Australian Cities: Issues, Strategies and Policies for Urban Australia in the 1990s*, ed. Patrick Troy (Cambridge: Cambridge University Press, 1995), p. 26.
25. Alan Barcan, *Two Centuries of Education in New South Wales* (Sydney: UNSW Press, 1988), pp. 238–40.
26. Terry Irving, David Maunders, and Geoff Sherington, *Youth in Australia: Policy Administration and Politics: A History since World War II* (Melbourne: Macmillan, 1995), William C. Radford, *School Leavers in Australia 1959–60* (Melbourne: Australian Council for Educational Research, 1962), pp. 5–7.
27. C. Sanders, "Student Selection and Academic Success in Australian Universities," in *Education Series No. 1* (Sydney: Commonwealth Office of Education, 1948).
28. M. S. Brown, "The Holding Power of High Schools in Sydney," *The Forum of Education* 13, no. 2 (1954).
29. "Crisis in the Secondary Schools," *Current Affairs Bulletin* 20, no. 1 (1957).
30. Alan Barcan, *A History of Australian Education* (Melbourne: Oxford University Press, 1980), pp. 297–300. See also J. S. Maslin, *Hagley: The Story of a Tasmanian Area School* (Melbourne: Georgian House, 1948).

31. Michael White, *Thomas Logan Robertson, 1901–1969: A Biographical Study* (Perth: Curtin University of Technology, 1999).
32. Kaye Tully, "State Secondary Education in Western Australia 1912–1972," *Education Research and Perspectives* 29, no. 2 (2002), pp. 87–108.
33. H. S. Wyndham (Chair), "Report of the Committee Appointed to Survey Secondary Education in New South Wales" (Sydney: Government of New South Wales, 1957) (henceforth *Wyndham Report*), p. 9.
34. B. Bessant and A. D. Spaull, *Politics of Schooling* (Melbourne: Pitman, 1976), pp. 159–67, Jill Duffield, "The Making of the Wyndham Scheme in New South Wales," *History of Education Review* 19, no. 1 (1990).
35. Kevin Smith, "Political Influences Behind the Delayed Implementation of the Wyndham Report in New South Wales," in *Education Policy Making in Australia*, ed. R. F. Broadbent (Melbourne: Australian College of Education, 1982), pp. 179–81.
36. John Hughes, "Harold Wyndham and Educational Reform in Australia 1925–1968," *Education Research and Perspectives* 29, no. 1 (2002).
37. Jill Duffield, "Independent Advice: A Comparative Study of Secondary Education Policy-Making, Scotland and New South Wales" (M. Ed., University of Edinburgh, 1990). See also J. Gray, A. F. McPherson, and D. Raffe, *Reconstructions of Secondary Education: Theory, Myth and Practice since the War* (London: Routledge & Kegan Paul, 1983).
38. Hughes, "Harold Wyndham and Educational Reform in Australia 1925–1968," pp. 130–32.
39. *Wyndham Report*, pp. 29–30.
40. Ibid., pp. 34–39.
41. Ibid., pp. 40–55.
42. Hughes, "Harold Wyndham and Educational Reform in Australia 1925–1968," p. 146.
43. *Wyndham Report*, pp. 56–62.
44. Ibid., p. 63.
45. Ibid.
46. Ibid., p. 69.
47. Ibid., p. 80.
48. G. W. Bassett, "The Wyndham Report—a General View," in *Secondary Education in New South Wales: Lectures and Discussions on the Wyndham Report* (Armidale: Department of Adult Education, University of New England, 1961), p. 8.
49. *Wyndham Report*, p. 81.
50. Helen Proctor, "Gender, Merit and Identity at Parramatta High School, 1913–1919," *History of Education Review* 31, no. 1 (2002).
51. *Wyndham Report*, pp. 82–84.
52. Ibid., p. 85.
53. Ibid., p. 86.
54. Ibid., pp. 94–98.
55. R. W. Connell et al., *Making the Difference: Schools, Families and Social Division* (Sydney: George Allen & Unwin, 1982), pp. 122, 169–71. See also Bessant and Spaull, *Politics of Schooling*, pp. 159–66.

56. Hughes, "Harold Wyndham and Educational Reform in Australia 1925–1968," p. 146.
57. Evidence to be Presented by The New South Wales Teachers' Federation to the Survey of Secondary Education Committee, New South Wales Teachers' Federation Archives, Document 442.
58. *The Crowther Report*, pp. 24–25.
59. George Howie, "The Case for Comprehensive Schools," *Current Affairs Bulletin* 26, no. 5 (1960), pp. 66–67.
60. Ibid., pp. 67–70.
61. Ibid., pp. 77–78.
62. Lesley Johnson, *The Modern Girl: Girlhood and Growing Up* (Sydney: Allen & Unwin, 1993), pp. 73–75.
63. Patricia Jenkings, "Australian Political Elites and Citizenship Education for 'New Australians' 1945–1960" (Ph.D. University of Sydney, 2001), Jean Martin, *The Migrant Presence, Australian Responses, 1947–1977: Research Report for the National Population Inquiry* (Sydney: George Allen & Unwin, 1978).
64. *Wyndham Report*, pp. 89–90.
65. Ibid., p. 92.
66. Hughes, "Harold Wyndham and Educational Reform in Australia 1925–1968," pp. 170–75.
67. See Rodney Barker, *Education and Politics 1900–1951: A Study of the Labor Party* (Oxford: Clarendon Press, 1971), "Labor Governments and Comprehensive Schooling 1945–51," *History Workshop*, no. 7 (1979).
68. *Sun Herald* (Sydney) August 2, 1959, p. 17.
69. J. L. Mackie, "The Case for Selective Schools," *Current Affairs Bulletin* 26, no. 6 (1960). Mackie and Howie had earlier debated the question in the Sydney press. Editorials and many correspondents favored retaining some selective high schools. See *Sydney Morning Herald*, August 7, 1959, p. 2; August 10, 1959, p. 2; April 18, 1960, p. 2; April 22, 1960, p. 2; April 25, 1960, p. 2; April 26, 1960, p. 2.
70. H. S. Wyndham, "The Need for Change," Sydney, 1960, pp. 12–13, New South Wales Teachers Federation Archives, Document 441.
71. See *Sydney Morning Herald*, April 18, 1960, p. 2, April 20, 1960, p. 2.
72. Evidence to be Presented by the New South Wales Teachers' Federation to the Survey of Secondary Education Committee, p. 11.
73. *Sun Herald*, February 10, 1957, p. 2.
74. Ronald S. Horan, *Fort Street: The School* (Sydney: Honeysett, 1989), pp. 283–84.
75. Catherine Brown, " 'Little Bastions of Privilege': NSW ALP Policy on Selective Schools" (B. Ed. Hons, University of Sydney, 1998).
76. *New South Wales Parliamentary Debates* (*NSWPD*), vol. 38 (November 9, 1961), p. 2389.
77. Wyndham to Minister, June 26, 1963, cited in Hughes, "Harold Wyndham and Educational Reform in Australia 1925–1968," p. 174.
78. Ibid.
79. Ronald Fogarty, *Catholic Education in Australia, 1806–1950*, 2 vols. (Melbourne: Melbourne University Press, 1959), vol. 2, Thomas A. O'Donoghue, *Upholding*

the Faith: The Process of Education in Catholic Schools in Australia, 1922–1965 (New York: Peter Lang, 2001).

80. "The Catholic School in Australia," *Current Affairs Bulletin* 22, no. 9 (1958). See Michael Charles Hogan, *The Catholic Campaign for State Aid: A Study of a Pressure Group Campaign in New South Wales and the Australian Capital Territory, 1950–1972* (Sydney: Catholic Theological Faculty, 1978), pp. 35–36.
81. Brown, "The Holding Power of High Schools in Sydney," pp. 54–55.
82. Judith Brett, *Australian Liberals and the Moral Middle Class: From Alfred Deakin to John Howard* (Cambridge: Cambridge University Press, 2003), pp. 35–40.
83. Hogan, *The Catholic Campaign for State Aid*, pp. 9–17.
84. Ross Fitzgerald, *The Pope's Battalions: Santamaria, Catholicism and the Labor Split* (Brisbane: University of Queensland Press, 2003).
85. Robert Murray, *The Split: Australian Labor in the Fifties* (1970: F. W. Cheshire, 1984), Tom Truman, *Catholic Action and Politics*, Rev. ed. (Melbourne: Georgian House, 1960).
86. Hogan, *The Catholic Campaign for State Aid*, pp. 9–17 and p. 42.
87. Smith, "Political Influences Behind the Delayed Implementation of the Wyndham Report in New South Wales," pp. 185–94; Hughes, "Harold Wyndham and Educational Reform in Australia 1925–1968," pp. 166–70.
88. Hogan, *The Catholic Campaign for State Aid*, pp. 63–91.
89. W. F. Connell, *Reshaping Australian Education 1960–1985* (Melbourne: ACER, 1993), pp. 51–55.

3 GOING COMPREHENSIVE

1. David Crook, "Edward Boyle: Conservative Champion of Comprehensives," *History of Education* 22, no. 1 (1993); Brian Simon, *Education and the Social Order, 1940–1990* (London: Lawrence & Wishart, 1991), pp. 271–341, 405–29 and Denis Dean, "Circular 10/65 Revisited: The Labour Government and the 'Comprehensive Revolution' in 1964–1965," *Paedogogica Historica* 34, no. 1 (1998). For an analysis of earlier explanations of comprehensive schools as official policy see David Reynolds and Michael Sullivan, *The Comprehensive Experiment: A Comparison of the Selective and Non-Selective Systems of School Organization* (London: Falmer, 1987), pp. 4–28.
2. In particular see C. B. Cox and A. E. Dyson, eds, *Black Paper Two: The Crisis in Education* (London: Critical Quarterly Society, [1969]). See also Simon, *Education and the Social Order, 1940–1990*, pp. 396–404.
3. Geoffrey Sherington, "Citizenship and Education in Postwar Australia," *Paedagogica Historica: Supplementary Series* 4 (1998). See also Nicholas Brown, *Governing Prosperity: Social Change and Social Analysis in Australia in the 1950s* (Cambridge: Cambridge University Press, 1995).
4. Judith Brett, *Robert Menzies' Forgotten People* (Sydney: Macmillan Australia, 1992). See also A. W. Martin, *Robert Menzies: A Life*, 2 vols. (Melbourne: Melbourne University Press, 1993, 1999).

5. Bob Bessant, "Robert Gordon Menzies and Education in Australia," *Melbourne Studies in Education 1977* (1978).
6. Don Smart, *Federal Aid to Australian Schools* (Brisbane: University of Queensland Press, 1978), pp. 33–49.
7. Don Smart, "The Industrial Fund: a Highly Successful Model of Big Business Collaboration with the Headmasters Conference in the Interests of School Science," *Melbourne Studies in Education 1984* (1984).
8. I. F. K. Birch and D. Smart, eds, *The Commonwealth Government and Education 1964–1976: Political Initiatives and Development* (Melbourne: Drummond, 1977).
9. Alan Barcan, *A History of Australian Education* (Melbourne: Oxford University Press, 1980), Rupert Goodman, *Secondary Education in Queensland, 1860–1960* (Canberra: Australian National University Press, 1968).
10. Heather Radi, Peter Spearritt, and Elizabeth Hinton, *Biographical Register of the New South Wales Parliament, 1901–1970* (Canberra: Australian National University Press, 1979), pp. 9–10.
11. See Katharine West, *Power in the Liberal Party: A Study in Australian Politics* (Melbourne: Cheshire, 1965).
12. Gerard Henderson, *Menzies' Child: The Liberal Party of Australia, 1944–1994* (Sydney: Allen & Unwin, 1994), pp. 136–37.
13. B. Bessant and A. D. Spaull, *Politics of Schooling* (Melbourne: Pitman, 1976), pp. 65–67, Alan Barcan, *Two Centuries of Education in New South Wales* (Sydney: UNSW Press, 1988), pp. 214–15; Radi, Spearritt, and Hinton, *Biographical Register*, pp. 79–80.
14. Radi, Spearritt, and Hinton, *Biographical Register*, p. 67.
15. Ibid., p. 69, John Power, *Politics in a Suburban Community: The N.S.W. State Election in Manly, 1965* (Sydney: Sydney University Press, 1968). See also Darby, *New South Wales Parliamentary Debates* (*NSWPD*), vol. 117 (August 12, 1975), pp. 207–11 and *NSWPD*, vol. 82 (October 29, 1969), pp. 2051–56.
16. *NSWPD*, vol. 38 (November 14, 1961), pp. 2458–59.
17. John Hughes, "Harold Wyndham and Educational Reform in Australia 1925–1968," *Education Research and Perspectives* 29, no. 1 (2002), pp. 175–85.
18. *NSWPD*, vol. 57 (September 22, 1965), pp. 805–06; vol. 57 (September 28, 1965), pp. 949–50.
19. *NSWPD*, vol. 72 (December 6, 1967), p. 4276.
20. Audrey Armitage, *Newcastle High School: The First 75 Years* (Newcastle: Newcastle High School, 1983).
21. Ibid., p. 160.
22. *NSWPD*, vol. 186 (February 20, 1986), p. 163.
23. Ronald S. Horan, *Fort Street: The School* (Sydney: Honeysett, 1989).
24. Eddie J. Braggett, "The Education of Gifted and Talented Children: Australian Provision" (Canberra: Commonwealth Schools Commission, 1985), p. 258.
25. R. T. Fitzgerald, *The Secondary School at Sixes and Sevens: A Review of the Sixties and a Prospect of the Seventies* (Melbourne: ACER, 1970).
26. Ibid., p. 2.

27. *NSWPD*, vol. 38 (October 31, 1961), pp. 1963–65.
28. Fitzgerald, *The Secondary School at Sixes and Sevens*, p. 84.
29. *Sydney and the Bush: A Pictorial History of Education in New South Wales*, (Sydney: New South Wales Department of Education, 1980), pp. 244–45.
30. R. A. Reed, "Curriculum Reform in Victorian Secondary Schools in the Late Sixties," *Melbourne Studies in Education 1975* (1975), Sheila Spear, "Secondary Education for All: The Evolution of Policy and Practice in Victorian Secondary Schools, 1968–1978," *Melbourne Studies in Education 1983* (1983).
31. Directorate of Studies, "Aims of Secondary Education in N.S.W" (Sydney: New South Wales Department of Education, 1973). See also *Education* 54, no. 8 (1973).
32. Secondary Schools Board, "Base Paper on the Total Curriculum" (1975). (Reproduced as Appendix 3 in "Report of the Select Committee of the Legislative Assembly Upon the School Certificate") (Sydney: New South Wales Parliament Journal and Votes and Proceedings, 1980–1981).
33. Alan Barcan, "After Wyndham, What?" *Australian Quarterly* 46, no. 3 (1974).
34. Fitzgerald, *The Secondary School at Sixes and Sevens*, p. 35.
35. Bruce Mitchell, *Teachers Education and Politics: A History of Organizations of Public School Teachers in New South Wales* (Brisbane: University of Queensland Press, 1975).
36. John O'Brien, *A Divided Unity! Politics of Nsw Teacher Militancy since 1945* (Sydney: Allen & Unwin, 1987).
37. Bruce Mitchell, "In the Public Interest? The New South Wales Teachers' Strike of 1968," in *Strikes: Studies in Twentieth Century Australian Social History*, ed. John Iremonger, John Merritt, and Graeme Osborne (Sydney: Angus and Robertson, 1973).
38. Report of the Committee Appointed to Investigate and Advise of Class Sizes and Teaching Loads in Government Secondary Schools in New South Wales, 1969, p. 24 in *New South Wales Parliamentary Papers*, 1969–1971, vol. 3.
39. Ibid., p. 35.
40. Ibid.
41. Ibid., pp. 37–39.
42. O'Brien, *A Divided Unity!*, pp. 148–62.
43. *NSWPD*, vol. 152, (February 28, 1980), pp. 4959–60.
44. David Crook, "Local Authorities and Comprehensivisation in England and Wales, 1944–1974," *Oxford Review of Education* 28, no. 2 & 3 (2002). See also Alan C. Kerkhoff et al., *Going Comprehensive in England and Wales: A Study of Uneven Change* (London: Woburn Press, 1996).
45. Kerkhoff et al., *Going Comprehensive in England and Wales*.
46. Fitzgerald, *The Secondary School at Sixes and Sevens*, p. 98.
47. Peter Spearritt, *Sydney since the Twenties* (Sydney: Hale and Iremonger, 1978), pp. 203–08.
48. Ibid., pp. 90–93.
49. Carolyn Allport, "The Castles of Security: The New South Wales Housing Commission and Home Ownership," in *Sydney: City of Suburbs*, ed. Max Kelly (Sydney: University of New South Wales Press, 1987), p. 103.

50. A. A. Congalton, *Status and Prestige in Australia* (Melbourne: Cheshire, 1969).
51. Ibid., p. 211.
52. New South Wales. Department of Education, "First Report of the Committee, Appointed by the Minister for Education, to Inquire into Various Aspects of Higher Education in New South Wales" (Sydney: Committee on Higher Education, 1961), pp. 112–15.
53. Bruce Mansfield and Mark Hutchinson, *Liberality of Opportunity: A History of Macquarie University 1964–1989* (Sydney: Macquarie University, 1992).
54. Ian Burnley, "European Immigration Settlement Patterns in Metropolitan Sydney 1847–1966," *Australian Geographical Studies* 10 (1972).
55. Ibid., p. 252.
56. K. I. Turner, "A Profile of Manly," in *Politics in a Suburban Community: The N.S.W. State Election in Manly, 1965*, ed. John Power (Sydney: Sydney University Press, 1968), pp. 35–36.
57. John Patrick Hughes, "There Goes the Neighborhood School: A Case Study of Restructuring of Secondary Education on Sydney's Northern Beaches" (2001).
58. Interviews with school principals, see Craig Campbell and Geoffrey Sherington, "Public Comprehensive High Schools in New South Wales: School Principals Discuss the Challenges and Opportunities" (Sydney: Public Education Council of New South Wales, 2004).
59. *Davidson High School: The First Twenty Years* (Sydney: Davidson High School Parents' & Citizens' Association, 1992), p. 1.
60. Ibid., p. 2.
61. Helen Proctor, "Gender, Merit and Identity at Parramatta High School, 1913–1919," *History of Education Review* 31, no. 1 (2002).
62. Cumberland County Council (N.S.W.), "The Cumberland Plan: Progress Report 1955" (Sydney: Cumberland County Council, 1955).
63. *NSWPD*, vol. 88 (October 14, 1970), pp. 6662–64.
64. Diane Powell, *Out West: Perceptions of Sydney's Western Suburbs* (Sydney: Allen & Unwin, 1993), p. 63.
65. *NSWPD*, vol. 111 (August 7, 1974), p. 57.
66. Powell, *Out West*, pp. 63–67.
67. Ibid., p. 60
68. Kerkhoff et al., *Going Comprehensive in England and Wales*, pp. 260–73.
69. W. C. Radford and R. E. Wilkes, *School Leavers in Australia, 1971–1972* (Melbourne: Australian Council for Educational Research, 1975).
70. Fitzgerald, *The Secondary School at Sixes and Sevens*, p. 9.
71. New South Wales Department of Education and Training, *Government Schools of New South Wales 1848–2003* (Sydney: The Department, 2003), Appendix 1, Geoffrey Sherington, R. C. Petersen, and Ian Brice, *Learning to Lead: A History of Girls' and Boys' Corporate Secondary Schools in Australia* (Sydney: Allen & Unwin, 1987), Appendix II and Alison Nation, "Selective Growth: An Examination of the Expansion of Academically-Selective Schooling During the Metherell Era of Education in New South Wales 1988–1990" (M. Teach Hons, University of Sydney, 2001), Appendices A and B.

4 IN RETREAT

1. Caroline Benn and Brian Simon, *Half Way There: Report on the British Comprehensive School Reform* (London: McGraw-Hill, 1970).
2. John McLaren, *A Dictionary of Australian Education* (Brisbane: University of Queensland Press, 1974), p. 66.
3. Terry Irving, David Maunders, and Geoff Sherington, *Youth in Australia: Policy Administration and Politics: A History since World War II* (Melbourne: Macmillan, 1995), pp. 223–35.
4. Ibid., p. 252.
5. Simon Marginson, *Educating Australia: Government, Economy and Citizen since 1960* (Cambridge: Cambridge University Press, 1997).
6. C. B. Cox and A. E. Dyson, eds, *Fight for Education: A Black Paper* (London: The Critical Quarterly Society, 1969).
7. Peter Gordon, Richard Aldrich, and Dennis Dean, *Education and Policy in England in the Twentieth Century* (London: Woburn Press, 1991), pp. 196–99; Brian Simon, *Education and the Social Order, 1940–1990* (London: Lawrence & Wishart, 1991), pp. 472–525.
8. David T. Gordon, *A Nation Reformed? American Education 20 Years after 'a Nation at Risk'* (Cambridge Mass.: Harvard Education Press, 2003). See also David L. Angus and Jeffrey Mirel, *The Failed Promise of the American High School, 1890–1995* (New York: Teachers College Press, 1999).
9. Bengt Henkens, "The Rise and Decline of Comprehensive Education: Key Factors in the History of Reformed Secondary Education in Belgium, 1969–1989," *Paedagogica Historica* 40, nos. 1 & 2 (2004).
10. See Gough Whitlam, *The Whitlam Government 1972–1975* (Melbourne: Penguin, 1985).
11. On the process of persuasion, see Graham Freudenberg, *A Certain Grandeur: Gough Whitlam in Politics* (Melbourne: Macmillan, 1977), pp. 24–32.
12. Peter Karmel (Chair), "Schools in Australia: Report of the Interim Committee of the Australian Schools Commission" (Canberra: AGPS, 1973).
13. Ibid. See also Ronald T. Fitzgerald (Commissioner), "Poverty and Education in Australia: Australian Government Commission of Inquiry into Poverty," (Canberra: Australian Government Printing Service, 1976).
14. Karmel (Chair), "Schools in Australia," p. 101.
15. R. W. Connell, *Schools and Social Justice* (Philadelphia: Temple University Press, 1993).
16. Committee on Social Change and the Education of Women, "Girls, School and Society: Report by a Study Group to the Schools Commission" (Canberra: Schools Commission, 1975), Jane Kenway and Sue Willis, *Answering Back: Girls, Boys and Feminism in Schools* (London: Routledge, 1998).
17. Irving, Maunders, and Sherington, *Youth in Australia*, pp. 226–27. See also R. W. Connell et al., *Making the Difference: Schools, Families and Social Division* (Sydney: George Allen & Unwin, 1982), Peter Dwyer, Bruce Wilson, and Roger Woock, *Confronting School and Work: Youth and Class Cultures in Australia*

(Sydney: George Allen & Unwin, 1984), Peter Gilmour and Russell Lansbury, *Ticket to Nowhere: Education, Training and Work in Australia* (Melbourne: Penguin, 1978), Ian Watson, *Double Depression: Schooling, Unemployment and Family Life in the Eighties* (Sydney: George Allen & Unwin, 1985).

18. Irving, Maunders, and Sherington, *Youth in Australia*, pp. 236–44.
19. Schools Commission, "Schooling for 15 and 16 Year-Olds" (Canberra: Schools Commission, 1980).
20. Commonwealth Schools Commission, "In the National Interest: Secondary Education and Youth Policy in Australia" (Canberra: The Commission, 1987), p. 29.
21. Peter Karmel (Chair), "Quality of Education in Australia: Report of the Review Committee" (Canberra: Commonwealth of Australia (AGPS), 1985).
22. Karmel (Chair), "Schools in Australia," ch. 2. See also Marginson, *Educating Australia*, pp. 46–70.
23. Jean Martin, *The Migrant Presence, Australian Responses, 1947–1977: Research Report for the National Population Inquiry* (Sydney: George Allen & Unwin, 1978), pp. 113–45.
24. See James Jupp, ed., *The Australian People: An Encyclopedia of the Nation, Its People and Their Origins*, 2nd ed. (Cambridge: Cambridge University Press, 2001), pp. 812–15.
25. Paul Kringas and Frank Lewins, *Why Ethnic Schools? Selected Case Studies* (Canberra: Australian National University Press, 1981).
26. DOGS mounted a High Court challenge to state aid for nongovernment schools; see M. J. Ely, *Erosion of the Judicial Process: An Aspect of Church-State Entanglement in Australia, the Struggle of Citizens to Be Heard in the Australian Full High Court on the State Aid Issue, 1956–1980* (Melbourne: Defense of Government Schools, 1981).
27. Marginson, *Educating Australia*, p. 47.
28. Peter Tannock (Chair), "Funding Policies for Australian Schools" (Canberra: Commonwealth Schools Commission, 1984), p. 10. (Calculated from Table 1.2.)
29. Chris Ryan and Louise Watson, "The Drift to Private Schools in Australia: Understanding Its Features" (Canberra: Centre for Economic Policy Research, Australian National University, 2004). For the debate in the 1980s see Michael Hogan, *Public Versus Private Schools: Funding and Directions in Australia* (Melbourne: Penguin, 1984).
30. Marginson, *Educating Australia*, Ross A. Williams, "The Economic Determinants of Private Schooling in Australia" (Canberra: Australian National University Centre for Economic Policy Research, 1984), Ross A. Williams, "Interaction between Government and Private Outlays: Education in Australia 1949–50 to 1981–82" (Canberra: Australian National University Centre for Economic Policy Research, 1983).
31. D. Anderson, "Is the Privatisation of Australian Schooling Inevitable," in *Australia Compared*, ed. F. Castles (Sydney: Allen & Unwin, 1991), Don Anderson, "The Interaction of Public and Private School Systems," *Australian Journal of Education* 36, no. 3 (1992).
32. Jean Blackburn (Chair), "Discussion Paper: Ministerial Review of Postcompulsory Schooling" (Melbourne: Ministerial Review of Postcompulsory

Schooling (Victoria), 1984), Jean Blackburn (Chair), "Report: Ministerial Review of Postcompulsory Schooling" (Melbourne: Ministerial Review of Postcompulsory Schooling (Victoria), 1985). See also Irving, Maunders, and Sherington, *Youth in Australia*, pp. 247–56.

33. *NSWPD*, vol. 101 (October 12, 1972), pp. 1737–38.
34. Roger Wescombe, *Schools Community and Politics in NSW: Ideas and Strategies in the Schools Councils Controversy 1973–1976* (Sydney: University of Sydney, 1980).
35. C. L. MacDonald (Chair), "The Education of the Talented Child: Report of the Committee Appointed by the Minister for Education to Enquire into the Education of the Talented Child" (Sydney: New South Wales Department of Education, 1977), p. 2.
36. Eddie J. Braggett, "The Education of Gifted and Talented Children: Australian Provision" (Canberra: Commonwealth Schools Commission, 1985), pp. 1–7.
37. MacDonald (Chair), "The Education of the Talented Child," p. 2.
38. Uldis Ozolins, *The Politics of Language in Australia* (Cambridge: Cambridge University Press, 1993), p. 130. See also Multicultural Education Centre, "Multicultural Perspectives to Curriculum: A Support Document to the Multicultural Education Policy 1983" (Sydney: Directorate of Special Programs, New South Wales Department of Education, 1983), "Multicultural Education Policy Statement 1983" (Sydney: New South Wales Department of Education, 1983).
39. Braggett, "The Education of Gifted and Talented Children," p. 259.
40. MacDonald (Chair), "The Education of the Talented Child," p. 13.
41. Ibid., pp. 45–75.
42. Braggett, "The Education of Gifted and Talented Children," p. 260.
43. *NSWPD*, vol. 149 (October 11, 1979), p. 1752. See also Winifred Mitchell and Geoffrey Sherington, *Growing up in the Illawarra: A Social History 1834–1884* (Wollongong: University of Wollongong, 1984), pp. 127–29.
44. Interview with Eric Bedford 1998 cited in Catherine Brown, " 'Little Bastions of Privilege': NSW ALP Policy on Selective Schools" (B. Ed. Hons, Sydney University, 1998).
45. Susan Susskind, "Public Schools? They're All Mediocre," *Sydney Morning Herald*, May 29, 1987.
46. Marginson, *Educating Australia*, pp. 130–31. An example from the media: "Mickey Mouse Subjects Invade Schools," *Bulletin*, January 24, 1976.
47. Braggett, "The Education of Gifted and Talented Children," pp. 25–91.
48. *NSWPD*, vol. 173 (February 17, 1983), pp. 4307–08.
49. *NSWPD*, vol. 179 (May 17, 1984), pp. 1127–28.
50. B. McGowan (Chair), "Report from the Select Committee of the Legislative Assembly Upon the School Certificate" (Sydney: New South Wales. Parliament. Legislative Assembly. Select Committee upon the School Certificate, 1981), Appendix 4.
51. Ibid. Terms of Reference and Introduction.
52. Ibid., p. 34.
53. Ibid., pp. 3–10.
54. See Alan Barcan, "Proposals to Reorganize N.S.W. Secondary Education," *ACES Review* 9, no. 3 (1982).

55. D. Swan and K. McKinnon, "Future Directions of Secondary Education: A Report" (Sydney: NSW Government Printer, 1984).
56. R. Mulock, "Official Opening Address," in *The Future of Secondary Education: A Symposium Held at the University of Sydney 17th September, 1983*, ed. Alan T. Duncan (Sydney: University of Sydney Department of Adult Education, 1983).
57. Alan Barcan, "The Future of Secondary Education in N.S.W," *ACES Review* 11, no. 4 (1984).
58. Alan Barcan, *Two Centuries of Education in New South Wales* (Sydney: University of New South Wales Press, 1988), p. 309.
59. Interview with Rodney Cavalier, October 24, 2002.
60. *NSWPD*, vol. 179 (May 10, 1984), pp. 561–63; Interview with Rodney Cavalier and Brown, "Little Bastions of Privilege," pp. 64–65.
61. Alison Nation, "Selective Growth: An Examination of the Expansion of Academically-Selective Schooling During the Metherell Era of Education in New South Wales 1988–1990" (M. Teach (Hons), University of Sydney, 2001).
62. Swan and McKinnon, "Future Directions of Secondary Education."
63. Ibid, pp. 9–29.
64. Barcan, *Two Centuries of Education in New South Wales*, p. 313.
65. Susan Susskind, "Education's Architect Is Not Disappointed," *Sydney Morning Herald*, October 8, 1987.
66. Nick Greiner, *Australian Liberalism in a Post-Ideological Age, The Twenty-Fourth Alfred Deakin Lecture* (Melbourne: The Alfred Deakin Lecture Trust, 1990).
67. Martin Laffin and Martin Painter, eds, *Reform and Reversal: Lessons from the Coalition Government in New South Wales 1988–1995* (Melbourne: Macmillan, 1995), pp. 2–4.
68. Geoffrey Sherington, "Education Policy," in *Reform and Reversal: Lessons from the Coalition Government in New South Wales 1988–1995*, ed. Martin Laffin and Martin Painter (Melbourne: Macmillan, 1995), pp. 173–74. See also Nation, "Selective Growth."
69. Quoted in Sherington, "Education Policy," p. 174.
70. Nation, "Selective Growth."
71. Ibid., p. 57
72. Ibid., p. 67.
73. B. W. Scott (Director of Review), "Schools Renewal: A Strategy to Revitalise Schools within the New South Wales State Education System" (Sydney: NSW Education Portfolio, 1989). See also P. West, "Politics and Education in NSW 1988–91: Management or Human Values?" *Australian Educational Researcher* 18, no. 3 (1991).
74. J. Carrick (Chair), "Report of the Committee of Review of New South Wales Schools" (Sydney: New South Wales Government, 1989).
75. Sherington, "Education Policy," pp. 173 and 179.
76. Marian Sawer, *The Ethical State? Social Liberalism in Australia* (Melbourne: Melbourne University Press, 2003).
77. Carrick (Chair), "Report of the Committee of Review of New South Wales Schools," pp. 7 and 20.

78. Ibid., p. 103.
79. Ibid., p. 160.
80. Ibid., p 206.
81. Ibid., p. 208.
82. Ibid., p. 210.
83. Geoffrey Riordan and Sam Weller, *The Reformation of Education in N.S.W.: The 1990 Education Reform Act* (AARE, 2000) [http://www.aare.edu.au/00pap/rio00358.htm].
84. Sherington, "Education Policy," pp. 178–85.
85. John Patrick Hughes, "There Goes the Neighbourhood School: A Case Study of Restructuring of Secondary Education on Sydney's Northern Beaches" (2001), p. 22. See also NSW Department of Education and Training, "New Horizons: A Plan to Improve Education and Training on the Northern Beaches," (Sydney: Author, 2000).
86. Brown, "Little Bastions of Privilege," p. 70.
87. Australian Bureau of Statistics, "Schools: Australia," [cat. 4221.0] (Canberra: Commonwealth of Australia).

5 The Market

1. "Class We Failed," *Daily Telegraph*, January 8, 1997.
2. See Estelle Morris, "Why Comprehensives Must Change," *The Observer*, June 23, 2002.
3. Alan Laughlin, *Mount Druitt High School: Review of 1996 Higher School Certificate Performance* (Sydney: Department of School Education (NSW), 1997).
4. The median weekly individual income for the statistical district of Blacktown (South-East) was $384 which was 13.5% below the median for Sydney as a whole. The ratio of single parent families with children to couple families with dependent children was 1 : 2.4. For Sydney as a whole it was 1 : 3.5. Australian Bureau of Statistics, "Selected Social and Housing Characteristics for Statistical Local Areas: New South Wales and Jervis Bay Territory, 2001," in *2015.1 Census of Population and Housing* (Canberra: The Bureau, 2002).
5. Laughlin, *Mount Druitt High School*, p. 5.
6. Ibid., p. 24
7. Ibid., p. 6. For a more general analysis, see Richard Teese, *Academic Success and Social Power: Examinations and Inequity* (Melbourne: Melbourne University Press, 2000).
8. New South Wales Department of Education and Training, *Government Schools of New South Wales 1848–2003* (Sydney: The Department, 2003); Australian Bureau of Statistics, "Selected Social and Housing Characteristics."
9. Craig Campbell, "State Policy and Regional Diversity in the Provision of Secondary Education for the Youth of Sydney, 1960–2001," *History of Education* 32, no. 5 (2003).

10. On real estate, end of zoning and school choice, see Jennifer Stynes, "Smart Choice," *Sydney Morning Herald*, July 14–15, 2001. p. 6H.
11. $542 in the Baulkham Hills area as opposed to $359 in Southwest Blacktown. Australian Bureau of Statistics, "Selected Social and Housing Characteristics."
12. "Crestwood High School: 2000 Annual Report" (Sydney: NSW Department of Education and Training, 2001), Interview with Principal, Crestwood High School, (2001).
13. "Glebe High School: 2000 Annual Report" (Sydney: NSW Department of Education and Training, 2001), Interviews with Principals, Glebe High School and Balmain High School (2001).
14. Interview with Principal, Young High School (2001), "Young High School: 2000 Annual Report" (Sydney: NSW Department of Education and Training, 2001).
15. Craig Campbell and Geoffrey Sherington, "Public Comprehensive High Schools in New South Wales: School Principals Discuss the Challenges and Opportunities" (Sydney: Public Education Council of New South Wales, 2004).
16. For example, Catherine Armitage, "Too Clever by Half?" *The Australian*, March 6–7, 1999, Catharine Lumby, "Class Distinction," *The Bulletin*, August 22, 2000.
17. Gerard Noonan, "Local High Schools Fall from HSC Honour Roll," *Sydney Morning Herald*, December 21, 2000.
18. See New South Wales Department of Education and Training, *Building the Future: An Education Plan for Inner Sydney: Draft Proposal* (Sydney: The Department, 2001), p. 13, Geesche Jacobson, "Public School Exodus as Suburbs Grow Richer," *Sydney Morning Herald*, October 17, 2000.
19. Gerard Noonan, "Dr Boston . I Presume," *Sydney Morning Herald*, November 1, 1999.
20. Ken Boston, "The Educational Building Blocks of a Better Tomorrow," *Sydney Morning Herald*, March 23, 2001.
21. Ken Boston, "Reshaping Comprehensive Secondary Education," *Inform: Public Education in New South Wales*, July 21, 1999. See also John Polesel, "The New South Wales Multi-Campus Schooling Model: The Sydney Experience," (Sydney: NSW DET, 2001).
22. Interviews with school principals reported in Campbell and Sherington, "Public Comprehensive High Schools in New South Wales," pp. 35–37.
23. Summary of changes, see Tony Vinson, "Inquiry into the Provision of Public Education in New South Wales" (Sydney: NSW Teachers Federation & Federation of P & C Asociations of NSW, 2002). Report no. 2, p. 7.
24. Department of Education and Training (NSW), "Entry to Selective High Schools in 2005," *Sydney Morning Herald*, March 31, 2004.
25. Vinson, "Inquiry into the Provision of Public Education in New South Wales" Report no. 2, p. 22.
26. See New South Wales Department of Education and Training, *Building the Future: An Education Plan for Inner Sydney: Draft Proposal*, New South Wales. Parliament. Legislative Council. General Purpose Standing Committee No 1, "Inquiry into the Proposed Closure and Restructuring of Government Schools in Inner Sydney" (Sydney, 2002).

27. Ibid., p. 4.
28. Alex Mitchell and Miranda Wood, "Carr's Deputy Rallies against School Axing in Master Plan," *Sun-Herald*, June 10, 2001.
29. John Patrick Hughes, "There Goes the Neighbourhood School: A Case Study of Restructuring of Secondary Education on Sydney's Northern Beaches," (2001), NSW Department of Education and Training, "New Horizons: A Plan to Improve Education and Training on the Northern Beaches" (Sydney: The Department, 2000).
30. See Gerard Noonan and Stephanie Peatling, "Class Moves," *Sydney Morning Herald*, April 11, 2001, and "Class Rules," *Sydney Morning Herald*, March 24, 2001.
31. For example, Gerard Noonan, "Non-Believers Flock to Catholic Schools," *Sydney Morning Herald*, March 28, 2000, p. 9.
32. Barry McGaw "Securing Their Future: The New South Wales Government's Reforms for the Higher School Certificate" (Sydney: Department of Training and Education Co-ordination, 1997), p. 7. (Henceforth *McGaw Report*.)
33. Interviews with school principals reported in Campbell and Sherington, "Public Comprehensive High Schools in New South Wales," pp. 32–33.
34. *McGaw Report*, p. 64
35. Ibid., p. 116
36. Interviews with school principals reported in Campbell and Sherington, "Public Comprehensive High Schools in New South Wales," pp. 30–34.
37. "The Future of Public Education: Reaffirming the Primacy of Comprehensive Education," *Education (NSWTF)*, August 30, 2004, pp. 18–19.
38. Vinson, "Inquiry into the Provision of Public Education in New South Wales." Also http://www.pub-ed-inquiry.org/ (retrieved January 13, 2005).
39. Gerard Noonan, "Bipartisan Backing," *Sydney Morning Herald*, July 25, 2002.
40. See government web-site: http://www.dest.gov.au/schools/ses/index.htm (retrieved January 5, 2005).
41. Samantha Maiden, "Howard Slams Public Schools," *The Australian*, January 20, 2004, but see also Louise Dodson, "PM: I Didn't Slate Public Schools," *Sydney Morning Herald*, August 13, 2004; Linda Doherty, "Class Divide: Why Parents Are Choosing Private," *Sydney Morning Herald*, January 24–25, 2004, Linda Doherty, "Push for Values Drives Public School Exodus," *Sydney Morning Herald*, August 9, 2004.
42. Ken Boston, "No Losers, Just the Risk of a National Asset Lost," *Sydney Morning Herald*, October 10, 2000, Jennifer Buckingham, "School Funding for All: Making Sense of the Debate over Dollars," *Issue Analysis*, no. 17 (2000).
43. Warren A. Grimshaw, "Review of Non-Government Schools: Report 1," (Sydney: Department of Education and Training (NSW), 2002), Table 2.7, p. 33.
44. Linda Doherty, "School Fees up but Drift Gathers Pace," *Sydney Morning Herald*, January 5, 2004. pp. 1 and 4
45. For example, Stephen O'Doherty, "Why Supporters of Public Education Can Applaud the Growth of Faith," *Sydney Morning Herald*, January 1, 2004.
46. Grimshaw, "Review of Non-Government Schools: Report 1."

47. Michael Pusey, *The Experience of Middle Australia: The Dark Side of Economic Reform* (Cambridge: Cambridge University Press, 2003), pp. 75, 68–75, 92–101.
48. R. W. Connell, "Working-Class Families and the New Secondary Education," *Australian Journal of Education* 47, no. 3 (2003), p. 249.
49. For this aspect of the study, the Australian Bureau of Statistics was commissioned by the authors to make sets of tables for New South Wales and selected regions, for every second census from 1976 to 2001. The 1976 census was the first to have its data electronically digitized.
50. See Anne Davies, "Latham Warns Labor to Hitch Itself to the New Outwardly Mobile Voter," *Sydney Morning Herald*, March 19, 2002, Anne Davies, "Newest Sanctuary for 'White Flight' Buyers," *Sydney Morning Herald*, March 19, 2002, Tom Morton, "Up the Greasy Pole," *Sydney Morning Herald*, June 16, 2001.
51. The clerical and service categories are divided into advanced, intermediate, and elementary levels.
52. For example, Chris Ryan and Louise Watson, "The Drift to Private Schools in Australia: Understanding Its Features" (Canberra: Centre for Economic Policy Research, Australian National University, 2004).
53. Interviews with school principals reported in Campbell and Sherington, "Public Comprehensive High Schools in New South Wales," pp. 21 and 39.
54. On youth and ethnicity, especially in the outer western suburbs of Sydney, see Jock Collins, *Kebabs, Kids, Cops and Crime: Youth Ethnicity and Crime* (Sydney: Pluto Press, 2000), Diane Powell, *Out West: Perceptions of Sydney's Western Suburbs* (Sydney: Allen & Unwin, 1993). On sensational journalism, for example, see the article by Les Kennedy, "Machetes Fly in Schoolboy Street War," *Sydney Morning Herald*, March 28, 2002.
55. For example, on alleged racism in such schools, Ebru Yaman, "Private School Fees Are Protection against Racism: Black Leader," *Australian*, April 19, 2001, p. 1.
56. On regionalism and the comprehensive school, see Campbell, "State Policy and Regional Diversity in the Provision of Secondary Education for the Youth of Sydney, 1960–2001."
57. Paola Totaro, "Gifted Students Told: Pick Any High School," *Sydney Morning Herald*, January 28, 2003.
58. Fenton Sharpe, "Education without the Cringe Factor," *Sydney Morning Herald*, December 28, 2000.
59. Pusey, *The Experience of Middle Australia*.
60. For example, Linda Doherty, "It's Private—Madison's Part in the Class Revolt," *Sydney Morning Herald*, October 28, 2002. See also Craig Campbell, "Changing School Loyalties and the Middle Class: A Reflection on the Developing Fate of State Comprehensive High Schooling," *The Australian Educational Researcher* 31, no. 1 (2005).
61. For example, Diana Bagnall, "Tying up Values-Added Education," *Bulletin*, August 24, 1999, pp. 20–25.

62. On developments in the Anglican church in particular see David Marr, *The High Price of Heaven* (Sydney: Allen & Unwin, 1999).

CONCLUSION

1. Ken Boston, "Reshaping Comprehensive Secondary Education," *Inform: Public Education in New South Wales*, July 21, 1999, p. 6.
2. Ibid., p. 6.
3. Ibid., p. 7.
4. Ibid., p. 7.
5. Ibid., p. 6.
6. Department of Education and Training (NSW), *Parents' Guide to Schools* (Sydney: The Department, 2001).
7. Geoffrey Sherington, R. C. Petersen, and Ian Brice, *Learning to Lead: A History of Girls' and Boys' Corporate Secondary Schools in Australia* (Sydney: Allen & Unwin, 1987).
8. For example, A. R. Crane and W. G. Walker, *Peter Board: His Contribution to the Development of Education in New South Wales* (Melbourne: ACER, 1957).
9. Michael Pusey, *Economic Rationalism in Canberra: A Nation-Building State Changes Its Mind* (Cambridge: Cambridge University Press, 1991).
10. See Bob Lingard, John Knight, and Paige Porter, eds., *Schooling Reform in Hard Times* (London: Falmer, 1993), Simon Marginson, *Markets in Education* (Sydney: Allen & Unwin, 1997), Geoff Whitty, "Creating Quasi-Markets in Education," *Review of Research in Education* 22 (1997).
11. Craig Campbell and Geoffrey Sherington, "Public Comprehensive High Schools in New South Wales: School Principals Discuss the Challenges and Opportunities" (Sydney: Public Education Council of New South Wales, 2004), for example, p. 41.
12. Stephen Ball and Carol Vincent, "New Class Relations in Education: The Strategies of the 'Fearful' Middle Classes," in *Sociology of Education Today*, ed. Jack Demaine (Houndsmills (UK): Palgrave, 2001), Craig Campbell, "Changing School Loyalties and the Middle Class: A Reflection on the Developing Fate of State Comprehensive High Schooling," *The Australian Educational Researcher* 31, no. 1 (2005), Sally Power et al., *Education and the Middle Class* (Buckingham: Open University Press, 2003).
13. Rob Gilbert and Pam Gilbert, *Masculinity Goes to School* (Sydney: Allen & Unwin, 1998), Jane Kenway and Sue Willis, *Answering Back: Girls, Boys and Feminism in Schools* (London: Routledge, 1998).
14. Brian J. Caldwell and Don K. Hayward, *The Future of Schools: Lessons from the Reform of Public Education* (London: Falmer, 1998), Brian Caldwell and John Roskam, "Australia's Education Choices" (Canberra: Menzies Research Centre, 2002).
15. Pat Thomson, *Schooling the Rustbelt Kids: Making the Difference in Changing Times* (Sydney: Allen & Unwin, 2002), see also Margaret Vickers, "Markets

and Mobilities: Dilemmas Facing the Comprehensive Neighbourhood High School," *Melbourne Studies in Education* 45, no. 2 (2004).
16. Richard Teese, *Academic Success and Social Power: Examinations and Inequity* (Melbourne: Melbourne University Press, 2000), Richard Teese et al., "Who Wins at School? Boys and Girls in Australian Secondary Education," (Melbourne: Department of Education Policy and Management, University of Melbourne, 1995).
17. Teese, *Academic Success and Social Power*, p. 189.
18. Simon Marginson, *Educating Australia: Government, Economy and Citizen since 1960* (Cambridge: Cambridge University Press, 1997).

EPILOGUE

1. Barry M. Franklin and Gary McCulloch, eds, *The Death of the Comprehensive High School? Historical, Contemporary, and Comparative Perspectives* (New York: Palgrave Macmillan, 2007).
2. See Geoffrey Sherington and Craig Campbell, "Comprehensive Secondary Schools," in *Routledge International Encyclopaedia of Education*, ed. Gary McCulloch and David Crook (London: Routledge, 2008), pp. 118–121.
3. Pavla Miller, "'My Parents Came Here with Nothing and They Wanted Us to Achieve': Italian Australians and School Success", pp. 185–198, and Thomas C. Pedroni, "The End of the Comprehensive High School?", pp. 111–128, in *The Death of the Comprehensive High School?* ed. Franklin and McCulloch.
4. Rene Antrop Gonzalez and Anthony De Jesus, "Breathing Life into Small School Reform," in *The Death of the Comprehensive High School?* ed. Franklin and McCulloch, pp. 73–92.
5. Jose R. Rosario, "Soul Making in the Comprehensive High School," in *The Death of the Comprehensive High School?* ed. Franklin and McCulloch, pp. 93–109.
6. Franklin and McCulloch, *The Death of the Comprehensive High School?*, p. 4.
7. David Gonski (Chair), "Review of Funding for Schooling: Final Report" (Canberra: Australian Government, 2012).
8. Craig Campbell, Helen Proctor, and Geoffrey Sherington, *School Choice: How Parents Negotiate the New School Market in Australia* (Sydney: Allen & Unwin, 2009).
9. Ibid.
10. "My School: NSW schools ranked", *Sydney Morning Herald*, February 27, 2012, Supplement.
11. Kim Arlington, "Big day out", *Sydney Morning Herald*, March 15, 2012.
12. Campbell, Proctor, and Sherington, *School Choice*.
13. Anna Patty and Andrew Stevensen, "Migrant pupils top the entry tests for selective schools," *Sydney Morning Herald*, July 3, 2010.
14. Anna Patty and Andrew Stevensen, "Arabic-speaking children have the smarts but shun selective system," *Sydney Morning Herald*, June 28, 2011.

15. Anna Patty, "White flight leaves system segregated by race," *Sydney Morning Herald*, March 10, 2008. Following the initial newspaper articles on this topic there was vigorous correspondence in the letters pages, and other articles and opinion pieces, for up to a fortnight.
16. For example, see the blog belonging to the education editor of Sydney's daily tabloid newspaper, and the multitude of responses: Maralyn Parker, "My School evidence—NSW selective schools have been hijacked", 10 February 2010. http://blogs.news.com.au/dailytelegraph/maralynparker/
17. Campbell, Proctor, and Sherington, *School Choice*.
18. We are indebted in the following paragraphs to the unpublished research carried out on Pennant Hills High School by an Honors student in the Faculty of Education and Social Work at the University of Sydney, Renell Lope.
19. On the education policies of the state Labor government, 1995–2011, see Geoffrey Sherington and John Hughes, "Education," in *From Carr to Keneally: Labor in Office in NSW 1995–2011*, eds David Clune and Rodney Smith (Sydney: Allen & Unwin, 2012), pp. 138–149.
20. Campbell, Proctor, and Sherington, *School Choice*, especially pp. 160–178.
21. Media release, Premier Barry O'Farrell and Minister for Education, Adrian Piccoli, "Local schools, local decisions," March 11, 2012. Retrieved from https://www.det.nsw.edu.au/, March 22, 2012.
22. See Trevor Fletcher, "Schools should lead classroom reform," and Stephen Dinham, "Steep learning curve on path to more freedom," *Sydney Morning Herald*, March 19, 2012, p. 13; and the forum, Raewyn Connell, Chris Bonnor, Kevin Donnelly, and Marian Spencer, "The Question: Will local autonomy improve public schools," *Sydney Morning Herald*, News Review, March 17–18, 2012, p. 12.
23. Andrew Stevenson, "Principals fear education the loser in school reforms," *Sydney Morning Herald*, March 17–18, 2012, p. 7.
24. For a brief Australian discussion of the devolution of financial control and managerial responsibility in public school systems, see Anthony Welch, "Making Education Policy," in Raewyn Connell, Craig Campbell, Margaret Vickers, Anthony Welch, Dennis Foley, Nigel Bagnall and Debra Hayes, *Education, Change and Society*, (Melbourne: Oxford University Press, 2010), pp. 262–264.
25. Martin Forsey, *Challenging the System? A Dramatic Tale of Neoliberal Reform in an Australian High School* (Charlotte, NC: Information Age Publishing, 2007).
26. "NSW axes outdated School Certificate," *Sydney Morning Herald*, August 2, 2011.
27. See Kim Arlington, "Inner-city parents want a high school that is close to home," *Sydney Morning Herald*, August 6, 2011.
28. "Selection, choice and schools," Editorial, *Sydney Morning Herald*, March 16, 2012, p. 10.

Bibliography

Ainley, John and Michael Sheret. *Progress through High School: A Study of Senior Secondary Schooling in New South Wales*. Melbourne: ACER, 1992.

Anderson, D. "Is the Privatisation of Australian Schooling Inevitable." In *Australia Compared*, edited by F. Castles. Sydney: Allen & Unwin, 1991.

———. "The Interaction of Public and Private School Systems." *Australian Journal of Education* 36, no. 3 (1992): 213–36.

Angus, David L. and Jeffrey Mirel. *The Failed Promise of the American High School, 1890–1995*. New York: Teachers College Press, 1999.

Armitage, Audrey. *Newcastle High School: The First 75 Years*. Newcastle: Newcastle High School, 1983.

Austin, A. G. and R. J. W. Selleck. *The Australian Government School 1830–1914*. Melbourne: Pitman, 1975.

Ball, Stephen J. *Class Strategies and the Education Market: The Middle Classes and Social Advantage*. London: RoutledgeFalmer, 2003.

Barcan, Alan. "After Wyndham, What?" *Australian Quarterly* 46, no. 3 (1974): 65–75.

———. "The Future of Secondary Education in N.S.W." *ACES Review* 11, no. 4 (1984): 16–19.

———. *Two Centuries of Education in New South Wales*. Sydney: University of New South Wales Press, 1988.

Benn, Caroline and Brian Simon. *Half Way There: Report on the British Comprehensive School Reform*. London: McGraw-Hill, 1970.

Benn, Caroline and Clyde Chitty. *Thirty Years On: Is Comprehensive Education Alive and Well or Struggling to Survive?* 2nd ed. London: Penguin Books, 1997.

Bessant, Bob. "The Emergence of State Secondary Education." In *Australian Education in the Twentieth Century: Studies in the Development of State Education*, edited by J. Cleverley and J. Lawry, 124–41. Melbourne: Longman, 1972.

Bessant, B. and A. D. Spaull. *Politics of Schooling*. Melbourne: Pitman, 1976.

Birch, I. F. K. and D. Smart, eds. *The Commonwealth Government and Education 1964–1976: Political Initiatives and Development*. Melbourne: Drummond, 1977.

Boston, Ken. "Reshaping Comprehensive Secondary Education." *Inform: Public Education in New South Wales*, July 21, 1999, 6–7.

Braggett, Eddie J. "The Education of Gifted and Talented Children: Australian Provision." Canberra: Commonwealth Schools Commission, 1985.

Brett, Judith. *Australian Liberals and the Moral Middle Class: From Alfred Deakin to John Howard*. Cambridge: Cambridge University Press, 2003.

Brown, Nicholas. *Governing Prosperity: Social Change and Social Analysis in Australia in the 1950s*. Cambridge: Cambridge University Press, 1995.

Butts, R. Freeman. *Assumptions Underlying Australian Education*. Melbourne: Australian Council for Educational Research, 1957.

Caldwell, Brian and Don K. Hayward. *The Future of Schools: Lessons from the Reform of Public Education*. London: Falmer, 1998.

Caldwell, Brian and John Roskam. "Australia's Education Choices." Canberra: Menzies Research Centre, 2002.

Campbell, Craig. "Changing School Loyalties and the Middle Class: A Reflection on the Developing Fate of State Comprehensive High Schooling." *The Australian Educational Researcher* 31, no. 1 (2005): 3–24.

———. "Secondary Schooling, Modern Adolescence and the Reconstitution of the Middle Class." *History of Education Review* 24, no. 1 (1995): 53–73.

———. "State Policy and Regional Diversity in the Provision of Secondary Education for the Youth of Sydney, 1960–2001." *History of Education* 32, no. 5 (2003): 577–94.

Campbell, Craig and Geoffrey Sherington. "Public Comprehensive High Schools in New South Wales: School Principals Discuss the Challenges and Opportunities." Sydney: Public Education Council of New South Wales, 2004.

———. *The Comprehensive Public High School*. New York: Palgrave Macmillan, 2006.

Campbell, Craig, Carole Hooper, and Mary Fearnley-Sander, eds. *Toward the State High School in Australia: Social Histories of State Secondary Schooling in Victoria, Tasmania and South Australia, 1850–1925*. Sydney: ANZHES, 1999.

Carey, Howard K. "Revolution in the Secondary School: The Wyndham Scheme in New South Wales." In *It's People That Matter: Education for Social Change*, edited by Donald McLean. Sydney: Angus & Robertson, 1969.

Cathie, Ian. *The Crisis in Australian Education*. Melbourne: F. W. Cheshire, 1967.

Chitty, Clyde and Brian Simon, eds. *Promoting Comprehensive Education in the 21st Century*. Stoke on Trent: Trentham Books, 2001.

Collins, Jock. *Kebabs, Kids, Cops and Crime: Youth Ethnicity and Crime*. Sydney: Pluto Press, 2000.

Commonwealth Schools Commission. "In the National Interest: Secondary Education and Youth Policy in Australia." Canberra: The Commission, 1987.

Conant, James B. *The Comprehensive High School: A Second Report to Interested Citizens*. New York: McGraw-Hill, 1967.

———. *Slums and Suburbs*. New York: McGraw-Hill, 1961.

———. *The American High School Today: A First Report to Interested Citizens*. New York: McGraw-Hill, 1959.

Connell, R. W. "Making the Difference, Then and Now." *Discourse: Studies in the Cultural Politics of Education* 23, no. 3 (2002): 319–27.

———. *Schools and Social Justice*. Philadelphia: Temple University Press, 1993.

———. "Working-Class Families and the New Secondary Education." *Australian Journal of Education* 47, no. 3 (2003): 235–50.

Connell, R. W., D. J. Ashenden, S. Kessler, and G. W. Dowsett. *Making the Difference: Schools, Families and Social Division*. Sydney: George Allen & Unwin, 1982.

Connell, W. F. *Reshaping Australian Education 1960–1985*. Melbourne: ACER, 1993.

———. *The Foundations of Secondary Education*. Melbourne: ACER, 1961.

Crane, A. R. and W. G. Walker. *Peter Board: His Contribution to the Development of Education in New South Wales*. Melbourne: ACER, 1957.

Crook, David. "Local Authorities and Comprehensivisation in England and Wales, 1944–1974." *Oxford Review of Education* 28, nos. 2 and 3 (2002): 247–60.

Crook, David, Sally Power, and Geoff Whitty. *The Grammar School Question: A Review of Research on Comprehensive and Selective Education*. London: Institutute of Education, University of London, 1999.

Cunningham, K. S., ed. *Education for Complete Living: The Challenge of To-day*. Melbourne: Melbourne University Press, 1938.

Dorn, Sherman. *Creating the Dropout: An Institutional and Social History of School Failure*. Westport (Conn.): Praeger, 1996.

Duffield, Jill. " 'Blissfully Unaware': Gender and Secondary Education Reform, New South Wales, 1953–61." *Australian Studies* 9 (1995): 70–85.

———. "Independent Advice: A Comparative Study of Secondary Education Policy-Making, Scotland and New South Wales." M. Ed., University of Edinburgh, 1990.

———. "The Making of the Wyndham Scheme in New South Wales." *History of Education Review* 19, no. 1 (1990): 29–42.

Dunlop, E. W. "The Public High Schools of New South Wales, 1883–1912." *Journal of the Royal Australian Historical Society* 51, no. 1 (1965): 60–86.

Durkheim, E. (1938/1977). *The Evolution of Educational Thought: Lectures on the Formation and Development of Secondary Education in France*. London: Routledge and Kegan Paul.

Fitzgerald, R. T. *The Secondary School at Sixes and Sevens: A Review of the Sixties and a Prospect of the Seventies*. Melbourne: ACER, 1970.

Floud, J. E., A. H. Halsey, and F. M. Martin, eds. *Social Class and Educational Opportunity*. London: William Heinemann, 1956.

Frost, Lionel and Tony Dingle. "Sustaining Suburbia: An Historical Perspective on Australia's Urban Growth." In *Australian Cities: Issues, Strategies and Policies for Urban Australia in the 1990s*, edited by Patrick Troy. Cambridge: Cambridge University Press, 1995.

Goodman, Rupert. *Secondary Education in Queensland, 1860–1960*. Canberra: Australian National University Press, 1968.

Gordon, David T. *A Nation Reformed? American Education 20 Years after 'a Nation at Risk.'* Cambridge Mass.: Harvard Education Press, 2003.

Gordon, Peter, Richard Aldrich, and Dennis Dean. *Education and Policy in England in the Twentieth Century*. London: Woburn Press, 1991.

Gray, J., A. F. McPherson, and D. Raffe. *Reconstructions of Secondary Education: Theory, Myth and Practice since the War*. London: Routledge & Kegan Paul, 1983.

Hammack, Floyd M., ed. *The Comprehensive High School Today*. New York: Teachers College Press, 2004.

Hampel, Robert L. *The Last Little Citadel: American High Schools since 1940*. Boston: Houghton Mifflin, 1986.

Hogan, Michael. *The Catholic Campaign for State Aid: A Study of a Pressure Group Campaign in New South Wales and the Australian Capital Territory, 1950–1972*. Sydney: Catholic Theological Faculty, 1978.

———. *Public Versus Private Schools: Funding and Directions in Australia*. Melbourne: Penguin, 1984.

Horan, Ronald S. *Fort Street: The School*. Sydney: Honeysett, 1989.

Howie, George. "The Case for Comprehensive Schools." *Current Affairs Bulletin* 26, no. 5 (1960).

Hughes, John. "Harold Wyndham and Educational Reform in Australia 1925–1968." *Education Research and Perspectives* 29, no. 1 (2002).

Irving, Terry, David Maunders, and Geoff Sherington. *Youth in Australia: Policy Administration and Politics: A History since World War II*. Melbourne: Macmillan, 1995.

Johnson, Lesley. *The Modern Girl: Girlhood and Growing Up*. Sydney: Allen & Unwin, 1993.

Johnson, Martin. *Failing School, Failing City: The Reality of Inner City Education*. Charlbury (UK): Jon Carpenter, 1999.

Jupp, James, ed. *The Australian People: An Encyclopedia of the Nation, Its People and Their Origins*. 2nd ed. Cambridge: Cambridge University Press, 2001.

Kenway, Jane and Sue Willis. *Answering Back: Girls, Boys and Feminism in Schools*. London: Routledge, 1998.

Kerkhoff, Alan C., Ken Fogelman, David Crook, and David Reeder. *Going Comprehensive in England and Wales: A Study of Uneven Change*. London: Woburn Press, 1996.

Kyle, Noeleen. *Her Natural Destiny: The Education of Women in New South Wales*. Sydney: NSWU Press, 1986.

Labaree, David. *The Making of an American High School: The Credentials Market and the Central High School of Philadelphia, 1838–1939*. New Haven: Yale University Press, 1988.

———. *How to Succeed in School without Really Learning: The Credentials Race in American Education*. New Haven: Yale University Press, 1997.

Laffin, Martin and Martin Painter, eds. *Reform and Reversal: Lessons from the Coalition Government in New South Wales 1988–1995*. Melbourne: Macmillan, 1995.

Laughlin, Alan. "Mount Druitt High School: Review of 1996 Higher School Certificate Performance." Sydney: Department of School Education (NSW), 1997.

Lingard, Bob, John Knight, and Paige Porter, ed. *Schooling Reform in Hard Times*. London: Falmer, 1993.

Mackie, J. L. "The Case for Selective Schools." *Current Affairs Bulletin* 26, no. 6 (1960).

Marginson, Simon. *Educating Australia: Government, Economy and Citizen since 1960*. Cambridge: Cambridge University Press, 1997.

———. *Education and Public Policy in Australia*. Cambridge: Cambridge University Press, 1993.

———. *Markets in Education*. Sydney: Allen & Unwin, 1997.

McCallum, David. *The Social Production of Merit: Education, Psychology and Politics in Australia 1900–1950*. London: Falmer Press, 1990.

McCulloch, Gary. *Educational Reconstruction: The 1944 Education Act and the Twenty-First Century*. London: Woburn Press, 1994.

———. *Failing the Ordinary Child? The Theory and Practice of Working-Class Secondary Education*. Buckingham: Open University Press, 1998.

Miller, Pavla. *Long Division: State Schooling in South Australian Society*. Adelaide: Wakefield Press, 1986.

Mitchell, Bruce. *Teachers Education and Politics: A History of Organizations of Public School Teachers in New South Wales*. Brisbane: University of Queensland Press, 1975.

Muller, Detlef K., Fritz Ringer, and Brian Simon, eds. *The Rise of the Modern Educational System: Structural Change and Social Reproduction 1870–1920*. Cambridge: Cambridge University Press, 1987.

O'Brien, John. *A Divided Unity! Politics of NSW Teacher Militancy since 1945*. Sydney: Allen & Unwin, 1987.

O'Donoghue, Thomas A. *Upholding the Faith: The Process of Education in Catholic Schools in Australia, 1922–1965*. New York: Peter Lang, 2001.

Ozolins, Uldis. *The Politics of Language in Australia*. Cambridge: Cambridge University Press, 1993.

Pedley, Robin. *The Comprehensive School*. Rev. ed. Harmondsworth: Penguin Books, 1969.

Peel, Mark and Janet McCalman. *Who Went Where in 'Who's Who 1988?': The Schooling of the Australian Elite*. Melbourne: University of Melbourne, 1992.

Polesel, John. "The New South Wales Multi-Campus Schooling Model: The Sydney Experience." Sydney: NSW DET, 2001.

Powell, Arthur G., Eleanor Farrar, and David K. Cohen. *The Shopping Mall High School: Winners and Losers in the Educational Marketplace*. Boston: Houghton Mifflin, 1985.

Powell, Diane. *Out West: Perceptions of Sydney's Western Suburbs*. Sydney: Allen & Unwin, 1993.

Power, Sally, Tony Edwards, Geoff Whitty, and Valerie Wigfall. *Education and the Middle Class*. Buckingham: Open University Press, 2003.

Proctor, Helen. "Gender, Merit and Identity at Parramatta High School, 1913–1919." *History of Education Review* 31, no. 1 (2002): 39–50.

Pusey, Michael. *Economic Rationalism in Canberra: A Nation-Building State Changes Its Mind*. Cambridge: Cambridge University Press, 1991.

———. *The Experience of Middle Australia: The Dark Side of Economic Reform*. Cambridge: Cambridge University Press, 2003.

Reese, William J. "Changing Conceptions of Public and Private in American Educational History." *In Public or Private Education? Lessons from History*, edited by Richard Aldrich, 147–66. London: Woburn Press, 2004.

Reynolds, David and Michael Sullivan. *The Comprehensive Experiment: A Comparison of the Selective and Non-Selective Systems of School Organization.* London: Falmer, 1987.

Riordan, Geoffrey and Sam Weller. *The Reformation of Education in N.S.W.: The 1990 Education Reform Act* AARE (Sydney), 2000. Available from http://www.aare.edu.au/00pap/rio00358.htm.

Rubinstein, David and Brian Simon. *The Evolution of the Comprehensive School, 1926–1972.* 2nd. ed. London: Routledge & Kegan Paul, 1973.

Rury, John L. "Democracy's High School? Social Change and American Secondary Education in the Post-Conant Era." *American Educational Research Journal* 39, no. 2 (2002): 307–36.

Ryan, Chris and Louise Watson. "The Drift to Private Schools in Australia: Understanding Its Features." Canberra: Centre for Economic Policy Research, Australian National University, 2004.

Sawer, Marian. *The Ethical State? Social Liberalism in Australia.* Melbourne: Melbourne University Press, 2003.

Sherington, Geoffrey. "Citizenship and Education in Postwar Australia." *Paedagogica Historica: Supplementary Series* 4 (1998): 329–42.

———. "Education Policy." In *Reform and Reversal: Lessons from the Coalition Government in New South Wales 1988–1995*, edited by Martin Laffin and Martin Painter, 171–87. Melbourne: Macmillan, 1995.

———. "Public Commitment and Private Choice in Australian Secondary Education." In *Public or Private Education? Lessons from History*, edited by Richard Aldrich. London: Woburn Press, 2004.

Sherington, Geoffrey, R. C. Petersen, and Ian Brice. *Learning to Lead: A History of Girls' and Boys' Corporate Secondary Schools in Australia.* Sydney: Allen & Unwin, 1987.

Simon, Brian. *Education and the Social Order, 1940–1990.* London: Lawrence & Wishart, 1991.

———. *Intelligence Testing and the Comprehensive School.* London: Lawrence & Wishart, 1953.

Smart, Don. "The Pattern of Post-War Federal Intervention in Education." In *Federal Intervention in Australian Education*, edited by Grant Harman and Don Smart, 15–34. Melbourne: Georgian House, 1982.

———. *Federal Aid to Australian Schools.* Brisbane: University of Queensland Press, 1978.

Smith, Kevin R. "Political Influences Behind the Delayed Implementation of the Wyndham Report in New South Wales." In *Education Policy Making in Australia*, edited by R. F. Broadbent, 179–94. Melbourne: Australian College of Education, 1982.

Spearritt, Peter. *Sydney since the Twenties.* Sydney: Hale and Iremonger, 1978.

Sutherland, Gillian. *Ability, Merit, and Measurement: Mental Testing and English Education, 1880–1940.* Oxford: Clarendon Press, 1984.

Swan, D. and K. McKinnon. "Future Directions of Secondary Education: A Report." Sydney: NSW Government Printer, 1984.

Taylor, Chris. *Geography of the 'New' Education Market: Secondary School Choice in England and Wales.* Aldershot (UK): Ashgate, 2002.

Teese, Richard. *Academic Success and Social Power: Examinations and Inequity.* Melbourne: Melbourne University Press, 2000.

Teese, Richard et al. "Who Wins at School? Boys and Girls in Australian Secondary Education." Melbourne: Department of Education Policy and Management, University of Melbourne, 1995.

Thomson, Pat. *Schooling the Rustbelt Kids: Making the Difference in Changing Times.* Sydney: Allen & Unwin, 2002.

Tully, Kaye. "State Secondary Education in Western Australia 1912–1972." *Education Research and Perspectives* 29, no. 2 (2002).

Vickers, Margaret. "Markets and Mobilities: Dilemmas Facing the Comprehensive Neighbourhood High School." *Melbourne Studies in Education* 45, no. 2 (2004): 1–22.

Vinson, Tony. "Inquiry into the Provision of Public Education in New South Wales." Sydney: NSW Teachers Federation & Federation of P & C Asociations of NSW, 2002.

Viteritti, Joseph. *Choosing Equality: School Choice, the Constitution and Civil Society.* Washington: Brookings Institution Press, 1999.

Vlaeminke, Meriel. *The English Higher Grade Schools: A Lost Opportunity.* London: Woburn Press, 2000.

Watson, Ian. *Double Depression: Schooling, Unemployment and Family Life in the Eighties.* Sydney: George Allen & Unwin, 1985.

Wescombe, Roger. *Schools Community and Politics in NSW: Ideas and Strategies in the Schools Councils Controversy 1973–1976.* Sydney: University of Sydney, 1980.

West, P. "Politics and Education in NSW 1988–91: Management or Human Values?" *Australian Educational Researcher* 18, no. 3 (1991): 53–67.

White, Michael. "Carnegie Philanthropy in Australia in the Nineteen Thirties—a Reassessment." *History of Education Review* 26, no. 1 (1997): 1–24.

Whitty, Geoff. "Creating Quasi-Markets in Education." *Review of Research in Education* 22 (1997): 3–47.

Wooldridge, Adrian. *Measuring the Mind: Education and Psychology in England, C. 1860–1990.* Cambridge: Cambridge University Press, 1994.

Wraga, William G. "A Progressive Legacy Squandered: *The Cardinal Principles* Report Reconsidered." *History of Education Quarterly* 41, no. 4 (2001): 471–519.

———. *Democracy's High School: The Comprehensive High School and Educational Reform in the United States.* Lanham (Ma.): University Press of America, 1994.

Wyndham (Chair), H. S. "Report of the Committee Appointed to Survey Secondary Education in New South Wales." Sydney: Government of New South Wales, 1957.

Index

Printed in the United States of America